The Bears of Yellowstone

Paul Schullery

The famous early twentieth century naturalist Ernest Thompson Seton called this photograph "the most remarkable wild animal photograph ever taken." It was taken by F. J. Haynes, an early park photographer, and was entitled "Madonna of the Wilds." Haynes Foundation, #16343, Montana Historical Society.

THE Bears OF Yellowstone

REVISED EDITION

by Paul Schullery

ROBERTS RINEHART, INC. PUBLISHERS
in cooperation with the
National Park Foundation

Books by Paul Schullery

author
> *The Bears of Yellowstone*
> *The Orvis Story* (with Austin Hogan)
> *Freshwater Wilderness: Yellowstone Fishes and Their World* (with John Varley)
> *Mountain Time*

editor
> *Old Yellowstone Days*
> *The Grand Canyon: Early Impressions*
> *American Bears: Selections from the Writings of Theodore Roosevelt*
> *The National Parks*
> *Theodore Roosevelt: Wilderness Writings*

contributing author
> *Sierra Club Guide to the National Parks: Rocky Mountains and the Great Plains*
> *Wildlife in Transition: Man and Nature on Yellowstone's Northern Range*

Published by Roberts Rinehart, Inc. Publishers
Post Office Box 3161 Boulder, Colorado 80303
International Standard Book Numbers 0-911797-20-3
(cloth) and 0-911797-21-1 (paper)
Library of Congress Catalog Card Number 85-63521
Printed in the United States of America
Designed by Linda Seals

Some short portions of the revised edition of this book
have appeared, in different form, in *Field & Stream*,
National Parks, and *Safari*

The Bears of Yellowstone
is dedicated to my friends
Dick Follett and John Whitman

"This whole episode of bear life in the Yellowstone is so extraordinary that it will be well worth while for any man who has the right powers and enough time, to make a complete study of the life and history of the Yellowstone bears."

Theodore Roosevelt, 1904

"The grizzly is a massive and powerful statement of the evolutionary history of circumpolar northern environments. The grizzly symbolizes the power, dynamism and productivity of the ice ages. Grizzly bears are a well-tuned way of capturing and utilizing a broad range of available energy. But the omnivorous grizzly ultimately competes with omnivorous man, and human beings through their technology have what our primitive ancestors lacked— the power to exterminate the grizzly.

We should preserve grizzly bear populations, not because their ecological function is critical, but because of what they can do for human imagination, thought and experience."

Steve Herrero, 1976

Contents

Preface to the Revised Edition

It is immensely satisfying to be preparing a new edition of *The Bears of Yellowstone*, for several reasons. I finished the first edition of this book late in 1978; I made a few revisions in the manuscript in 1979, and the book was finally published in 1980. Since then much has been learned about the ecology of the Yellowstone grizzly bear, and I have rewritten the grizzly bear natural history section to reflect those findings. The Interagency Grizzly Bear Study Team, under Richard Knight, is now producing major reports and publications that summarize the findings of their first twelve years of study, and their work is an important part of this new edition.

The story of management of grizzlies in and around Yellowstone Park is seven years longer than when the first edition was completed, and I have completely rewritten the story of grizzly bear management in Yellowstone since 1959. The story is important, and I think instructive, because it is a complex interweaving of science, philosophy, personality, and politics. I have devoted more than a third of this book to considering past struggles to manage the bears because without an understanding of that past it is impossible to understand what we must do next. I think that in this new edition I have been able to explore the ways in which politics and science intertwine (and too often become confused in people's minds), and the ways in which those intertwinings affect the bears, much more completely than I could in the first edition.

The fundamental messages of the book have not changed: these bears are extraordinarily interesting creatures, their future is unassured until we assure it, and their contribution to American culture is enormous. This new edition merely offers additional evidence in support of these messages. The bears of Yellowstone are important. They are an American institution. They have amused, entertained, instructed, and bewildered us for well over a century, during which about 80 million people have visited the park in the hopes of seeing, feeding, or doing something else to a bear. People will continue to come to Yellowstone, and my goal for this new edition is to illuminate the possibilities of what a Yellowstone bear is good for.

For that reason I suppose that my favorite part of the book is Part III, in which I share the best of the bear stories from more than a century of bear-human encounters in Yellowstone. There, as much as I am fascinated by bear ecology, and as much as I am intrigued by the political workings of bear management, is where we really get to the heart of what the bears of Yellowstone have meant to America. It is the part of the book that required the least revision for this new edition, because a good bear story, once told, endures. It is almost always funny, it is often a little scary, and it may even be tragic, but in any case it has an attraction for us that does not diminish. In that way it is like the bears themselves, who we never seem to tire of.

Like politics and religion, the bears of Yellowstone have inspired a vast assortment of opinions, beliefs, and emotions. There are huge disagreements over bear management, and almost equally large disagreements over bear science. I give you my interpretation of some of these disagreements in this book, but I encourage you to read more; like anyone else who has written about the bears of Yellowstone, I am not uniformly approved of for my views. At the end of this book I provide a sizeable bibliography for those wishing to pursue any particular topic. Because this book is not written for a technically oriented audience, I have not used footnotes or otherwise documented each piece of information in the text. In the first edition I used a light system of parenthetical documentation, but have discarded it in this new edition because the scientific reader will already know how to find more information. If you are unable to find your way to a certain piece of information that I refer to in the text, you are free to write to me in care of the publisher, and I will provide you with the source or sources in question.

I write this in my home, about an hour north of Yellowstone Park. It is 21° below zero tonight, and the subjects of this book are probably all bedded down for the winter. Any who aren't must have hibernation foremost in their thoughts on a night like this. There is something reassuring in thinking of them out there, settling in, boars alone, sows with cubs, other sows with cubs on the way, all of them free from human attention until spring. There is a bear season, and then there is the rest of the year. In the spring, researchers will anxiously listen for certain radio signals from certain collars, and will just as anxiously watch to see who has new cubs. But for the moment the bear season is over. The tourists go home, the researchers go to their labs to write up their year's data and observations, and the bears go about their lives without a thought to all the care, worry, and conversation we spend on them.

They're worth it all. The bears of Yellowstone belong to all of us, and they are a precious possession. Let's enjoy them, and let's take care of them.

Paul Schullery
Livingston, Montana
December, 1985

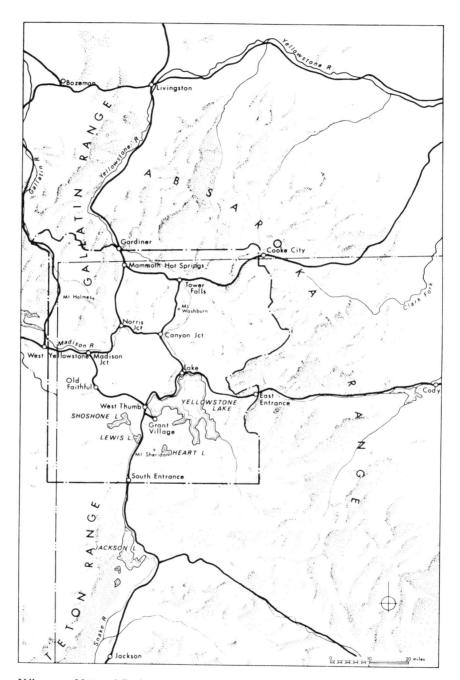

Yellowstone National Park.

Introduction

The bears of Yellowstone have long been the park's most popular animals. Indeed, they may be the most famous wild animals in the country. They are part of one of North America's most glorious and famous wilderness reserves, Yellowstone. The most famous wild animals and the most famous park have no doubt had a good deal to do with each other's popularity.

Yellowstone National Park, in the northwest corner of Wyoming (with a small sliver of land in Idaho and a larger border strip in Montana), protects over 2 million acres of wilderness. Elevation varies from one to two miles, but the average is over 7,000 feet. Approximately 80% of the park is covered by forest, predominantly lodgepole pine but with considerable amounts of spruce and fir. Average precipitation varies dramatically, from less than twenty inches in arid lower areas to over forty in the mountains. The mean annual temperature at park headquarters, Mammoth Hot Springs, is 39.8 F°. For the rest of the park the average is about five degrees cooler. Frederic Remington once said that Yellowstone has three seasons: July, August, and Winter. The park includes or neighbors the headwaters of a number of major river systems, including the Snake, which flows to the Pacific, and the Yellowstone and Madison, which flow eventually to the Gulf of Mexico. Over 95% of the park is completely undeveloped, virtually as wild as when modern man first saw it.

Bears are present throughout the park and in the surrounding country. Grizzlies inhabit more than 5,000 square miles in and around Yellowstone, moving across lands with many ownerships and a variety of local, state, and federal jurisdictions. This large area, generally known as the "Yellowstone Ecosystem," has in recent years come under a sort of unified interagency management coordination. Though I will at some stages concentrate on the bears and their story in the park, the ecological portrayal of the bears applies to the entire region, and the story of management is in fact a slow progress toward managing the grizzlies of all the region as one population.

Yellowstone and the surrounding country is one of the finest wildlife areas in North America, including even Alaska. The park has a host of large mammals. The numbers vary depending upon environmental conditions, but there may be 2,000 bison, 1,000 moose, 25,000 summering elk, and hundreds of mule deer, bighorn sheep, and pronghorn in any given year. Other animals include cougar, beaver, coyote, wolverine, and a variety of smaller mammals. With the possible exception of the wolf, the park retains populations of all the wild mammals it had before the area became a park in 1872. Much the same is true of its populations of birds, fishes, reptiles, and plants, though in the cases of fishes and plants there are additional species that have been introduced. One other animal, native humans, no longer inhabit the area; it appears from the archeological record that at times in the past their use of the area was significant, and we are not well informed on the extent to which they may have altered Yellowstone's prehistoric ecology.

Not unlike Caesar's Gaul, this book is divided into three parts. The first is devoted to natural history; thanks to a number of studies done over the past twenty-five years, especially the Craighead study (1959-1970) and the Interagency Grizzly Bear Team Study (1973-1986) of the grizzly bears, we are blessed with a great amount of information about the ecology of Yellowstone bears. The second tells the story of how Yellowstone's bears have been managed and studied from the establishment of the park until now. The third is an appreciation of the bears of Yellowstone—a gathering of stories, lore, and misadventures that add what I think is an essential element to our understanding of these animals.

Altogether this book is an introduction to a very involved story, a story of ecological relationships, of scientific investigations, and of human ignorance, good intentions, and hope. It is a study of the bear's place in Yellowstone, but it is also, and with no apologies to those who just wanted a book about bears, a study of our place in Yellowstone too.

PART I

The Wild Bears of Yellowstone

Chapter 1

The Black Bear/
Physical Description

 No two bears live exactly the same life. They are nearly as different in physical appearance and in personality as are people. In attempting to summarize their lives, it is easy to speak of norms, averages, and probabilities, but one of the marvels of an animal as complex as the bear is its endless capacity to surprise us.

There is a wealth of scientific information available on bears, most of it the result of the past twenty years, in which excellent studies of black and grizzly bears have been conducted in many parts of North America. The black bears of Yellowstone have been studied much less than many other black bear populations, but from studies in other areas we know much about how Yellowstone's black bears live. Yellowstone's grizzlies, on the other hand, have been the object of two of the most famous and long-running bear research projects in the world, studies that have totalled more than twenty years of intensive work in the wild. Yet even here the bear can still surprise us. It is hard to overstate the complexity of the natural world of which bears are a part.

The ecology of any animal is based on a shifting foundation of circumstances. The bear is among the most adaptable of large mammals, existing in an impressive variety of conditions. Indeed, in the course of its year, it exhibits tremendous flexibility of food and habitat use, and then closes the year with an even more memorable encore, the metabolic wonder of winter denning. Because of this unusual life cycle, I've adopted an approach to telling the bear's story that differs from most popular animal books, which simply tell an animal's story in a simple chronology, usually following some individual or family from birth to death. Instead, I've broken the portrait into individual topics.

To speak of the bears of Yellowstone, when speaking to the average visitor,

A black bear sow, showing the plantigrade foot. The small ears, placed well back on the head, probably do more than any other feature to make the bear's face appear comic. N.P.S. photo.

is to speak of the black bear. The black bear, who is often not black, is the one most frequently seen and photographed; the one remembered from the not-so-good old days when a drive through Yellowstone turned up several dozen begging bears. The grizzly bear is seldom seen from the road, and has practically never begged there. So we begin with the bear so many have seen, the black bear.

The black bear, *Ursus americanus,* is Yellowstone's most common bear. A few hundred live in the park and surrounding wild country, where they have long been objects of great interest and considerable misunderstanding. Specific physical characteristics and abilities will be dealt with throughout the book, but first we must have at least an overview of the physical appearance of the black bear.

"Black bear" is more a label than a description, since the animal comes in many shades, from black to brown to almost-blonde. In the eastern United States most are black, but in the Rockies many more, perhaps as many as half, are brown. The black ones occasionally have white marks on their chests, usually one small patch of varying shape. Excepting seasonal changes due to fading, color rarely changes from the time of cubhood (of 285 bears studied in Minnesota, nine changed color during the study). One litter often contains a mixture of cubs, each a different shade.

The hair is shed in summer, especially July, at which time the coat's appearance is shaggy and uneven. Shedding is encouraged by rubbing the loose hair off against trees and other objects, but we do not know if this is done to remove the hair or simply to relieve itching. Perhaps because it is almost covered by hair, and because of the interest always inspired by the other end, the bear's four to six-inch tail is rarely noticed.

The black bear, as imagined by the visitor, is larger and stockier than life. An adult standing on all fours is rarely more than 30 to 32 inches at the shoulder and 5½ feet from nose to tail. Only extremely rare individuals weigh 500 pounds. Most males weigh 250 pounds or less, and most females 150 pounds or less. The largest black bear weighed in a study done in Yellowstone in the late 1960s was 479 pounds.

The legs, especially the front ones, appear long to the visitor accustomed to animated bears and outdoor magazine artwork. The black bear quite often can be described as "lanky," especially in the spring.

The bear is a "plantigrade" animal, meaning it is one who walks on the flat of the foot, like man, rather than on the toes, like dogs. The foot has nearly hairless toe pads and soles, usually dark brown or black, and five clawed toes. Black bear claws, an inch and a half long at most, are deeply curved for digging and scraping. Rear claws, used more for climbing than digging, are not so sharply curved as front ones.

It is said, usually in an attempt to differentiate blacks from grizzlies, that the back of a black bear has a straight profile with no hump at the shoulder. This is a good general rule, but individual animals will break it, especially when shoulder hair is thick and bristling.

The black bear's head is long with a flat brow—almost a straight line from top of head to nose. The brown snout ends in a pig-like nose, the pad of which extends a short distance up the snout.

The nose of the bear is legendary. Carrion is scented miles away, cubs are identified, buried materials located, and all manner of unknown commodi-

The most common climbing technique involves holding the tree with the forelegs and step-climbing with the rear legs; the sign provides a convenient ladder rung in this case. N.P.S. photo.

ties are investigated. As we will see, the nose provides the leading sense in the search for nourishment.

Like its sense of smell, the bear's hearing is more acute than human hearing. The ears are small and rounded, set well back on the head. They also do more than any other facial feature to make the bear appear comic.

Bears are very nearsighted, but sight is an important sense. Bear eyesight, so long regarded as hopelessly poor, has recently been the subject of intense scientific investigation. The results indicate that not only does the bear have some color vision, but its eyesight is a useful tool in feeding. Good, or at least functional, eyesight is also indicated by the almost dainty way in which bears have been observed feeding on single berries. Distance vision, though poor, is often aided by the bear's ability to stand on its hind legs.

Standing on the rear legs is a stationary activity. Outside of circuses and television bears do not often walk about in this fashion. Even when attacking, they stay down until right on the target. Bear fights have been observed where neither combatant raised up at all—the teeth were the main weapon, accompanied by powerful swats from the front paws.

Black bears are strong and durable. Drugged bears have frequently (though not always) survived falls of twenty or more feet from trees. The very fact that the bear was able to haul itself up into the tree in the first place proves its strength.

Black bears are quick—they can turn or strike with alarming swiftness— and they are fast. Twenty-five miles per hour is not unusual for them over a short distance.

In the wild the black bear often remains healthy for fifteen or more years. Twenty-year-olds are rare, though they have been known to live past thirty in captivity. Under natural circumstances the animal gradually wears out, much like a human: teeth wear down, senses weaken, and old age reduces efficiency until the bear no longer survives. Interestingly, there does not seem to be an extended period of infertility in the elder years. The system of the bear appears capable of reproduction as long as it is capable of maintaining good health.

Chapter 2

The Black Bear/ Eating Habits

As a forager the black bear is the consummate opportunist. It thrives by being flexible in its appetites, so it is drawn to those places that afford the greatest variety of opportunity, or to the unusual place with an especially rich food source. Black bears in Yellowstone concentrate more heavily in a mixed forest blessed with numerous open meadows, bare hillsides and watering places than in a uniform closed forest. In a 1966 study in the Gallatin range in Yellowstone Park, an estimate of one black bear per 1.4 square miles was made for the best habitat, while the concentration of bears in neighboring areas of lodgepole pine forest was much less, perhaps as low as one bear per 20 square miles.

In this desirable habitat, a mixed forest of Engelmann spruce, lodgepole and whitebark pine, fir, and aspen, with frequent meadows, the bear can be a creature of edges, moving from forest to field (always near the safety of trees), from food to food, as season and food availability dictate.

The bear's feeding habits, from the time of spring emergence, are investigative. Unless some favorite and abundant food causes it to settle in, the bear spends much of its time slowly roaming. The impression this gives observers is a mistaken one. As the hunter-naturalist William Wright put it, "You never watch Black Bear when they are quite at home and undisturbed without being made to feel that they are hard put to know what to do with themselves." Their seemingly aimless meandering is actually purposeful. With such a wide diet, exploration is always a promising enterprise.

The black bear is well outfitted for its diet. A fully equipped adult has forty-two teeth, though often some are missing. Front teeth, incisors and canines, are for cutting, and rear teeth, premolars and molars, are for crushing; a standard arrangement for omnivores, who must be able to handle both vegetation and meat. The claws, described earlier, complete the bear's complement of utensils.

Vegetation

By far the most common form of nourishment for all of Yellowstone's bears is plant matter. An examination of bear droppings (known as scats) done in 1944 revealed an average of about 81% vegetation. This, in addition, was from bears who also had access to garbage feeding. Grasses and sedges made up 47% of the plant matter, and the rest was a variety of herbaceous plants, berries, and nuts. Though the figures vary from year to year (and this 1944 study did not include a proper proportion of spring scats) depending on the success or failure of specific crop types, the overall figure is reasonable. The black bear is primarily a vegetarian, taking other food when available to supplement its basic diet.

The newly emerged black bear sometimes can not be choosy about food. When he arrives on the open meadows he at first can rely on leftovers—dead grasses and sedges, mixed with unpalatable "accidentals" like pine needles and wood chips, until more succulent food appears. Succulence is important, so bears seek out moist areas, and mix the new grass shoots with roots of spring-beauty and wild onion. In digging out the roots and tubers, of course, bears encounter rodents and rodent food caches. Both are welcomed.

Another occasional meal during the spring shortage, and even in early summer, is cambium, the tender layer below the bark of lodgepole pines, Douglas fir, and spruce trees. Bears strip the bark with their teeth to reach this soft chewy layer of wood, leaving long strips of outer bark hanging loose, and occasionally girdling the tree completely and killing it. In some parts of the country, particularly the Pacific Northwest, bear-killed trees run into the hundreds in some areas. In Yellowstone bears kill few trees, but are entitled to.

It is the unglamorous truth that black bears pass much of the summer grazing. Yellowstone's meadows are rich in white clover and grasses, so the bears, like the elk and bison, take advantage of them.

Though Yellowstone is not known for the tremendous berry crops produced elsewhere in the Rocky Mountains, some years the bears do quite well. Usually berry hunting becomes profitable in August, when small sweet strawberries ripen under the lodgepole cover. Later, in these same forests, bearberries and grouse whortleberries will also appear.

The grouse whortleberry, also called the low red huckleberry, was rated as the number one berry in availability by Murie in 1944. His scat analysis indicated it made up 5% of the total sample. In some years and locations the figure would undoubtedly be much higher. Bears are exceptionally fond of berries. Among the other favorites are serviceberries, snowberries, red raspberries (found on rocky slopes as early as July), and chokecherries. These last two have accounted for many a surprise meeting between person and bear in the Mammoth Hot Springs area. The dense foliage often screens fellow berry-pickers until they practically collide.

Though bears are capable of feeding neatly on single berries, and have been observed to do so in other parts of the country, their enthusiasm rarely permits it. A more common approach is to grab a branch (or several) with paws and either strip off leaves and berries into the open mouth or feed at random while holding the branches. The amount of non-berry material consumed varies with the style. Some scats have contained mostly twigs and leaves, while others were almost pure berry. Very little chewing is done; the smaller berries are often bolted whole. Bear scat is easily recognizable at this time; a runny mixture of pulp and seeds. Such scat, obviously, is not durable, and scientists have difficulty estimating the importance of berries to the bear diet because berry scats, which deteriorate or are consumed by scavengers very quickly, are not as lasting as scats made of other food materials, and so are perhaps not found as often as the others.

Berries are often available well into fall, and will draw a number of bears into a surprisingly small feeding area. Even the following spring bears are on the lookout for a few remaining tidbits.

In fall the nut of the whitebark pine is a favorite of black bears. The agile black has an advantage over the non-climbing grizzly, since it can go up into the trees while the cones are still hanging. Such activity commences in August, when the blacks climb to break off branches and bring them back to the ground. Holding the cone in its mouth, the bear tears it apart with its teeth to get the nuts. Also, bears make life rough for red squirrels by uncovering carefully stored caches of nuts and gobbling down several hours' accumulations in a few seconds. Whitebark pine is available at higher elevations in Yellowstone, above 8,000 feet.

Animals

Though vegetation comprises the bulk of the bear's diet, there are times when meat has considerable significance, and it is always of interest. The black bear eats what nature offers, from buffalo to bird egg, but there are certain meats that it has regular chances to obtain.

The meat of large mammals is most available in the spring. Bears are most apt to have it as carrion, the remains of some animal that did not survive the winter, but they will occasionally hunt standing meat, seeking out the winter-weakened elk or deer. Later they have some success taking elk calves and deer fawns. Though not generally known as big-game hunters, black bears are known to prey successfully on moose calves in Alaska and elk calves in Idaho.

Much has been made of cannibalism in bears. To a wild animal dead meat is dead meat, so the carcass of a bear that succumbed to disease, old age, or battle is cleaned like any other carcass. Too, there are several documented cases in Yellowstone of members of the same bear family, loyal during life, consuming one of their number that has died. And a cub is prey of adult male bears until it is grown.

The popular literature has taken to the idea that bears (both grizzlies and blacks) prefer a rank carcass to a fresh one, as if this indicates some deficiency in the bear's appetite or character. If there is a preference, and there is little evidence to prove one, it might be based on the increased odor, and therefore increased detectability/locatability of the putrid meat, or on the presence of maggots. The maggots in an elk carcass are a prize among scavengers. Even songbirds have been observed venturing into the body cavity of a dead elk to get them.

Spring is also the best time to get fish. Around Yellowstone Lake, and in other areas where cutthroat trout spawn, bears find fishing good. The black bear, however, has a poor reputation as a fisher, and seems to lack the patience and skill of the grizzly, who is known to fish seriously for some weeks in the tributaries of the lake. The black takes advantage of the occasional stranded trout, and may succeed in getting one from the water, but fish are not recognized as an important part of their diet in Yellowstone. Ranger Dale Nuss has twice observed black bears fishing in creeks, and in both cases the bears were quite successful.

The black bear's attitude toward meat, especially in great quantities, is more casual than the grizzly's. A black bear may drag meat to a more convenient spot to eat it, but blacks do not "cache" meat, that is they do not formally hide it by concealment or burial to save it for later. When we turn to the grizzly bear we will see several examples of this contrast between blacks and grizzlies, with the grizzly generally appearing more systematic and forward-looking in its arrangements.

Most of the black bear's meat comes from small animals. It is adept at flipping rocks and logs to uncover mice. The technique has been observed: a paw is hooked underneath the near side of the rock, and it is flipped away from the bear, who is poised to grab or slap whatever dodges out. The hunting efforts of the black bear, even for these small animals, are not as determined as the grizzly's. The black bear will take a marmot it happens to catch in the open, but is not inclined to excavate the marmot's burrow. The digging bear will now and then unearth a vole or pocket gopher, or perhaps a Uinta ground squirrel.

Frogs and salamanders are intentionally hunted, and must also be encountered accidentally by bears that come to water to drink, bathe, or fish.

Black bears eat practically any insect, even ones so tiny there would seem no point in making the effort. Ants are a favorite. A study in northern Montana reported ants in over 30% of all spring and summer scats. It has been suggested that their acidic taste is appealing (just as some anglers claim it is appealing to trout), but for whatever reason, bear interest has inspired a charming bit of lore. Early naturalists claimed that the bear, on discovering an ant hill, would remove its top, stick its nose into the center tunnel, and inhale the inhabitants. The real approach, as observed in Yellowstone and elsewhere, is much more practical. A quick swipe of the paw wrecks the hill, and the paw is then laid on the center of turmoil. Once a sufficient number of ants have swarmed onto the paw to "defend" their home, the bear licks them off.

Ants and other colonizing insects live in rotting and down trees. Bears use their powerful forepaws and claws to rip the trees apart in search of the insects, speeding up the processes of decay while they are at it.

Bears also frequent snowbanks, any time of the year, to lick off insects that have mistakenly landed on the snow and become immobilized by the cold. This happens often to aquatic insects, hatching from nearby streams, who are later drawn to the bright snow.

In fact, any time cold weather chills insects bears gather them. In 1935, for example, northern Yellowstone Park experienced a great abundance of crickets. Adolph Murie, hiking the ridges in the upper Lamar River valley, observed eleven bears in one day feeding on the crickets, and grasshoppers, which were sluggish and easily captured. He examined sixty-four scats, fifty-eight of which were composed entirely of crickets and grasshoppers. The most unusual part of the report was not the insects, however; it was their chosen hiding place. Old dried buffalo chips were common in the area, and bears were flipping chips to find the insects:

Most of the crickets were picked up in the grass, but some were taken under bison chips. With a paw the chip was delicately tipped on one edge and held poised while she peered beneath to see what was uncovered.

Murie believed some of these bears were accustomed to feeding at park garbage dumps, which were then regularly used by bears. He was impressed that the bears were so fond of the insects that they were ignoring the easy garbage to get them.

The diet of the bear, like that of the human, does not benefit him equally in all its parts. Though no study of the digestive system of Yellowstone's black bears has been undertaken, such a study has been done of the park's grizzlies, and is summarized later. Some of that summary can be applied, with caution, to the black bear.

Eating habits, of course, involve more than what is eaten. They involve when, how often, and at what pace. These matters will be attended to in the final part of the black bear natural history, under the heading of "Lifestyle."

Chapter 3

The Black Bear/ Denning

The food habits of the bear are unlike those of most mammals in one important respect; they are not intended to merely maintain the body in as best condition as the season will allow. The bear is a winter denner, denning being an environmental adaptation to a seasonal shortage of food.

The bear's eating habits can be divided into three stages. First, post-denning, when bears are eating to regain lost weight and to strengthen themselves for an active summer of feeding and mating. Second, a steady summer and fall of feeding, to build up a reserve of fat in preparation for the third stage, denning. Denning is a several-months-long abstinence from any feeding or drinking.

Denning cannot be considered without reference to the other stages, the one being a recovery from it, the other a preparation for it, so we will begin with the preparations.

Usually by the end of July black bears begin to store up fat for the winter. Studies done around North America reveal what really capable over-consumers bears are. From August to early November, some Montana black bears were able to average about one pound weight gain per day for two or more months. Females studied in Wisconsin gained as much as 75 pounds in this period, males as much as 130.

There are three uses for this layer of fat, often four inches thick, that the bears so industriously store. The first is the one we all think of: energy to be used during winter sleep. The second is a bit less frequently mentioned but just as obvious; the layer of fat is fine insulation against the cold. The third is perhaps the most surprising since it involves the time after the bear has left the den. In those first few weeks food is often scarce, so stored fat provides energy to last until the plenty of summer.

The time of denning varies greatly over the bear's range. In some extreme southern areas, denning may not happen at all. Even in a limited area like Yellowstone there is variety, depending on elevation, the weather, the condition and the sex of the bear, and its family status. A pregnant female usually dens earlier, and stays denned longer, than a lone male. She is also more careful about preparing her den. Young bears also den earlier and emerge later than adults.

Denning usually begins in Yellowstone in mid to late October. Most black bears are denned by mid-November. Adult bears, except for sows with cubs, den alone.

As the first staying-snow falls in Yellowstone, and food crops of the late season are depleted or dried, black bears begin a gradual process of denning preparation. For some, several weeks of sporadic effort go into choosing a site, gathering bedding, and even excavating a little soil to improve the fit. Others, especially lone males, let it go until late in the season. Their preparations are limited to a quick search, it seems.

A den is essentially a secure shelter. It may or may not be entirely "out of the weather"; the bear may sleep in a true cave or out in relative open. In some parts of the country bears "den" simply by bedding down in a thicket. In Yellowstone they often seek partial shelter under a log or tree root, digging it out to suit, or may adopt another animal's den. The black bear's den is not as sophisticated as the grizzly's, but some black bears do show great energy and ingenuity in their den work. The den site may be visited many times in a few weeks, showing a degree of premeditation most people do not associate with the seemingly easygoing black bear.

It is not yet established for certain what finally causes the bear to den up. Food shortage is a factor, as is severe cold, heavy snow, or a glutted bear who is no longer hungry. It may well be that all the factors listed, as well as metabolic mechanisms not entirely understood yet, contribute to the decision to move into the den.

Bears in cartoons are portrayed in spacious dens, some with several chambers. It is to the advantage of the bear to have a den only slightly larger than body size, since it will hold heat better. Bears do not normally use what is known as the classic hibernation position: "a curled up position with the top of the skull pressed against the bedding and the nose near the tail." Denning bears sleep in a variety of positions, but however they choose to sleep it is clearly to their advantage to keep as compact as possible to conserve heat. Just as mittens keep your hands warmer than gloves because the fingers share their heat and have less surface exposed, the curled-up bear concentrates his heat by joining body and limbs in one close unit.

For some years the term "hibernation" was not popular to describe bear denning because the bear did not seem to hibernate in the way "true" hibernators did. Unlike some small mammals, like mice, ground squirrels, and marmots, the bear can be easily awakened. Its sleep is not the coma-like torpor of the others. Recently, however, studies of denning bears have encouraged the use of the word hibernator to describe the bear.

The typical small hibernator drops very quickly into its dormant state. Reduced heart rate, slight oxygen use, and a deep unconsciousness are the result. However, these animals frequently revive (every two to ten days for some mice). During their short waking periods they feed, drink, urinate and defecate. They store food for the waking period, or they go and forage.

Bears, on the other hand, take as much as several weeks to get into their dormant state. Remarkably, they then stay in it for as much as six months. We have grown up hearing about bear denning, and are perhaps dulled to the real wonder of it. The undisturbed Yellowstone black bear sleeps, without eating, drinking, or passing any substance through its system, for four or five months. This is the equivalent of getting up from Thanksgiving dinner and taking a nap until Easter. And maybe giving birth in the meantime. We must be impressed, if not awed, by such an achievement.

Shortly before the bear enters its den it stops feeding. In some cases it appears lethargic for a few days prior to denning. There have been reports that the bear will eat fibrous materials at this time in order to form an "anal plug" at the bottom of its digestive tract; such plugs have occasionally been found in the abandoned dens of all three species of North American bears. It now appears, however, that the plug actually forms during hibernation as the bear's digestive tract passes not only remnants of food but dead cells from inside the tract. It remains unclear if this plug has any physiological value.

The summer sleeping heartbeat of the adult bear is about forty beats per minute. In the deepest winter sleep that drops to eight. The decline from forty to eight takes three or more weeks, and is subject to change if the bear is disturbed.

Body temperature also drops, from four to seven degrees Centigrade below normal. The body temperature of the bear will fluctuate along with the temperature of the den. It seems, however, that the black bear's body has some

The almost breathtaking cuteness of a black bear cub has gotten it into trouble with thousands of park visitors. N.P.S. photo.

mechanism for preventing its temperature from dropping below a certain point. The lowest measured body temperature is thirty-one degrees Centigrade, a drop of slightly more than seven degrees.

Combined with these lethargic characteristics is, naturally, a decrease in oxygen use, sometimes as much as 50%. The metabolism of the bear truly gears down. It appears also that blood circulation is lessened to some parts of the body. The front of the body (brain and chest) gets a higher than usual proportion of blood, while the lower body and limbs get less. Winter fat provides the only source of the liquid essential to keep water content of the blood normal. In fact, it seems that the lean underbody changes little; the fat is the key to successful hibernation.

Black bears have been observed abroad in Yellowstone in the winter. Their roaming at this time, though not typical, is revealing. They are occasionally roused; perhaps the den caved in, perhaps their fat layer was inadequate, or maybe the den was appropriated by a larger bear. Usually they will den up again quickly, as there is little or no food for them after December.

There is a longstanding legend that bears suck sustenance from their paws. It may have originated from observations of curled-up bears, who hold their paws near their mouths, but it has an unusual twist. Bears sometimes shed the outer layer of skin from their footpad while in the den, and one study (not in Yellowstone) revealed that these pads are occasionally eaten by the animal before it leaves the den area in the spring.

The post-denning period is a time of gradual adjustment. The bear begins to stir as warmer temperatures reach into the den. Snow is not necessarily a factor in how soon the bear leaves the den, since it can wander to lower elevations, but of course a thick snow blanket will insulate the den and cause it to stay cold longer, thus allowing the bear to sleep longer.

In Yellowstone, emergence can be expected in early April, with young bears and sows with young coming out as much as a month later.

Hunters have often remarked that newly emerged black bears appear fat and healthy, but that the fat is "spongy" and contains little oil. More scientific observations show that the black bear loses from 15 to 25% of its weight before emerging, whatever its appearance may be. Also, both hunters and researchers agree that the first few weeks of activity thin the animal down considerably.

The bear, even given the opportunity, does not gorge itself like a starving man at first emergence. There may be several short exploratory jaunts, over a week or two, establishing daybeds near the den, and light feeding, before emergence is complete. As noted, spring is not a good food time, so it is suitable that the bear is not immediately ravenous. Usually in about two weeks the digestive system is functioning well and the bear is building up energy for that *other* big event in its metabolic schedule, mating.

Chapter 4

The Black Bear/
Mating and Cub Growth

Adult bears customarily live alone, disinclined to the sociability of the other large vegetarians. When they do keep company it is for mating. Though breeding often becomes a biological possibility (for both males and females) at age three and a half, females rarely mate successfully before four and a half—their fifth summer. The male black bear's reproductive system begins to activate late during winter denning. His gonads become active, and production of sperm begins at this time. He is fully potent both prior to and after the female is able to mate with him.

The female's ovaries also become active in March and April (follicular growth begins in April or May), though it will be two months before her system is prepared for estrus. The duration of estrus (the popular term is being "in heat") is up to two months. An unusual observation was made in Yellowstone (by Skinner) of mating black bears in September, but the peak of activity is late June and early July. Barnes and Bray observed the most activity between June 8 and June 22.

Promiscuity, mating with more than one partner, is often quite common. When Yellowstone's bears were concentrated near dumps and along roads, the likelihood of multiple encounters was probably even greater, but even in the wild it appears that a few dominant males manage to take care of fertilizing most of the available females. On the other hand, it has happened that a male-female pair may travel together throughout the mating season, evidently concentrating only on each other. Dominant males are more than willing to defend females from other males.

At the height of the breeding season the female is the least affected. She will follow more or less normal daily habits of feeding, travel, and resting, while the male follows *her*, awaiting her acceptance. He eats less, and will

21

spend much time attending her, nosing her, and generally hanging around. He is, in short, distracted.

There is great variation in the number of times black bears copulate. The chance meeting, or one-time encounter, may occur, where the bears spend only a few hours or less together, but more often there are extensive preliminaries.

Most of the "courtship" is during the period that the female is unwilling to mate. The male follows her closely, nosing or licking her genital area, emitting low grunts, and even attempting to mount. If she is not ready, she may drive him away or simply sit down. The two can travel for some days this way, in relative peace and good humor, but when she is at last receptive copulation occurs quickly. The male mounts from the rear, staying mounted for as long as 30 minutes. During copulation the male intersperses pelvic thrusting with resting, sometimes letting the female support most of his weight. He might gently bite her about the ears, and she in turn bites at him. It is awkward, but coupled pairs do move around, the female even grazing.

To those offended by the female's seeming indifference to the male's advances it will be some comfort to know that the arrangement is biologically

Black bear cubs are interested in almost everything. N.P.S. photo.

sound. The male must travel to her, while her primary role is to keep fit and fed for the term of her pregnancy. Thus she continues to feed through the courtship.

Copulation occurs repeatedly; if a strong bond has been formed the pair may remain together until the female is no longer in heat. There is no especial drive in the male to be polygamous, but his continued interest may lead him to other females. It seems likely that promiscuity in bears, who do not reproduce very quickly or frequently, is a trait that helps guarantee that all available breeding stock will be taken advantage of.

The male has no further involvement in the lives of the pregnant sow or young bears. He has no role in cub-rearing and will even pose a threat to his offspring when they emerge from the den with their mother the following spring.

Bear pregnancy is adapted to the long winter dormancy. The cubs are born in the winter den, so the mother must be prepared to nurse them for two months without any nourishment for herself. This set of circumstances has generated in bear physiology the remarkable phenomenon of delayed implantation, or "embryonic delay."

The principle is beautiful. After fertilization, the embryo develops only slightly, to what is known as the blastocyst stage. At this point growth either stops or is retarded to imperceptibility until November. At that time one of two things may happen.

If the sow has not had a good year and is in poor condition or has not put on enough weight to nourish herself and her cubs through the winter, her body will abort the blastocyst to ensure that at least she survives the winter to breed again in future years. But if her condition is good, the blastocyst implants in the uterine wall and resumes normal growth. In this case, though the total gestation of the bear is between 200 and 220 days, only about half of that time is devoted to fetal development. This retarded prenatal growth is the key to successful winter birth of young bears. The embryo has only been growing normally since November, so the cubs are tiny at birth, only eight to ten inches long and weighing from ten to twenty ounces. Here is the advantage of delayed implantation. Had the cubs developed through a full pregnancy, they would weigh ten or more pounds each and would require a great deal more milk than their mother could provide them during two months in a snowed-up den. Born the size of a squirrel, their needs are manageable.

As noted, the pregnant female is among the first to den up and among the most careful in her den preparations. She will also be among the last to emerge the following spring. We know relatively little about what pregnancy does to affect her sleep, and little about her exact physiological state at the time of birth. In late January or early February, seven months after conception, she gives birth. A first pregnancy is likely to result in only one cub, but after that the litter is most often two. Three is not unusual, but four is rare. There is one reported case of six cubs in one litter in all of North America, but such an event is extraordinarily rare.

The cubs are helpless for weeks. They can crawl enough to find their mother's nipples (there are six of these), but little more. They are blind, have no teeth, and almost no hair. It must be assumed that the mother is semiconscious, or her tremendous bulk would be fatal to such fragile creatures. We do not know how many die from being crushed or suffocated, but it seems to be very few.

Nursing is done by the mother lying on her side. When the cubs are larger she can nurse them while on her back or sitting, perhaps propped against a tree.

Growth in the den amounts to several pounds per cub by emergence time. After five weeks their eyes are open (though they may not be well focused), their first coat of real hair develops, and their first teeth appear. They still are not strong enough to walk, but crawl with some authority.

When they follow their mother from the den they weigh about five pounds. They are wobbly, but can both run and climb. As soon as she leads them from the den, and even before she has readjusted to normal activity, the cubs have embarked on an intensive survival training course.

There is no way to write about bear cubs that does not reflect their playful rambunctious character. The coldest, more thoroughly scientific monograph, no matter how technical (or dry) the language, evokes in the reader the same lively image; bear cubs are frolicsome eager young animals. The naturalist who dreads anthropomorphism—the equating of animal behavior with human character traits—will become hopelessly entangled in his own language, for the similarities between child-rearing and cub-rearing are too great to be ignored. A misbehaving cub is swatted by a not-quite all-enduring mother, a frightened cub runs to mother for protection, and a mother bear's devotion to her young, though overrated in the popular literature, is legendary. Certainly restraint is in order when discussing wildlife, but anthropomorphism is less of a concern now than it was a few decades ago. Humans

The mother bear is teacher, disciplinarian, and guardian of the cubs until they are more than a year old. N.P.S. photo.

seem to be more willing to acknowledge their own animal nature, and so are less defensive when compared to their fellow creatures.

The cubs' immediate concern is food. Newly emerged cubs can eat small solids (buds, or maybe insects), but prefer their mother's milk for several weeks. There is evidence of a remarkable, instinctive food-finding ability in cubs. A cub taken captive (not in Yellowstone) while still in its den was released some months later in the forest. It demonstrated an uncanny ability to locate succulent roots in several inches of soil, smelling them out and digging directly to them. Studies in Michigan revealed that some cubs as small as eighteen pounds (five-and-a-half months of age) could survive to adulthood with no additional guidance. Fall hunters in some states are asked to not kill cubs, even if they have killed a mother. The cubs may well survive.

The role of the mother is to coach the cubs in feeding (without her guidance they may not develop such wide tastes, especially if there are unusual techniques she has herself learned with difficulty) and to protect them.

Teaching seems to be a process of example. The cubs watch her flip rocks, or tear apart wood, or feed on vegetation. At first they may only play at such activities, but after a time the lesson takes hold. Non-feeding activities, such as swimming, also may be taught by example.

For protection the best defense is to send the cubs up a tree. This the sow will do at any risk, even if it involves a stay of several hours. She might also do it to allow herself a leisurely and worry-free feeding spree. Sow black bears in Yellowstone in the 1960s were known to leave their cubs up trees for two hours or more while they begged along the roads.

In Yellowstone the cub has few natural enemies. The most dangerous is the adult bear, both the grizzly and the black. A small lone cub could fall prey to other predators, such as coyotes, cougars, and eagles, but as long as the mother is near the chances are slim.

Cubs spend many of their waking hours playing—with each other, with their mother, and with inanimate objects or small animals they might capture. Social encounters of comparable frequency and intensity will be limited when they are adults, but bears are not the uncommunicative hermits they have often been made out to be. Studies of captive black bears in the southeast indicate that the bears develop a surprisingly sophisticated communication system to serve them during cubhood, involving sounds, facial expressions, and body postures, all of which express some basic attitude to family members and to anyone else they encounter. It is not a language, but it is a significant means of expression that bears have never been given full credit for in the past.

As the summer passes the cubs learn to feed on everything the mother does. By late fall they weigh up to forty pounds and have learned most of what she can teach them. The family dens together, again entering the den earlier than mature loners. In the spring, usually shortly before mating season, she abandons them. Sometimes this is not easy, as they tag along after she has lost interest in them. It may not finally happen until an adult male appears to court her. He might even chase them off himself.

The lone yearling is the most vulnerable of bears. A Montana study showed as many as half of the yearling age group succumbing to a variety of natural causes. The annual attrition (disappearance by death) from any adult age group is less than 15%.

Black bears continue to grow in stature for two or three years after they reach sexual maturity, and in some circumstances may continue to put on weight after that. By fall, yearlings have often doubled their weight from the previous fall, though yearling weights vary greatly; a Vermont study reported a weight range of dressed yearling black bears from 50 to 138 pounds. Thus it is difficult to give a good "average" weight for two- or three-year-old bears. These young animals fare so differently from one another that their sizes and personalities are widely dissimilar. However well or poorly they do, though, they are entered into the lone life and challenging world of the wild bear.

Their mother, too, continues. She is capable of rearing a new family every other year for as long as she remains healthy.

Chapter 5

The Black Bear/
Lifestyle

I actually mean, by that rather trendy title, that this section of the book will suggest how the various components already considered—physical capacities, denning, mating, cub rearing, and so on—add up to a pattern of movements and habitat use.

Except during mating, a black bear's habits are primarily the result of diet. The search for food directs its movements, leading it as far as necessary. Terms like "range" and "territory" must be used carefully with bears. Their range is flexible, so that in poor forage they may travel many miles in a day, but in a good berry season may spend a week in a two-acre space. The many studies done in North America show great variations in range. In some areas the bears roamed over an area with a rough radius (the areas are not round, of course) of fifteen miles. In others the radius was only two. The Barnes and Bray study in Yellowstone revealed some interesting things about bear movements in the park.

Adult males were more mobile, even twice as mobile as adult females. (Males are the mate-finders, remember, and the females often have cubs.) Some males traveled as much as twenty miles in the course of the summer from the point of original live-capture, but most stayed within ten miles of their original capture site (capture/release/recapture studies are often used to determine movements of wild animals that are difficult to observe steadily). Females moved about half as far as males. Such figures are only the roughest sort of information, since they define the movements of only a few bears, some of whom were also affected by the availability of garbage.

For many years it was believed that black bears are not territorial in the sense that they did not seem to defend a set of boundaries. More recent research has suggested that bears may be aware of some territorial limits at some times, however, so it isn't yet possible to speak with total confidence about this. Recent research on bear-marked trees, for instance, suggests that a sense of territoriality may have something to do with this well-known bear activity. Adult black bears studied in Minnesota have been observed chasing immi-grating younger bears from the adult's known range. Another study, in northern Montana, revealed a subtler form of territoriality, if that's what it may be called. Young bears, once separated from their mothers, were seen to adopt portions of her range as their own and then gradually expand from it. An intriguing result was a kind of "group territoriality" that resulted in all bears in a given area, say a large drainage, showing hostility to strange bears that wandered in but showing tolerance to other resident bears in the area.

As mentioned earlier, black bears do not spend much time in the lodge-pole pine forests that dominate much of Yellowstone. The bears favor a mixed habitat. Yellowstone, therefore, has only a limited supply of truly first-rate black bear country. Within this country the black bear's habits develop. In many areas black bears are nocturnal, but in Yellowstone the black bear seems to choose its hours to suit the circumstances. We already have the example of the early-morning insect-eaters, but a more vivid (if somewhat dishearten-ing) example was the beggar bear. Until the 1970s, dozens of Yellowstone black bears lined the park road during the daylight hours chowing down on candy wrappers and kosher dills. They were demonstrating their versatility to the wrong audience. Day-night activities are affected by many things, not the least of which may be the presence of grizzly bears, who generally are avoided by the blacks. When grizzlies and blacks share a range, the blacks may adjust their own habits to avoid contact with the bigger bear.

Like many other animals, bears "shade up" on hot days. Resting periods occur in most weather, as the bears establish day beds or just plop down in a likely looking spot. Pregnant females rest less than lone males, probably because the former have greater nutritional needs. Younger bears rest more than old ones, and often nap in trees.

Two non-feeding activities which must not be passed by are rubbing (already discussed in the chapter on physical description) and bathing. Rub-bing, besides removing hair, is also done to relieve itching and because it feels good. Bears do, indeed, back up against a tree and go at it, but many other approaches are popular. Among the most novel is belly-scratching, done some-times by walking over a very small tree, bending it until it goes underneath them and springs up behind.

Bears in Yellowstone, as elsewhere, are fond of water. Bathing both cleans and cools them. Black bears have been observed swimming in Yellowstone Lake, miles from shore. They also have shown fondness for park thermal features, resulting in some of the stories included in Part III of this book.

One of the most fascinating aspects of bear movement is their homing ability. It is more developed in adults, who can return across seemingly new country to their familiar haunts. The whole process poses important questions, and not just to managers of bear populations. How well do bears remember terrain, and how sophisticated is their innate sense of direction once they are removed from familiar range? It appears their memory does play a role in homing, for an older, more experienced bear is much more adept at it than a young one. At the same time, their sense of topographical orientation transcends simple familiarity with specific features. They can find their way home from country they have never before visited.

Bears become habituated to certain trails within their home range, even stepping in the same footprints until a double rut is created. This would appear to be in contrast to other bear traits. For one thing, it differs from the meandering habit mentioned earlier, but that is probably not an important difference, because bears, like cows, ducks, people, and many other animals, are at times going somewhere purposefully and at other times just wandering around. Well established bear trails in Yellowstone have traditionally been associated with park dumps; bears on those trails were not looking for random food sources, they were headed toward a specific known food source.

Bears all using the same trail does not suggest that they are maintaining exclusive territories of their own, but it does not prove they are not. Territoriality may be a seasonal instinct, as during mating or during the peak of some food crop, and a given bear trail probably leads to some communal food source where there is more food than one bear could reasonably defend (or eat). Usually when bears concentrate at a food source, whether it is a dump, a salmon stream, or a berry patch, real or imagined competition for food results in a hierarchy of privilege that serves the same purpose that territoriality would elsewhere. The biggest and most aggressive bears get the most food, though the biggest may not always be the most aggressive. Fights occur, but much more common are showdowns of bluffs, and fatalities from fights are rare.

Bears do not "hug" their prey to crush it. The bear may hold an animal with its forelegs during a struggle, but reliable records of bears using such a grip to crush the animal do not exist. It appears that a black bear may "hug" an opponent in an attempt to bite it.

One of the most fascinating and still mystifying elements of bear behavior is the famous "bear-tree," supposedly scratched or bitten by a bear as a mark of territorial claim. Legend had it that bears would reach as high as they could in order to show other passing bears, by the height of their claw-marks, just how large they were. That part of the story may not be true, but marking is clearly an important form of communication between bears. A recent study in Great Smoky Mountains National Park showed that marked trees are both visual and chemical (scented) signs, which give bears a fair number of options for reading the message, whatever it is, that has been left on a tree. It remains unclear exactly what all the messages may be. Among the suggestions: a warning system so that bears know where other bears are and avoid them; a sort of reassurance to the bear making the mark that his (most marks are made by males) chosen area is secure; a means of orienting a bear that is still learning an area and needs a few personal landmarks; some communication system between bears during mating season. The last one may help explain why, in Yellowstone, several bears have been observed marking the same tree from time to time with no noticeable regard to other marks. It could be that these "community" trees serve as signs of belligerence only a few weeks of the year (the study in the Smokies showed that marking was particularly common during mating season), and as some other communication sign the rest of the year.

Trees have another important function for bears, as refuges. There are two common climbing techniques. The most popular relies on the front legs to grasp the trunk while the hind legs, pushing in unison, move the bear upward. The other involves a "walking" motion, wherein all legs grab and lift in the same order as they move in walking. Descent, usually accompanied by "walking," is made head-up, even among inexperienced cubs (who, it might be added, climb with no apparent training).

Another part of adult bearhood is play. We have seen how it figures in the education of young bears, providing instructive social interaction, but it is evidently part of the life of adult bears, though in a more controlled way. There are even popular writers who claim the bear has a sense of humor (science has not gone quite that far yet).

The relations of black bears with other animals have been discussed in the chapters on food and cub growth. About the only serious natural enemy of an adult black bear in Yellowstone is another bear, either a larger bear or a grizzly. Blacks avoid grizzlies as a rule, but the rule is not ironclad. Large

Depending upon how great the danger, the mother black bear may send or accompany her cubs up the tree, and is willing to stay there for hours if necessary. N.P.S. photo.

The relationship between black bear and grizzly bear is not constant. A photograph taken during a black bear study in Yellowstone in the late 1960s shows a large black bear confronting an equally large grizzly in a dump. N.P.S. photo.

black bears, whose temperament allowed it, have been known to chase grizzlies from food. The black bear does not know it is not supposed to be as aggressive as grizzlies, nor does the grizzly bear know *its* reputation.

There are other natural enemies of the black bear, but they are much smaller than the bears. Bears in Yellowstone are attacked by ticks, mosquitos, lice, and other small pests, but rarely is a healthy bear seriously hurt by them. In the natural history of the grizzly bear I will discuss a number of other parasites that infect Yellowstone bears. Most of those that attack grizzlies also attack blacks, but on the average the blacks are not as seriously affected.

Bears produce several vocal sounds. Though not a true vocalization, the "jaw-popping," or teeth snapping, that often accompanies bluffs is an intentional bear noise that heightens the effect of the presentation. Sounds, at least in adult bears, are usually associated with actions; part of a communication system we need to study more. Perhaps the most often written-about bear sound, next to the cries of cubs, is the sudden expulsion of air that frequently occurs when the bear suddenly senses danger. Whether it is used to chase cubs up a tree or to warn an intruder, it is usually described as a "woof." It could be the result of surprise. In any case, it has often been mentioned by surprised hikers as their only warning of the bear before it fled or attacked. Sounds and other social behavior of bears are being studied nowadays for the very practical reason that the more we understand the way they communicate the better we will be prepared to react to them.

The aforementioned bluff is perhaps the most misunderstood trait of the black bear. The false charge, accompanied by growls, woofs, feet-stamping, and jaw snapping, is used against other wild animals and man. Bluffing often serves the bear's needs. Most bear-to-bear encounters can be settled by this sort of energetic conversation. Bear populations are rarely large enough to survive wholesale physical combats, and vocal showdowns are an acceptable alternative. One should not assume, however, that the black bear is a "coward," or a phony, because it pretends to do something it doesn't really plan to do. Not only can the bluff turn into a real charge, but bluffing itself is a fascinating and specialized activity, almost the equal of the birds who pretend to have a broken wing in order to lead predators from a nest.

People are inclined to judge wild animals by their own standards. A slow, fat, nearsighted individual is ridiculed, and so, at first glance, the bear is treated the same way. The black bear is slow for a good reason, and fast when it needs to be. It has equally good reasons for its other characteristics, and is, in fact, much better suited to its world than humans are to theirs. Furthermore, it is able to adjust itself to the human world and to survive the ceaseless spread of that world over its range. That adjustability may be the biggest single difference between the black bear and its entirely unlaughable cousin, the grizzly.

Chapter 6

The Grizzly Bear/ Physical Description

The grizzly bear, *Ursus arctos,* is a seldom-seen resident of Yellowstone Park and the surrounding wild lands. As of 1985, the Interagency Grizzly Bear Study Team, which has been studying the grizzly in Yellowstone since 1973, believed that there were at least 200 grizzly bears in the 5 million acres of land in and around the park. The bears are unaware of jurisdictional boundaries, and move from federal to state to private land in order to make use of the habitat's offerings of food and shelter.

Being a plains and mountain animal, the grizzly bear did not come to the notice of European settlers as early as did the black bear. Variations on the name began to appear in the late 1700s when accounts of a "grizzled" or "grizzle" bear were brought from what is now western Canada. It would appear that the first naming was inspired by the animal's coat colors rather than by its personality. By the time of the Lewis and Clark expedition, 1804-1806, partly because of that expedition's reports, the term "grizzly" had taken on its double meaning: grizzled hair and grizzly (often interchanged with grizly or grisly in the nineteenth century, all meaning gruesome or gory) character. The dictionary definition of "grizzled" includes such terms as "streaked," "flecked," and "mixed with gray."

The grizzled hair of the bear consists of dark brown fur with long "guard hairs" extending beyond the mat of fur. The guard hairs, whose tips are pale, give the coat a grizzled, or mixed, appearance. For this same reason the bear is often called the silvertip. This coat is not a predictable pattern, however, since grizzlies may be anything from almost-cream to black. Darker colors predominate, and quite a few bears are not uniform. They have lighter, grizzled, patches variously placed on the face, shoulders, saddle, or legs. As with black bears, a sow grizzly may give birth to three different-colored cubs in one litter.

Perhaps the most famous series of grizzly bear photographs in Yellowstone history, these show a large grizzly near a park dump. The three views provide an excellent portrait of a prime adult bear, an animal almost visibly confident in his world. N.P.S. photos.

Spring shedding, new growth, and the effects of climate cause noticeable change in an individual's color over a season. A dark new summer coat will often fade, another reason for pale shoulders and saddle. On the other hand, as the new coat grows and thickens, it may darken, so that a single bear might begin the season dark, shed its winter coat and appear lighter, then grow a new coat and darken again.

Adult Yellowstone grizzly bears stand 3½ to 4½ feet at the shoulders on all fours. The average nose-to-tail length of ten adult male grizzlies measured by the Interagency Study Team was 70.9 inches; the average of sixteen adult females was 62.7 inches. The back profile of a grizzly has two high points, one about midway between the tail and front shoulders, the other directly over the front shoulders. The shoulder hump, sometimes called the roach, is the result of a muscular arrangement that is different from that of black bears. It is prominent on most grizzly bears, and is a good means of identification.

Yellowstone grizzly bears were larger and more productive of young when the population was feeding regularly at dumps in the park. Pope, writing in 1923, reported a male Yellowstone grizzly weighing 916 pounds, and the heaviest grizzly handled by the Craighead research team in the 1960s weighed 1,120 pounds. Since the dumps have been closed, and possibly for additional environmental reasons including a drying climatic trend in the 1970s, the average size of Yellowstone grizzlies has decreased. The average fall weight of nineteen adult males handled by the Interagency Study Team was 489.8 pounds, and the average weight of twenty adult females was 319.3. The corresponding averages during the Craighead study were 674.7 and 367.4.

The grizzly's front legs appear longer than the hind ones. The body of the bear is smaller in diameter behind the front legs and grows thicker toward the belly, which seems almost to sag, giving the bear a bottom-heavy appearance.

The grizzly is plantigrade, walking flat-footed. The claws extend prominently beyond the hair of the feet, being especially visible on the front feet. Claws, rarely less than two inches long, curve sharply to serve in digging. Claw size is another distinguishing feature between grizzlies and blacks, whose claws are not easily seen from a distance.

First-time observers are often impressed with the size of the grizzly's head, which has a massiveness unlike the black's. The popular literature frequently refers to the "dish-shaped" profile of the grizzly, meaning that, when viewed from the side, the line from the brow to the nose is concave, with its low point in the middle. This is an unreliable indicator of species, as head shape varies from a very concave curve to a straight line similar to a black bear. Size, back profile, claws, and general massiveness are better guides to identification.

The nose, ears, and eyes benefit the grizzly about as they do the black. Under favorable conditions Yellowstone grizzlies are able to scent a ripe carcass from several miles away. The grizzly's ears are smaller and more rounded, in proportion to its head, than are the black bear's.

The grizzly has forty-two teeth, which take about two-and-a-half years to completely arrive in the head of a young bear.

The bear's tremendous complement of muscles permits amazing quickness and speeds in excess of twenty-five miles per hour. Bursts of such speed are useful to the adult animal both in hunting and fighting. Movement is on all four feet, and standing occurs only to improve vantage point or reach.

The strength and durability of the grizzly became legend in the nineteenth century, partly as a result of the primitive firearms of the day and partly because the bear is, indeed, very strong. Many stories have been told of grizzlies that "took a lot of killing," some even involving Yellowstone bears. Later we will turn to some of the stories, but for now we confine ourselves to natural examples. Grizzlies drag adult elk hundreds of yards, up and down rugged terrain. Their forelegs are powerful enough to break the neck of a steer or

The size of an adult grizzly bear is more easily appreciated when compared to these people preparing it for relocation. N.P.S. photo.

elk with one swat. And the bear is, in turn, strong enough to withstand those swats when directed at it by another bear.

Grizzly bears frequently live fifteen to twenty years in the wild. It appears that survival requires a level of health that usually includes the mating capacity; as with the black bear, and barring injury, once the animal no longer functions reproductively it has probably also lost the physical abilities it needs to live much longer. A European brown bear lived 47 years in captivity, but a Yellowstone grizzly 25 years old would be rare. The oldest bears reported by the Craigheads and the Interagency Study Team were 25.

The grizzly bear is superbly adapted to its world. None of its formidable equipment goes to waste. The animal is such a spectacular evolutionary achievement that it will always be regarded as one of Yellowstone's most exciting inhabitants. There is always the danger, in studying just one animal, of unconsciously removing it from its context. That danger is probably at its greatest with an animal like the grizzly. In the following account an effort has been made to resist glorification. The bear does not need to have its existence dramatized, and those who are interested in it will appreciate it best when it appears, in place, as part of the great Yellowstone wilderness.

Chapter 7

The Grizzly Bear/
Eating Habits

Bear food habits are inextricably bound up with bear habitat; bear use of available habitat is in great part the result of food availability, keeping always in mind the bear's need for certain kinds of shelter. Here I will concentrate on food for the moment, and turn to habitat use in the "lifestyle" section, but ecologists don't have the luxury of separating food preferences and habitat use so conveniently. One of the most revealing elements of modern grizzly bear research is that so much of it has concentrated not on studying the bears themselves but on painstaking study, including a careful mapping of the entire grizzly bear habitat in and around Yellowstone, of where the bears live.

Changes in management in Yellowstone have altered grizzly bear food habits in many ways. I've already mentioned that the closing of the garbage dumps (the largest were closed by 1971, and several smaller ones near the park were closed during the 1970s or early 1980s) deprived the bears of a food source they were quite accustomed to, one that appears to have allowed them to grow larger and produce more young than they do now. But the closing of the dumps was only one part of an overall change in management that will be discussed at length later in this book. Various elements of the Yellowstone wilderness setting were permitted to seek what are believed to be natural balances with their surroundings, and in several cases these other changes are affecting grizzly bears. The trout population of Yellowstone Lake was in a collapsed state in the 1950s and 1960s; stricter regulations have restored those fish to something more approaching historic levels, and huge numbers of fish are now available to bears in the spring when they move into the lake's many tributaries to spawn. Elk numbers were suppressed for many years in Yellowstone; throughout the 1960s the northern elk herd was

41

kept to 5,000 or less most of the time. That herd has been allowed to grow in an effort to restore it to some natural equilibrium with its range, and since 1970 it has increased more than threefold. Current bear research in Yellowstone shows that grizzlies are preying on elk and making heavy use of winter-killed elk carcasses in the spring. Bison, for many years also kept to a low number, have also increased, and grizzlies make good use of bison carcasses in the spring as well. A natural fire policy was adopted in Yellowstone in the early 1970s that has great promise for maintaining and improving grizzly bear habitat in the park.

The point of listing all these changes that have occurred in the last fifteen years is to make it clear that in many ways the grizzlies of Yellowstone are not yet in a stable relationship with their environment, and though the research project that has been going on since 1973 has provided a wealth of useful information, the portrait it provides of the bear is not a finished one. The elk are still adjusting. The fish population is not wholly recovered. The bison may have reached their practical limit, but other animal and plant populations are in flux. As important, human use of the Yellowstone area is changing. The summary of bear habits that follows is therefore somewhat tentative. Scientists have a pretty good idea now of what Yellowstone's grizzly bears do and how they live, but scientists are cautious about suggesting they have all the answers. There was great scientific disagreement over just what closing the dumps did to the bear population, and there is bound to be continued uncertainty over just what the new conditions—no dumps, more elk and bison, more fish, and so on—will bring to the grizzlies of Yellowstone. But, after twelve years of study, the Interagency Study Team has given us an extraordinarily valuable picture of what grizzly bear life is like now.

The Yellowstone grizzly is primarily a vegetarian. Some years more than 80% of its diet is plant matter, and it could probably survive on even more. Most of the year it is the location of various preferred plant foods that will dictate the location of the bears; sometimes a single plant food can have a tremendous effect on the movements of most of Yellowstone's bear population.

After a week or two of gradual adjustment to renewed activity after leaving the den, bears often seek out carrion or the first few available plants, whether they are dried plants from the previous year or new succulent ones. Succulence is the key factor in bear choice of plants, so bears are drawn, at each season, to plants at that stage of growth when their succulence is greatest. This has a number of implications, one being that as the growing season for plants ends, bears are drawn to the last fresh vegetation, which may be in areas of greater moisture, such as river banks, seeps, marshes, and springs.

One safe generalization about bear diet is that their choices increase as the season goes on. The Interagency Study Team has found that diversity of food types in the grizzly bear diet increases from emergence in March or April until September, when it begins to decrease slightly until denning.

Depending upon where the bear had denned, its first feeding will vary greatly. It may settle into Pelican Valley for a few weeks of feeding on freshly thawed bison carcasses, or it may be in the Firehole Valley feeding on elk carcasses, or it may be taking advantage of some other opportunity.

Yellowstone is blessed with an abundance of animal life, and it is in spring that the large mammals—elk, bison, moose, deer, sheep, and pronghorn—are most often available to bears. The animals provide essential protein to bears in several ways during this season. A harsh winter results in hundreds of dead elk and fewer (but larger) dead bison. The grizzly is only one of many scavengers who compete for this carrion. In some years, the bear's survival may depend in good part on this carrion supply, and in others the bears may ignore carrion in favor of an unusually good crop of some favored plant.

Grizzly bears share spring carrion, such as this elk, with other scavengers, including magpies and coyotes. N.P.S. photo.

THE GRIZZLY / EATING HABITS   43

As with the black bear, grizzlies do not seem to prefer a rank carcass, but it will perhaps be easier to find. If a rank and a fresh carcass are found side-by-side, the grizzly may use the rank one first because it will have the added attraction of maggots (the condition of the meat does not appear to be a major factor in the bear's decision). One grizzly was seen passing up carrion to hunt for standing elk, exhibiting a preference for meat it killed itself.

Another way the bears get animal protein in the spring is from live prey. Winter-weakened elk and newborn elk, bison, and other ungulates, fall prey to bears, sometimes in good numbers. A study of bear predation on elk in a western portion of the park showed that some years grizzly predation there accounted for as many as half of the spring elk deaths. Of course it isn't long before the elk that are too weak to recover are all gone, and the calves are either lost or grow strong enough to escape, so the bears have only a short time to get their share.

Grizzlies can be determined hunters. Individuals or pairs can chase a herd at an easy lope, identifying, and then taking, weak stragglers with a sudden burst of speed. Elk driven into deep snow or water are often too weak or frightened to resist. In some cases the elk is so weakened, from the winter or the chase, that the bear has only to walk up to it and kill it. Grizzly killing methods have been described by Glen Cole, who studied them in the early 1970s:

> Bears pulled down running elk by rearing on their hind legs, grasping an animal on or over the rump, and apparently allowing their weight to collapse the elk's hindquarters. Bears then grabbed and vigorously shook the elk's neck with their jaws, rolled the elk over on its back, and opened the abdomen. The neck was grabbed and shaken again if the elk continued to struggle.

Another approach was observed early one spring near Lava Creek, by a snowplow operator who surprised an elk and bear in mortal combat:

> The two combatants were fighting at close quarters, the elk fighting for his life, the bear endeavoring to kill, probably for food. The bear had the elk gripped around the neck with his forepaws and was endeavoring to throw the elk, after the fashion of a rodeo performer bull-dogging a steer. The elk in turn was endeavoring to get free and by so doing was shoving the bear backward along the road. Thus from my vantage point I had thought that the elk was being led by someone.
>
> I stopped the snowplow and taking my camera started to try and photograph the incident. This action on my part disrupted the battle

temporarily, for the elk broke loose from the bear and started running away. He seemed partially stunned from his encounter. The bear ran right beside him and kept reaching out his paw now and then to slap the elk on the side of the head. The elk by this time appeared to be about exhausted for his tongue was lolling out and he seemed wobbly.

The slapping action of the bear soon caused the elk to stop and fight again, this time charging the bear, which reared to his hind legs again. The bull's head struck the grizzly in the stomach and the bear then grabbed the elk around the neck. With all of his strength the elk would bunt the bear, each time raising the bear's hind feet from the ground. Shortly the elk became so tired that the bear's weight brought him to his knees.

While all of this was happening I had approached quite near the animals and suddenly the Grizzly sensed my presence. He reared up, sniffed, snorted, and allowed the elk to get up and stagger off into the woods. The Grizzly became frightened and ran away apparently suffering none from the elk's efforts to protect itself.

Yet another approach was observed by William Rush while watching elk on Specimen Ridge in the 1930s. He was watching a line of elk climb the snowy ridge near a forested slope:

> Without warning a great furry ball of grizzly bear hurtled out of the forest into the middle of the moving line. The terror-stricken elk tried to run but they could not. Some of them jumped to one side of the beaten trail. Their sharp hooves cut through the crusted snow and they floundered helpless, unable to go farther. Some crawled on top of those ahead in the trail, piling up in a frantic heap. Others turned and tried to go back. Panic held them in a milling throng while the bear picked out a cow that had fallen on her side. With a swift rush the grizzly was upon her, grabbing her nose with a long-clawed paw while it sank saber-like teeth into her neck and ripped open her belly with the other front paw.

Surprisingly, the bear then deserted its kill and carried off a calf, leaving the terrified elk to go on their way.

From these examples it is obvious the procedure varies greatly. An adult grizzly is strong enough to kill with blows from its forepaws, but more often it employs both teeth and forepaws.

The most effective hunters observed by Cole were young adults, not because they are more agile but because older, dominant bears have learned to wait until the younger ones have made a kill and then chase them from it.

Other large animals are also included in the bear diet. Mature bison and

Grizzly bear investigating bison carcass. N.P.S. photo.

moose have relatively little to fear from Yellowstone grizzlies, but are occasionally taken when weak or old. There is one reported case in Yellowstone of an adult bear killed by a bison, presumably the result of an unsuccessful attack by the bear. Encounters of this sort are probably rare, as the animals would more often steer clear of one another.

We can assume that mule deer are occasionally taken (at least one successful stalk has been observed in Yellowstone, by Dale Nuss), but bighorn sheep and pronghorn are probably rarely available to grizzlies, and would have little to fear if pursued. Sheep take refuge in cliffs, and pronghorn are much too swift to be caught in the open by bears. Any of the above would naturally be consumed as carrion, and their calves, lambs, and fawns would be a special treat for a bear who found one.

Grizzlies often save food for later, dragging a partially consumed carcass to a suitable location and covering it with brush or digging a hole and burying it. On rare occasions such "caching" involves quite a lot of work, as the hole may be several feet deep.

Once the spring meat-feeding has ended, the bear's protein diet is replaced with one more heavily based on carbohydrates. As May progresses, bears, which have been aware of early plants such as springbeauty, turn more exclusively to plant foods. Grasses are the most important of these, and it comes as a disappointment to many of the grizzly's more romantic admirers that the bear spends most of its time grazing. According to Steve Mealey's 1973-1974 study, grizzlies prefer "dense stands" at least three inches tall: "Grizzlies usually grazed with a sideways motion of the head which placed the muzzle perpendicular to the vegetation. The food appeared to be grasped and plucked." Other favorites are clover, horsetail, dandelion, and biscuitroot.

Throughout the season bears show great interest in whitebark pine nuts, an especially important food in the fall but one of interest to them whenever they can locate the nuts, whether in small mammal caches or when the pine cones disintegrate in October and November and the nuts are most available.

In fact, small mammals cache a variety of bear foods, including the pine nuts and an assortment of roots, corms, and forbs, that bears find in the process of their routine grazing and digging. The bear's good fortune is sometimes compounded when they find not only the cache but the animal that made it.

Throughout the summer bears also eat insects, especially ants and grasshoppers. All sorts of special opportunities present themselves, ranging from licking numbed insects from snowbanks where they mistakenly landed to concentrating on heavy emergences of moths, an activity reported from a grizzly bear study in western Montana.

Strawberries.

Whitebark pine cones.

Low red buckleberries.

Small mammals are highly prized by grizzlies when they can get them. Passing over such occasionals and accidentals as birds (and eggs), frogs, and small bears, we come to a few favorites. The yellow-bellied marmot, or rock-chuck, is a sizeable morsel. Marmots live in rocky burrows, but a grizzly may spend an hour or more excavating hundreds of pounds of earth and stone to get at a family of the chubby little animals. Smaller rodents, such as voles and pocket gophers, are another benefit of the grizzly's devotion to meadow grazing. The presence of the rodents, which rarely make up more than 3% of the bear's total diet, is enough to attract and hold grizzlies to an area as long as the succulent plants are common. The bear feeds on the plants while hunting the rodents, which serve as little more than an occasional treat. An enthusiastic grizzly will dig up thousands of square feet of ground if there are enough rodents to keep his interest. The "grazing" grizzly is actually an open-minded shopper.

In early June grizzly bears begin to concentrate along the tributaries of Yellowstone Lake to take advantage of one of the park's great protein concentrations, the spawning runs of cutthroat trout. Literally hundreds of tons of trout move into these streams much as salmon do into many rivers of Alaska where bears also concentrate. Fishing behavior has been studied in various parts of North America, so that some of the traditional beliefs about bears fishing have been disregarded. Bears rarely slap fish from the water, as they are often depicted doing in outdoor artwork. Slapping has been observed in Yellowstone but more often bears use their front feet to pin the trout to the bottom of the stream. Bears, unlike some animals, will use both paws and mouth to secure their food, and though large Alaskan salmon may be caught by bears using only their mouths, Yellowstone trout require quick stepping. The fish, usually less than eighteen inches long, are trapped by a quick paw (either on the bottom or against the bank) and then grasped with the mouth. An interesting sidelight of one Yellowstone study was that cubs seemed as skilled at fishing as adults, which is different from most other studies which reported that cubs go through an awkward training period.

Usually the trout have returned to the lake by the middle of August and bears have moved on to other foods or returned to the staples mentioned earlier. In August berries start to assume a more important role in bear diet. Yellowstone is not known for the quality of berry production of some other parts of the Rocky Mountains, but some years bears benefit from sugar-rich strawberries, huckleberries, buffaloberries, and grouse whortleberries.

By September and October, with the decline of succulent vegetation and the increased availability of pine nuts, grizzlies concentrate on the latter. Not since spring, when the meat of ungulates was the dominant food item, have the bears concentrated so single-mindedly on one type of food. The pine nuts are extraordinarily important to the bears, not only for the fat that will help prepare them for denning but because in years when the pine nut crop fails the bears amble off to find other food and frequently get in trouble with people. A direct correlation has been noticed in recent years between man-caused grizzly deaths in a given year and the quality of its pine nut crop.

Though primarily herbivores, bears are not able to use plant foods as efficiently as are elk or other grazers. They cannot get as many nutrients from the plants, nor can they use as much dried material, as can elk, bison, and so on. The bear's answer to its lower efficiency is increased consumption: running a great quantity of material through its system to satisfy its needs. And, of course, supplementing its diet with more highly digestible animal material. The key to the "success" of the Yellowstone grizzly as a feeder is

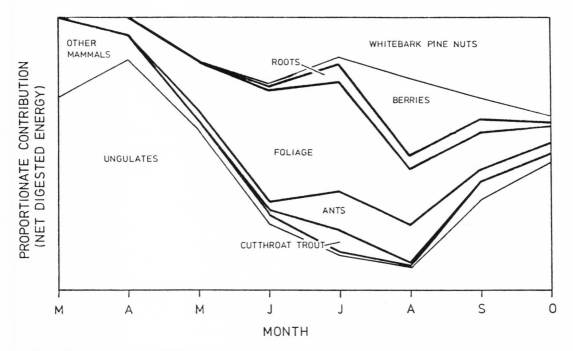

A layer diagram showing which food items contribute to the grizzly bear's net digested energy, month by month. Based on the research findings of the Interagency Study Team, the diagram reveals the bear's greater dependence, in spring and fall, on fewer types of food. Courtesy of the Interagency Grizzly Bear Study Team.

its flexibility. As long as there exists an ample supply of the succulent vegetation that serves as the foundation of its diet, the bear can fill in nutritional gaps from the smorgasbord of plant and animal foods Yellowstone provides in such great variety.

Though I'll pay more attention to bear movements and habitat use later, it's worth pointing out here that grizzlies, even in the best of feeding conditions, seem to have some interesting tendencies to look around. Like the black bear, it pays for the grizzly to keep moving, and unless the food is a carcass, or a particularly easy trout stream, or an exceptional berry crop, the bear may move on after a while. Dean Graham's 1975-1976 study of grizzly food habits in Pelican and Hayden Valleys in central Yellowstone reported other evidence of this mobility:

> Eighty-four percent of grizzly sign was associated with feeding activity. Although some dig sites were quite extensive (up to one-tenth hectares), most feeding sites covered less than 45 square meters. Bears would dig, grub and graze in these microsite locations and then move to an adjacent microsite or to a site a considerable distance away before resuming their feeding activity. On two occasions I observed a bear feeding in a clover patch of less than 35 square meters. After foraging about thirty minutes, the bears left the site which still supplied an abundance of readily available and highly nutritional clover. They traveled about 100m into a *Festuca idahoensis/Deschampsia caespitosa* habitat type where they began grubbing for yampa roots.

This urge to move, even though the next pasture is no greener than the one being abandoned, has been reported for bears in other parts of North America.

Chapter 8

The Grizzly Bear/
Denning

 The grizzly's food habits are designed to prepare it for several months of fasting. By fall the bear is putting on a layer of fat that approaches eight inches in thickness in places. The fat serves as it serves the black bear. In fact, grizzlies follow essentially the same course as blacks in the whole denning process—weight loss during denning, further loss in early spring, and then a summer and fall of feeding and weight increase until shortly before denning. In terms of the basic metabolic processes involved, grizzlies differ little from blacks in the character of their winter sleep. There are several differences in the actual practice of denning, however, and so it is well worth the time to examine the winter denning of the grizzly.

Grizzlies put a great deal of work and advance preparation into winter denning. Grizzlies are usually burrowing denners in Yellowstone—they create an entire cave to suit their purposes.

The first denning preparations have been observed in summer in some northern areas, but in Yellowstone bears do not begin to dig their dens until much later. The Interagency Study Team reported that the average entrance date of seventy radio-collared Yellowstone grizzly bears was November 9, the earliest being a pregnant female who denned on September 28 and the latest being a three-and-a-half-year-old female who did not den until December 21. This female, incidentally, provided an unusual record of denning behavior:

> This female denned with another slightly larger bear, possibly her mother. We are not aware of any documented precedents where 2 bears of this age denned together or where a bear was 4 years old before estrangement.

51

The Craighead study reported that grizzly bears seemed to den almost in unison during snowstorms, suggesting that among other things this helped obscure their location, but the Interagency Study Team's data suggested that bears were denning more individually. Pregnant females denned earliest.

Grizzly bears spend anywhere from one to three weeks near the densite. Bears often seem to return to the same general area each year to den; site selection might be an instinctive process, but it appears that younger, less experienced bears are less able to locate a good site.

Dens are usually dug into slopes, most of which are between thirty and sixty degrees. The slope site has several advantages. First, it is easier to remove the dug-out material because it just rolls downhill. Second, a moderate slope provides the bear with the easiest way of putting a reasonably thick "roof" over its head; digging a cave on level ground would require a much longer entrance tunnel, and digging on a very steep slope would be difficult because of the awkwardness of approach. Third, the sleeping chamber can hold its heat better if the tunnel does not rise from the chamber. Some bears actually build the entrance tunnel so that its mouth is lower than the sleeping chamber, thus creating a "heat trap," but only six of twenty-eight dens examined by the Interagency Study Team were of that type.

There are no absolute rules about where a bear will put its den, but generally they prefer northern exposures with at least a moderate tree cover of whitebark pine or subalpine fir. A few grizzlies in Yellowstone have used natural caves or even hollow trees. Dens have been observed at many elevations from 6,500 feet to over 10,000 but most fall between 8,000 and 9,000.

Grizzlies are energetic diggers, not only in feeding and in caching of food but in denning. Unlike black bears, who are opportunists about denning, grizzlies rarely take advantage of some other animal's burrow that they can modify. Even after the den is completed, the bear sometimes goes through a "ritualized" digging, arranging its bedding or just straightening whatever seems out of order. This apparent need to dig has been seen as an instinctive necessity, as has the grizzly's reluctance to reuse the same den, though that reluctance is probably also partly the result of the number of dens that cave in during spring thaws.

About half the time the bear digs its den under the roots of a tree, using the spreading root system as a sort of roof support. About the same number of dens are simply dug into slopes with no roof support, and a few are dug under fallen trees. The chamber of a dug den is usually just a little larger than the bear. Typically there is a small opening (perhaps between two tree

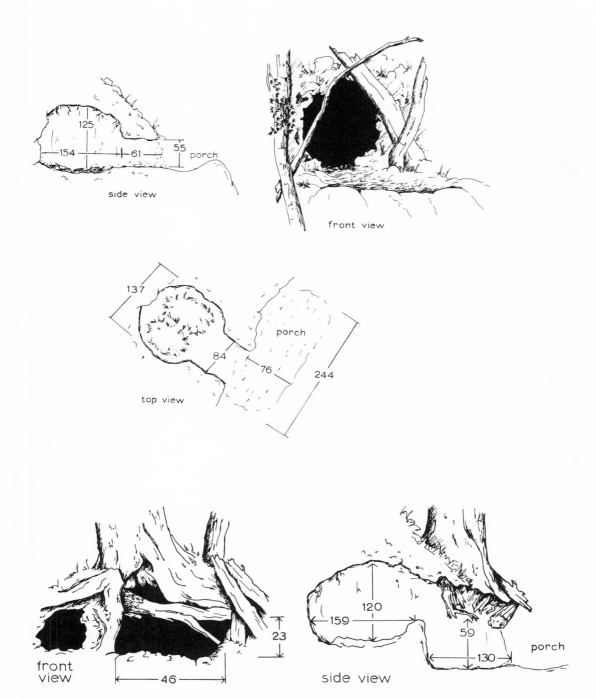

Den diagrams of grizzly bears. (All measurements in cm.) Courtesy of Interagency Grizzly Bear Study Team.

THE GRIZZLY / DENNING 53

roots), a short passageway (1 to 5 feet in length), and the chamber itself. The average size of ten chambers measured in the Craighead studies in the 1960s was 56 × 53 × 37 inches. The Craighead team determined that, though digging may go on intermittently for weeks, the biggest part is done in a short stretch of a week or less.

Once the den is completed, and the hundreds of pounds of soil and rock have been removed, final preparations include gathering of bedding. Spruce and fir boughs, mosses, and grasses are used to line the den floor. These materials are more than just an added comfort to the bear. They add warmth. Just as the air in loose pockets in thermal underwear hold small amounts of warmed air, the openings in the boughs hold air warmed by the bear's body, part of a very shallow "microclimate" that surrounds the bear in its den.

The metabolic changes that occur in the system of the grizzly do not differ significantly from those that occur in black bears. The bear ceases to consume, and heart rate, respiration, and body temperature are all reduced. Sleep is deep, but the bear can be roused.

Even in a subject where great variations in scientific findings seem to be the rule, the observations of weight losses by denning grizzlies are remarkably variable. Biologist Albert Pearson recorded losses of from 30 to 43% in southern Yukon grizzlies (who den a month or more longer than Yellowstone bears). A much lower percentage weight loss, more in agreement with figures already given for black bears, may be more typical for Yellowstone grizzlies. Unquestionably, much additional weight is lost in the first few weeks of post-emergence activity.

Length of denning time of grizzly bears varies by almost 100%. Radio-collared grizzlies in the 1970s stayed in the den as short as 86 days and as long as 211 days. The average for males was 113 days. For single females and those that denned with young it was 132 days, and for females who gave birth in the den it was 170 days. That means that males emerged first, usually in late February or the month following. Females with new cubs usually didn't appear until April. Though other studies have suggested that snow depth at the densite had a direct effect on when bears emerged, the most recent Yellowstone study does not show any such connection.

Emergence from the den should be of special interest to Yellowstone visitors because the springtime grizzly bear, the carrion seeker of magnificent appetite, is also the most visible grizzly bear. If you can get to the park in April and May, and if the snow will let you drive through, you have the best chance of seeing a grizzly in Yellowstone.

Though they seem devoted to expending lots of energy in constructing a den, grizzly bears sometimes do reuse an old den. Of thirty-five dens examined by the Interagency Study Team, ten had been reused. In two cases the den was used by the same bear two years in a row, in one case it was used by different bears in different years, and in seven cases there was no way of knowing if the same or different bears had reused the den.

Chapter 9

The Grizzly Bear/
Mating and Cub Growth

 The society of grizzly bears, widely advertised as being unhealthy for humans, is probably less healthy for the bears. Grizzlies kill many more of their own kind than they do humans (though both figures are quite low), under circumstances we will explore more fully later. The point is brought up here to introduce and illuminate the mating season, one truly social season in the life of an adult bear.

Grizzly bears in Yellowstone mate from late May to mid-July, with most activity occurring in June. We can assume that the same biological preparations take place in grizzlies as in blacks. Reproductive behavior of grizzlies has been studied in several places, but perhaps nowhere as exhaustively as in Yellowstone, so we have a wealth of information on the proceedings.

As is the case in our knowledge of bear sizes and weights, our understanding of bear mating habits has been broadened by the closing of the park's dumps. Grizzly bears do not mate as young, or produce as large litters, as they did when their diet was strengthened by available garbage. Later in this book the consequences of these changes will be considered, but for the moment some comparisons are in order.

During the Craighead study, nine of sixteen sow grizzlies first became pregnant in their fifth year. Some three-and-one-half-year-olds experienced estrus, and some of these even mated with males, but none gave birth to cubs. Some other sows did not have their first pregnancy until later, even their eighth or ninth year. During the more recent Interagency Study Team study, in its first nine years data was gathered on twelve bears. Only two became pregnant at age five, and seven more became pregnant at age six. The peak year for first pregnancy is now one year later.

Similar changes have occurred for size of litter. During the years of the

56

Craighead study (1959-1970), the average litter size was 2.24. From 1974 to 1982, the average litter size had dropped to 1.9.

There has been great disagreement over just what these numbers mean. Much of Part II of this book is devoted to considering the controversy over grizzly management and the science upon which it depends. I'm going to concentrate here on the process of mating, rather than on its effect on human attitudes and politics.

The grizzly bear is probably an induced ovulator, meaning that ovulation does not take place without some sexual stimulus. A sow that does not encounter a boar, even if she is not accompanied by cubs, might not ovulate at all. The male bear takes the initiative, seeking out the female and pursuing her until she is ready to mate or until he is chased off by another male. Males may accompany a female for a few days, or they may remain together throughout the entire estrus cycle of the female. The estrus cycle varies. Those three-and-one-half-year-olds that came into heat during the Craighead study were usually receptive only a few days. Older females remained in heat for two to four weeks. There appears to be a break in the middle of grizzly estrus, when the female is not of interest to males. The break lasts only a few days.

When given the opportunity grizzly bears are promiscuous. In circumstances where bears are concentrated by food, such as at a dump or a salmon stream, both sows and boars may mate with several bears. Since the dumps were closed, Yellowstone bears are less often concentrated during mating season than they used to be, and for this reason a lengthy pair-bond is probably more likely because other mates are less easily found. Only about one-third of the adult females are receptive in any given year, the others having cubs or yearlings to take care of. Under these circumstances, it has been suggested that the best interests of the population are probably served by a male and a female investing all their energy in each other rather than in exploring for new mates.

The receptive female, having attracted a mate who in turn has proven his ability to defend and breed her, exhibits certain behavior toward him. His approaches in the courtship stage include rubbing, licking, and smelling, and physical contact is evidently quite important to him, even if only to rest quietly at her side. Once she is receptive and he has become fully aroused, his behavior is predictable. Maurice Hornocker, who studied grizzly mating habits during the Craighead study, has described the male's activity:

> Sexually aroused males were easily recognized, even at a distance.
> Some variation in behavior existed, but generally they exhibited a charac-

teristic stiff-legged, swaggering walk. When approaching another bear this walk was exaggerated, the neck was bowed and the head was held low. They salivated profusely and frequently urinated on the belly and hind legs.

The female's response involves a demonstration of submission, usually accomplished by cowering—lowering of the head and shoulders in an obviously subordinate stance, not unlike scolded dogs behave.

A comparison with human mating is irresistible because the similarities are so great. Various individuals, with various personalities, drives, status in the "pecking order," and physical abilities, respond to the mating instinct in different ways. Chemical/metabolic functions add more dimensions, so that each participant is unique.

Actual copulation has been measured from five minutes to an hour, with an average between fifteen and twenty minutes. The boar, mounting the sow and grasping her sides with his front legs, may stay motionless for some moments. Nibbling and biting exchanges take place, which sometimes look more aggressive than they are. It is good to remember, though, how near these bears are to enmity. The mating season tolerance is a shaky contract; it works but it must not work too well, for the sow needs a sharply developed antipathy to the boar if her cubs are to survive.

The mating couple is mobile, the sow can graze or shuffle or kneel on her front legs, and the whole process may be repeated several times in one day. Free-roaming grizzlies have not been observed continuously (day and night) for several days during mating, so our knowledge of details is far from complete.

If the pair has joined for the duration of the female's estrus, the boar leaves as soon as she has gone out of heat. Until then he attends and even herds her, sacrificing his appetite for food to his greater urge to mate. Sows seem to be able to keep producing young as long as they remain healthy. The Craighead study, which produced more information on grizzly breeding habits than any study since, and upon which most of this discussion has been based, reported a Yellowstone sow giving birth at age twenty-two-and-one-half. The Interagency Study Team reported a sow giving birth to one cub at age twenty-five.

Grizzlies are very slow to reproduce. A grizzly bear population is more easily hurt by heavy mortality than a black bear population because grizzlies are slower to replace themselves. Black bear sows can rear another family every second year while many grizzly sows keep their cubs with them through two winters.

Upon completion of the mating season, the sow is once again alone. Embryonic delay occurs, and the sow carries the free blastocyst until November, at which time it implants in the uterine wall and normal fetal development resumes. The sow probably is in her den by the time the fetus begins to grow. As noted, pregnant sows den a few weeks earlier than lone adults, and take special care to provide soft bedding.

Unlike the black bear, the first litter of a sow grizzly is more often than not two cubs. They are born in late January or early February, not much larger than black bear cubs, less than a foot long and weighing about a pound or a pound and a half. They appear naked but in fact are covered by very fine short hair. Their eyes are closed, and stay closed for five or six weeks. In most respects the pre-emergence life of black and grizzly cubs is similar. The mother provides warmth and nourishment while the cub passes through its most helpless stage.

The average litter size in Yellowstone, as observed in the free-ranging population in the last several years, is about 1.9 cubs per sow. There is one reasonably well documented case of a sow with five new cubs in Yellowstone,

Grizzly cubs in their first summer. N.P.S. photos.

Young grizzly bears occasionally have a "collar" of lighter-colored hair. N.P.S. photo.

but two is most typical. Both Craighead and Interagency Study Team work revealed that there are usually more males than females. In the Craighead study, the ratio was about 59% males to 41% females. In the first few years of the Interagency Study Team study, 1975-1979, the ratio was 71% males to 29% females, but that has evened out considerably, so that from 1975 to 1984 the ratio was 55% male to 45% female. These figures are all subject to some uncertainty because they are based on relatively small sample sizes. By the time of adulthood, the ratio approaches one to one, so the imbalance seems to work itself out by the time the cubs are four or five years old. The imbalance may be nature's way of correcting for the greater mobility of the young males; they tend to travel farther and thus are more vulnerable to a variety of dangers.

Cubs weigh between five and ten pounds when, in April or May, their mother leads them from the den. Sows often establish daybeds near the den, and make forays to and from it for some days, taking the cubs along on gradually increasing trips.

Cub life is full of adventure and surprise. The cubs follow their mother's lead, striking off on small explorations of their own, tumbling into all sorts of mischief. Cub education was described for the black bear, as a training by example and experience. The scene is heartwarming and charming. The cubs play, fight, climb, and grow, stopping now and then to nurse contentedly (a humming noise has been heard from nursing cubs). The family association, with all its lessons, is at the heart of the adult bear's character. The sow's feeding habits become the cubs'. Her job is to find food for the whole family, and presumably each new food she introduces them to is a lesson for their future.

The cubs take quickly to a partial diet of solids, though these are not preferred to milk. In fact most cubs are not entirely weaned until sometime during their second summer. It seems that no feeding takes place during denning, but the sow is able to produce some milk the following year, and one Alaskan sow was observed nursing cubs following their second denning.

Grizzly cubs frequently stay with their mother for two winters, going on their own in the spring of their third year. The Craighead study showed that about 50% of Yellowstone's grizzly bear cubs remained the extra year with their mother. This obviously has some effects on the cubs. Cubs staying that extra year with the mother are going to be larger, when weaned and abandoned, than cubs left on their own a year earlier, since they have the advantages of mother's milk *and* her help with foraging. Too, an extra year of experience with the sow might make them better food-finders. One would expect, therefore, that the two-and-one-half-year-old weaners would dominate the population after a few years. It does not seem to work that way, perhaps because the sows who wean their cubs at one-and-one-half years are capable of breeding more often and therefore keep producing more cubs than the other sows can. In recent years, 50% of those bears weaned as cubs did not survive to adulthood.

There are other effects on individual cubs. A one-and-one-half-year-old on its own is likely to be less assertive, more wary, than the larger two-and-one-half-year-old, and can be expected to retain that trait for some years. Subtle differences like these are hard to measure, but we do know that an aggressive sow usually passes that trait along to her cubs. It also seems that a sow with only one cub forms a closer bond with it (and in fact serves as a playmate for it) than that same sow would if she had two or more cubs.

Yellowstone grizzly cubs have little chance of surviving if they are orphaned. Some may make it through their first winter alone, but very few will survive the yearling year.

By the end of their first summer, grizzly cubs begin to lose some of their cub appearance. N.P.S. photo.

The sow-cub bond is weakened by the time the cub becomes a yearling. As the young bear becomes more independent and self-sufficient, the sow is less solicitous and protective. The family may endure for two years as a group, but by the end of that time they have often grown apart enough that the final separation takes place quite casually.

Adoption and interchange of cubs, though not common, has been observed in some circumstances. Sometimes the cubs of two sows will have the opportunity to play together (not a common opportunity in Yellowstone now), and actually mix, leaving with the wrong mother (it has been seen, for example, along Alaskan salmon streams, where the mothers are busy fishing). One case of this sort in Yellowstone resulted in one of the two sows assuming responsibility for all cubs. Now that grizzlies do not learn to tolerate one another as they did at dumps, such an event is unlikely, and even then it was not typical. Orphaned cubs have been physically rebuked by strange sows they tried to follow.

Weaning and abandonment occurs in the spring, about a week before mating season begins. The cubs are often reluctant to part company with one another, so they may spend that summer together and even den together. One unusual case in Yellowstone, of a pair of cubs living together for eight years, was reported by naturalist Milton Skinner in the 1920s.

By their first fall, the cubs will weigh between 60 and 70 pounds. The following fall, their weight will have more than doubled. The average of ten yearlings weighed between 1975 and 1982 was more than 157 pounds. In the fall of the following year they will average more than 220, and the males will begin to weigh more than the females. Eight three-year-old males averaged 376.5 pounds, while three females averaged 230. Individual variations are considerable even at this age, as suggested by the average weight of five five-year-old males, which was only 289 pounds, a significant decline from the three-year-olds' average. One problem with such averages is that the number of bears measured is too small to make really accurate evaluations.

It appears that in the present grizzly population in Yellowstone the most dangerous time for a young bear is between the time it is weaned and the time it reaches four years of age. Its first year or two it has the protection and help of its mother. Once on its own it is without an established range of its own and is also without the savvy and experience needed to take care of itself as well as it should. The bears that survive those first two years alone are the ones who avoid getting into trouble with humans, bigger bears, and other predators, and who have best learned their mother's lessons about food and shelter.

From the time they are five until they enter their teens, Yellowstone grizzly bears are at their best. After age twelve their odds of not surviving a given year are greater. Very few reach their late teens.

Chapter 10

The Grizzly Bear/ Lifestyle

Grizzly bears spend almost all of their time searching for and consuming food. Though to the casual observer the bear's feeding behavior may appear random, it is not. Yellowstone offers the bear many foods in many places and at many times, and all the offerings vary from year to year. A mild winter means fewer winterkilled elk. A dry summer means a failed pine nut crop or a poor berry crop. Bears, through a combination of experience and instinct, have adapted to take as full advantage of their varying menu as possible. A grizzly bear may not know at some given time just exactly what it will be eating in an hour, but it is where it is that day for a very good reason, the reason being that the feeding opportunities are the best there of anywhere in its range.

The size and shape of a grizzly bear's range, that is, the area of land it uses in the course of its life over several years, is the result of nutritional need. When there were dumps in Yellowstone, grizzlies had far less need to move great distances in search of food. When the dumps ceased to contribute to the bear's nutritional budget, the bears had to move more. The average male grizzly in Yellowstone today has a home range 7.5 times as large as a similar male back when dumps were open. Females have ranges 2.5 times as large. The average home range of an adult male grizzly in the park, as reported by the Interagency Study Team, is about 761 square miles. Individual adult males have ranges as large as 1,250 square miles and as small as 291 square miles. The average range of adult females is about 337 square miles, with extremes of 565 and 142. Those range sizes are affected by many things, and the most important is how good the available food sources are. A grizzly bear with a huge range, say one of over 1,000 square miles, is not necessarily an unusually large bear; it is important that bear needs are not confused with human ambition for territory. It is just as likely that the bear with the largest range is one that must look the hardest in that range for good things to eat. In terms of survival chances, it is often the case that the bear with the small range is the best off; it obviously is finding what it needs to get along without having to travel great distances and increase the chances it will run into enemies or accidents. It is able to feed, sleep, reproduce, and den without as much risk-taking as the more mobile bear.

It takes scientists several years to develop a fairly reliable idea of a bear's home range because the bear does not use that range the same way each year; all the variables mentioned so far, including weather's effects on food availability, presence or absence of potential mates, and shelter opportunities, play a role in keeping bear life dynamic. Where the bear goes during its waking seasons is something not even the bear knows until the time comes to go.

The Interagency Study Team's many reports on bear activities have revealed some important general patterns in bear habitat use. Bears tend to use gradually higher elevations as the spring and summer progress. They traveled farthest in dry years, and least far in wet years. They were less mobile in spring and fall, and most mobile in summer. These general rules fit their food habits nicely. In spring, many bears emerge from their dens to find carrion, a food that requires less travel than most vegetation types (many bears now are selecting den sites in areas of spring carcass concentrations). In fall, once again bears concentrate heavily on a few food types, especially pine nuts, and once again they are set loose to wander great distances if those few food types are in short supply. As summer wears on, bears seek out succulent vegetation, which they find at progressively higher altitudes. Dramatic failure — or unusual success — of any given food can alter the movement pattern. For example, when pine nuts do not materialize in sufficient quantities, the bear's flexibility as a feeder is its best hope for survival on a day-to-day basis.

The daily habits of the bear are not as simple as is often reported in the popular literature. Grizzly bears have often been characterized as meadow animals that favor fairly open habitat. They do indeed favor meadows, but in a certain way. What bears often prefer most is a fairly small "mosaic" of habitat types that gives them regular access to non-forested habitats while keeping forested habitats close. Ecologists used to refer to this as the "edge effect," that is, a mixture of habitats that provides a richness of borders between contrasting types. For the grizzly bear the most important contrast seems to be between forest and non-forest.

Various Yellowstone studies disagree to some extent on when bears are active each day. There is a general increase in daytime activity in the spring and fall over that of the summer, when bears are more exclusively nocturnal. Some interesting if not necessarily conclusive studies and theorizing have been done about the effects of various kinds of weather on bear activities. For example, high humidity may increase bear activity because the scent of food is better carried on a wet day than a dry one. Rain may cause bears to seek shelter and sit still more than they would on a clear day. Windspeed (and direction) and cloud cover are other factors that must have some effect on individual bears, but safe generalizations are slow to come about these environmental factors. Temperature variations do have a noticeable effect, however, with a peak of activity occurring around fifty degrees Fahrenheit.

During their periods of activity, bears alternate feeding with resting. The exploratory nature of their feeding leads them on a twisted path; the straight-line distance from where they start the day to where they finish it may be quite short, but the distance they traveled to get there is probably quite long. It is rarely possible today to monitor a grizzly bear's activity over the course of an entire day or night; most radio-locations of bears are made from aircraft and do not chart the course of their activities for hours at a time.

In 1981 members of the Interagency Study Team used trained bear dogs to follow the trail of a grizzly bear outside the west boundary of Yellowstone Park near Hebgen Lake. The dogs were not pursuing the bear, which had moved through the area several hours earlier. The account of the tracking is wonderfully illustrative of how Bear #15 moved through his day. He spent the night of July 15, 1981, bedded in willows near the lake. The dogs found the daybed and followed the trail for several hours. The bear had wandered through the heavy vegetation with numerous turns, settling briefly in some lodgepole pines. He then moved on, repeatedly wading back and forth across a small creek. He followed various established roads and cattle trails, then crossed U.S. 191 and took a logging road through a lodgepole forest until he came to a small community, which he did not avoid (it was at night, remember). He left the homes, crossed a shallow pond, then turned back and again crossed U.S. 191, where he was probably seen at 2:30 a.m. by passersby. He then turned south, feeding as he wandered. At this point the dogs were losing the trail, and the bear was soon relocated by radiolocation, about two-and-one-half miles from where the dogs lost him. Had the researchers relied only on the radiolocations, they would have known only that the bear had moved at least four-and-one-half miles. The trail followed by the dogs was at least nine miles long. This is not an unusual distance, and in fact grizzlies have been known to occasionally "light out" from one location and move dozens of miles in only a couple days.

Cover is of great importance to them, wherever they are. Radiotracked grizzlies show high reliance on timber for much of the day, as reported recently by Interagency Study Team member Bonnie Blanchard:

> Instrumented grizzly bears were located in the timber 90% of the time (1635 of 1826 radio locations...). The majority (76%) of the locations in timber were either in scattered timber (6%) or less than 100m from an opening at least 100m² in size (70%)... Only 1% of the locations were in dense timber more than 1 km from an opening at least 100m² in size.
>
> Grizzly bears were observed in the open 191 times from 1977 through 1979... The majority (75%) of bears in the open were observed less than 100m from timber cover; over half of these were less than 30m from timber.

Here again we see the bear's commitment to edges. Whether in the timber or not, the bears were usually close to the forest-nonforest boundary.

Grizzly bears often maintain several daybeds in an area, and use them frequently. Their location should be of nearly urgent interest to anyone hiking in grizzly country. Of 149 grizzly daybeds examined by the Interagency Study Team, 115 were on moderate slopes. All but one were in timber and 83% were within a yard of a tree. The average distance of the daybeds to the edge of the timber was a little over 100 yards, and there was sufficient cover around the bed to conceal the bear from observers until they were within 20 yards. Bears didn't put much work into construction; the beds were usually just shallow depressions in the soil.

This assortment of lifetime, annual, seasonal, and daily movements has a strong cumulative effect on the bear. Grizzlies have a better ability to "home" in on its range than the black bear. It appears that the grizzly is a determined traveler when displaced, or when suddenly in the mood to explore some remembered food source, and it appears that its memory can be extraordinary. Their ability to return to home ranges is so strong that managers now recognize as impractical the transplanting of bears to new country if the transplanting distance is less than fifty miles, and even then the bear may well find its way home. Transplanting is still commonly used in national parks, often in the hope of getting the bear away from trouble before it becomes accustomed to a human food source, for example. But once a food source has been learned it may never be forgotten. After the Trout Creek Dump in central Yellowstone was closed and covered in 1970, one grizzly visited the site and dug for possible food every year up to at least 1979.

Other Activities and Traits

A few other activities of grizzly bears are gathered here in catch-all fashion. Grizzlies have many of the same behavioral traits as already described for black bears. One interesting difference is that grizzlies seem to use specific trails much more often than blacks, especially near feeding areas. Early writers commented occasionally on double-rutted trails left by bears. Again the Trout Creek Dump is a good example. It was situated in the middle of a large open valley, and from the dump site emanated straight bear trails that ran to the surrounding forests. So well packed were these trails that fourteen years after the dump was closed the ruts had not disappeared.

Bears of both species do what they can to make themselves comfortable. Grizzles enjoy swimming, and are known to bathe in order to cool themselves and relieve itching. For the same reasons they wallow in dust beds and rub against trees, rocks, and any other object sturdy enough to serve their needs.

A topic of great popular interest is play. Nature writers, for example, with some justification, characterize the otter as "carefree" and the beaver as "businesslike." Animal species do seem to have different capacities for enjoyment, at least the sort of frivolous enjoyment we think of as play—a nonproductive concept. Playing cubs are, in fact, learning cubs. As they frolic and scuffle they are developing coordination and social attitudes. The proof may be in adult bears, who play less often, for obvious reasons, but who are known to romp and sport not unlike cubs. Adult grizzlies, for example, have been observed sliding down snowbanks, climbing up and doing it again. Doubtless some bears never entirely lose their interest in play.

An often-mentioned character trait of bears is curiosity, which seems quite natural, important in fact, for an animal whose food habits are so exploratory. A bear is apt to investigate anything its nose can lead its eyes, claws, and teeth close enough to examine.

Ferocity is probably the trait most often associated with the grizzly. Here we are inclined to subject the bear's behavior to our own value judgments. If ferocity means "might react violently if made to feel it or its young are threatened," the word applies. If it means "is by nature malicious, and usually wishes to cause pain to its fellow creatures," we have gone too far. Conscious

Given the opportunity, grizzly bears are fond of bathing. N.P.S. photo.

premeditated malice is probably beyond the bear's mental capabilities. It acts as it has been conditioned to act and as it judges the circumstances. The grizzly bear is not capable of any more intense anger than, say, the blue jay. The bear, by virtue of its size and power, just happens to be able to assert itself more conclusively. Every animal acts as an individual, and no absolute predictions can be made about those actions, but the next time you encounter an enraged blue jay, imagine what he would do to you if he weighed 500 pounds.

Bears and Other Animals

Adult grizzlies are not preyed on by any other large animal except larger bears. Cubs may be threatened by adult bears, or by the other predators that also threaten black bear cubs.

If we wish to consider parasites predators, there are several rather serious attackers of the Yellowstone grizzly. Most adults, and about 40% of the cubs, carry intestinal worms. Close to half are infected by trichina worms. A number of other internal and external parasites, the latter including ticks and fleas, are occasionally present. Bears hardly ever die from such attacks, but it appears that their general health and behavior can be influenced, at least by the first two. If their life functions are impaired, life expectancy may be less because the animal has been weakened.

Even though a grizzly will prey on a large animal, instances of coexistence are not uncommon. Bears are known to graze in the same meadows as elk or bison, for example. There seem to be tolerances developed by all concerned that permit a cautious neutrality at times.

Bears' behavior with other bears has been observed extensively. Under circumstances of frequent encounters a complex social hierarchy can develop, with some animals having established dominance and therefore first rights to food or mates.

In the simplest of situations, two bears encounter each other on their daily rounds. If neither is defending food or young, and if it is not mating season, there may be, literally, no encounter at all. They may actually ignore each other. If one has reason to be defensive, or for some reason wishes to challenge the presence of the other, it may become necessary for one to establish its supremacy, either by a showdown of bluffs, vocalizations, and other displays, or by actual combat.

The bluff has been discussed for the black bear. Veteran researchers, and some hunter-naturalists, have remarked that practically all charges by grizzly bears they had experienced firsthand were false. Some did not terminate until the bear was within ten feet, but it is felt that many hunters who think they are facing a killing charge are shooting bears that are either bluffing or running up to get a closer look. These same researchers and hunters do not recommend that the sportsman wait to find out, and, quite often, under natural circumstances, the bear being charged does not wait either; it attacks or flees. As we will see in Part III, these two choices are not good ones for humans in the same situation.

Bear sounds include crying, snorting, growling, whining, and all the non-vocal noises described for black bears. Some figure in encounters, as do other actions such as pawing and head swinging. We do not know exactly what each action means, but there is a system to it that is consistent. Bear communication in an angry encounter can be quite intricate, with an assortment of feints and growls, snorts and stampings, reaching a climax either in one bear backing down or in actual fighting. Fighting, if it occurs, is mostly done with the mouth and front paws. Adult grizzlies, especially older males, are often scarred from battles. Serious injury is infrequent (crippling, for example), and death is rare.

Supremacy, once established, is remarkably final. In many encounters observed by the Craighead team, the triumphant bear turned his back on the conquered one and walked away. *Never* did the loser take advantage of his opponent's vulnerability and attack from behind. Furthermore, they discovered that long-dominant males who were accustomed to being "in charge" at the dumps disappeared quickly once they were defeated in battle. It seemed likely to the observers that the defeat broke their spirit and, though in good health, they soon died. Groupings with the intensity of the old dump days are now infrequent in Yellowstone, so such complex social behavior has less opportunity to occur.

There is one more matter to attend to before turning to the story of man and the Yellowstone bears. We have seen that there are some distinct differences between black and grizzly bear, and a great many more similarities. Our understanding of both will be greater if we look for a moment at how the two species came to be.

Chapter 11

Why Two Kinds of Bears in Yellowstone?

 The bears of North America all developed from one common ancestral species, *Ursus etruscus. Ursus etruscus* was Asian, and not terribly unlike the modern black bear in appearance and habit (though probably larger in its later forms). *Ursus thibetanus* (the Himalayan black bear of today) and *Ursus americanus* (our black bear) seem to have formed distinct evolutionary lines from *Ursus etruscus* more than 2 million years ago. Fossil remains indicate that the ancestors of our black bear have been present in North America (presumably having crossed the Bering Straits on an ice- or land-bridge) for about 250,000 to 300,000 years.

The modern grizzly, *Ursus arctos*, also developed from *Ursus etruscus*, probably about a million years after *Ursus americanus* did so. About the time the black bear was beginning to fill its present range in North America, a distinct ancestral form of modern *Ursus arctos* was living in China, but it did not cross to North America until relatively recent times. The continental ice sheet blocked its southern migration until the end of the last ice age, about 10,000 years ago.

In this way Yellowstone got its two species of bears, but this travelogue does not answer the question of why they are different. The question is being answered, however, by scientists.

It has to do with trees. *Ursus etruscus* was a forest animal, a climber. So, customarily, are *Ursus thibetanus* and our own *Ursus americanus*. The ancestors of the grizzly bear, by contrast, branched from *Ursus etruscus* much more dramatically than did the ancestors of the black bear. When *Ursus etruscus* moved to new forests it became the modern black bears of Asia and North America. When it moved *out* of the forest, it became *Ursus arctos*, an open-ground animal

Telling Them Apart.

Park visitors are not the only ones who have trouble knowing if what they're seeing is a grizzly bear or a black bear. Hunters accidentally shoot grizzlies near the park now and then. In order to tell one from the other, look at several features of the bear: claws, back profile, massiveness of head, and overall size. These pictures suggest some of the pitfalls and perspectives you may encounter. Usually, if you can accumulate enough information, it will be obvious which bear you are seeing. Just keep your distance and don't get close enough to ask.

Shape and massiveness of head usually distinguish black from grizzly.

Most guidelines for telling bears apart show you a nice profile, but chances are you won't get that view right away. This is a grizzly, and your best clues are the claws and the distinct hump over the front shoulders. Black bear claws never look this big.

And this is a black bear; the claws are much less prominent and there is virtually no shoulder hump. From this angle there is relatively little difference to be seen in head shape between these two bears, so keep looking until you find at least one of the distinguishing characteristics. N.P.S. photos.

WHY TWO KINDS OF BEARS   73

From this angle you can't see the claws, but there appears to be a distinct shoulder bump; is it a grizzly? No, it's a black. The "hump" is mostly hair, and the head has the smaller, less massive outlines of a black bear. N.P.S. photo.

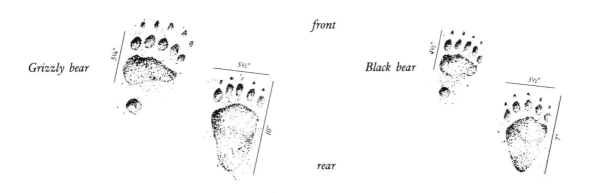

Grizzly bear   front   Black bear

5¼"   5½"   4½"   3½"

10"   7"

rear

that gradually lost most of its dependence on trees and developed a whole different nature as a result.

For black bears, trees are security. Young and adults seldom wander far from the forest haven. Grizzlies, having adapted to hunting food in the open (better digging equipment, for example), learned to find security in other ways. A sow black bear sends her cubs up a tree in a time of danger, and may even join them if the danger is great enough. A sow grizzly, whose cubs may retain their tree-climbing ability only for a couple years, has no such refuge, so she has become an aggressive defender of her young. She cannot send them anywhere, so she protects them where they are. They learn to do the same.

The distinction has numerous implications. The safety of trees may explain why black bear cubs are weaned as yearlings while grizzly cubs stay with their mother for two or three years. Over much of the grizzly's range the cubs cannot rely on trees and need her protection. It certainly helps to explain the size differences. Black bears need a body that can climb. Grizzlies lost their dependence on climbing and so could develop other abilities, which required greater size and strength (there are other considerations in grizzly size, of course).

Grizzly bears are much more feared and respected, by wild animals and man. Their options in an encounter are limited by the lack of an "absolute security" refuge. They are, therefore, more likely to defend young or possessions aggressively. The presence or absence of security must pervade the consciousness of an animal; witness the lengths to which sows go to find isolation while they raise their young. The overall effect of the stress of cub vulnerability—a constant nagging concern—is a change in the character and behavior of the grizzly mother. And *her* behavior is firmly imprinted on the cubs.

And so black and grizzly bears are adapted to different environments but often share common ranges. We have seen ample evidence of the flexibility of both species. Neither can be pigeonholed; "oh yes, the black bear—it lives in the woods." Bear life is too complex, and natural opportunities too diverse, for such simplifications. Yellowstone lacks the vast Asian arctic tundra that first changed a drifting population of *Ursus etruscus* into *Ursus arctos*, but the modern grizzly makes the best of it. Grizzlies do not thrive in the sizes and numbers they enjoy farther north, but they are successfully using a good part of the Yellowstone wilderness. And their smaller, less demanding, cousins the black bears cautiously share that part and eagerly exploit the rest.

PART II

Of Bears and Men

Chapter 12

The First 10,000 Years

Bears and humans have interacted for thousands of years in the Yellowstone country. Primitive human occupation of the area began shortly after the receding glaciers of the last ice age exposed it, and it was the disappearance of that ice farther north that opened the way for the spread of the grizzly into the present western United States. The climate of Yellowstone has undergone several major changes in the past 10,000 years. It remained relatively moist for the first 3,000, so that the area served as a hunting ground for nomadic tribes with the simplest of weapons; they were not even aware of the bow and arrow. A grizzly was a formidable adversary, not to be attacked by less than a party of men. The climate then dried in this part of the west by about 5000 B.C. The hunters were gradually replaced by bands of foragers, gathering whatever sorts of food were available, since the climatic changes had caused the disappearance of most of the big game.

If one measures human progress in terms of invention, the relative scarcity of food at this time caused some great leaps forward in the "civilizing" process. The people of the great plains and the northern Rockies, responding to the greater challenge of obtaining food, developed animal traps, and, by the time of Christ, the bow and arrow. As they progressed the climate reversed itself, the drought subsided, and large mammals again became abundant. Man now faced bear on slightly better terms, but the increasing sophistication of human culture added other dimensions to the contact. The bear, especially the grizzly, became a figure of reverence for many tribes—a "cousin," or even a god.

Most tribal groups in the Rockies were roamers, even as late as the arrival of white men. In fact, long after their first contact with Europeans, the tribes shifted as they vied for territory. The locations of the cultural/linguistic groups observed by early explorers were not based on generations of occupancy.

Whites then contributed to shifting tribal boundaries, not only by pushing eastern tribes westward but by supplying some tribes with warfare advantages in the forms of firearms and horses.

At the time of the first European visit to what is now Yellowstone (probably John Colter, a member of the Lewis and Clark expedition, who seems to have passed through what is now the park in 1807), the tribes in control of the region were the Crow, Blackfeet, and Shoshone. The only permanent occupants were a few members of a branch of the Shoshone tribe known as the Sheepeaters. Except for the advantage of an occasional horse or trapper's gun, they faced bears much as their ancestors had. Explorers in the Rocky Mountains reported that it was a much greater honor for a brave to have killed a grizzly than to have killed an enemy brave.

From 1810 to 1870 Yellowstone was visited by many whites. At first, trappers wandered the region, seeking beaver. By 1850 the heyday of beaver trapping was past, but prospectors, seeking a variety of precious metals, explored the region, eventually establishing a small settlement, the New World Mining District (present Cooke City) near the northeast corner of what is now the park in the late 1860s. Stories of Yellowstone's geologic and geothermal wonders were taken back to the settlements, but polite society disregarded the reports of trappers and similar disreputables. It was not until the 1860s that serious progress was made in formal exploration.

Many of these adventurers—trapper, prospector, and explorer—met Yellowstone's bears. We will turn to some of their tales in the third part of this book, but for now our subject is an adventure of a different sort: the 1872 Act of Congress that created Yellowstone Park, and the profound effect that act had on our concept of wildlife in general and bears in particular.

Chapter 13

1872-1916/
The First Park Bears

 The establishment of Yellowstone Park was one of the great milestones of early American conservation. The park's geological, geothermal, and biological riches, surviving today in remarkably good condition, are ample testament to the foresight of its founders. But much of what Yellowstone has become, including a magnificent wildlife sanctuary, was neither suspected nor intended by its creators. Yellowstone as a wilderness may have changed little, but as a concept—as an institution—it is radically altered from its original form.

The Yellowstone Park Act of March 1, 1872 specified that "the tract of land... lying near the headwaters of the Yellowstone River... is hereby reserved and withdrawn from settlement, occupancy, or sale under the laws of the United States, and dedicated and set apart as a public park or pleasureing ground for the benefit and enjoyment of the people."

The greatest concern of the sponsors of the park (excluding the overriding commercial interests of some of its most effective supporters) was to preserve the spectacular scenic and geothermal wonders of Yellowstone. There was no especial interest in wildlife, beyond the mandate to the secretary of the interior, who had charge of the park, to establish such "rules and regulations as he may deem necessary or proper" to protect the park, and to "provide against the wanton destruction of the fish and game found within said Park, and against their capture or destruction for the purposes of merchandise or profit." Hunting, for sport or provision, was regarded as a legitimate public use of Yellowstone Park in 1872.

The complex and even self-contradictory philosophies which now direct our management of national parks were not even foreseen in 1872. It was forty-four years before a comprehensive statement of modern park preservation received codification in the National Park Service Act of 1916. In the meantime, there were lessons to be learned, mistakes to be made, and, now and then, bears to be dealt with.

From 1872 to 1886 Yellowstone was administered by a series (five) of civilian superintendents. They were grossly underfinanced and received virtually no guidance from an understandably ignorant government. As a result of the inadequacies of this civilian administration, an assortment of political pressures resulted in the assignment, in 1886, of the U.S. Cavalry to the care and protection of the park. For over thirty years the army provided discipline, defense, and blessed order to Yellowstone Park. They initiated many management procedures that had lasting effects on Yellowstone's biological communities. Some were good and some were not, but most were continued by the National Park Service when that agency took over in 1916.

Yellowstone was subjected to some exciting scientific research in the nineteenth century, beginning with the first government explorations and continuing through several later survey parties, but most of the work was geological or topographical. Mapping and study of the park's wonders was complemented by some excellent work on botanical and zoological subjects, the latter especially with fish and invertebrates, but very little was learned about the bear or other large animals.

In 1880, Philetus Norris, second superintendent of the park, made an attempt at describing the "varieties" of bears. Norris, an avid if unschooled naturalist, named six: grizzly bear, silver-tipped bear, cinnamon bear, smutfaced bear ("with a brackled, impish-looking face—a true indicator of the character of the beast..."), black bear, and silk bear. All were simply individual variations on the two species we know the park contains, but at least Norris was showing some interest.

The public was showing a little interest too. In the park's first ten years about 10,000 people found their way to Yellowstone, and once there they were pretty much on their own. There were few hotels, and for some years virtually no roads. Visitors either brought provisions or shot what they needed. Many shot alot more than they needed.

In fact, the wildlife situation before 1886 was dangerously out of control. Market hunters, concentrating on elk and bison, ignored regulations (as well as hopelessly ineffective officials) and killed thousands of animals. Visiting sportsmen, from the east and Europe, were more moderate but just as deadly. A dawning of awareness was occurring, however, among sportsmen and nature-lovers; the wildlife of the west was not an inexhaustible resource. The park's staunchest defenders, voicing their displeasure through magazines like *Forest and Stream* urged elimination of hunting. Thus within a very few years Yellowstone took on a new role. It became a wildlife sanctuary of unparalleled size.

In 1883, by order of the Secretary of the Interior, hunting became illegal. At first, only the grazing animals and others deemed harmless by the standards of the day were protected. Predators, including cougars, coyotes, wolves, and bears, were still fair game. Of these, bears had only three more years before their reprieve. The others faced a full half-century of additional, and increasingly intense, persecution at the hands of park managers.

The ecological balances we now appreciate in a wilderness were only dimly perceived by a few naturalists before 1900. Animals, to most people, were "good" or "bad" as they fit the human plan. Judging from contemporary accounts, bears, though respected and coveted by hunters, were not considered game in the same class as elk or deer. Bears stood somewhere between the noble ungulates (elk, moose, deer, and so on) and the evil wolves. Wolves were not game animals at all—they were vermin. Additionally, bears were still annoyingly abundant throughout the west. Grizzlies still thrived in parts of the Sierras, in the Pacific Northwest, and in New Mexico and Colorado in 1880. There was little or no concern for their numbers beyond how to reduce them.

Some accounts of Yellowstone's bears have suggested that bear populations, both grizzly and black, were substantially reduced during the first lawless years. The available evidence, though too sketchy to be absolutely conclusive, indicates that the bears remained reasonably common until protected. In 1885, for example, a correspondent to *Forest and Stream* reported that Yellowstone's bears were "numerous."

That same year the *Livingston* (Montana) *Enterprise* informed its readers that H.A. Pearson, of San Francisco, who had bagged three grizzlies and two blacks while hunting in the park, was so excited about the excellent sport that he was considering setting up a guide service. Surely, if park bears were thinned out by hunting, no good businessman would want to count on them for income. It seems more likely that later writers, especially Skinner, accustomed to judging bear numbers in terms of visibility (at roadside, in camps, or in dumps) mistook a lack of visibility for a lack of presence.

When the Cavalry arrived in August of 1886 the struggling young park turned a corner and within a few years was transformed from a questionable experiment in government stewardship into a secure American institution. The strong and stable army administration responded to the most crying needs;

Acting superintendent Captain George Anderson, U.S. Cavalry, with captive bear cub at Fort Yellowstone, Mammoth Hot Springs, in the 1890s. N.P.S. photo.

vandals were arrested, poachers were apprehended, and haphazard fortune was replaced by regimented process. The officers who were appointed acting superintendent took their assignment very seriously. They immediately began to protect the park in every imaginable way.

Bears, in fact all animals, were brought under the protection of the 1883 hunting prohibition. Never again would Yellowstone's visitors be legally entitled to kill its wildlife (and often yet park rangers must answer the difficult ques-

OF BEARS AND MEN

tion of why fish are not "wildlife"). Killing would occur, but it would be either clandestine or administratively sanctioned. In a very short time the animals began to lose their wariness. By the 1890s visitors were delighted by the sight of elk and deer calmly grazing on the grounds of park developments. Not tame, these wild animals had simply responded to protection by losing their shyness.

Bears were no exception. Within three years (1889) black bears were gathering at night at garbage piles near the hotels. Garbage disposal being a very informal matter in the park, open pits were located near all the hotels, and smaller ones occurred wherever camping was popular. The idea of open piles of decaying refuse is repulsive to us now, but then it seemed an entirely satisfactory arrangement; if the bears were willing to dispose of some of it, all the better. Just how acceptable it was became clear when the garbage and camp food attracted enough bears to cause problems. The only solution even considered was removal of the bears. Garbage was here to stay.

By 1891 there *was* a problem. Acting Superintendent Anderson reported that "bears have become very troublesome at all the hotels, camps, slaughter-houses, and other places in the Park where there is anything for them to eat. They have not proved at all dangerous, but it is impossible to keep provisions anywhere within their reach." He mentioned also capturing four, and suggested that it might become necessary to kill "an occasional one" if they were too destructive.

The same year bears from Yellowstone became available to zoos, with one being shipped to Washington at the beginning of a long and flourishing relationship between the park and the National Zoological Gardens. In 1911, for example, a total of twelve bears (ten grizzlies and two blacks) were shipped to zoos in Philadelphia, Toronto, Kansas City, and Iowa. A notion of "surplus" animals was established, ones that the park could spare, and another management philosophy congealed: Yellowstone could be relied on to overproduce its wildlife, from bears to elk to trout, so the administration was justified (later the word would be obligated) to manage this harvest.

Bears appeared at the dumps in increasing numbers. By the early 1890s the blacks were joined by a few grizzlies, who seemed more cautious about associating with man and his food.

If they needed it, bears got added protection under the National Park Protective Act of 1894, which at last put legislative teeth in the park's feeble regulations (the civilians had had little recourse to punish offenders; all they were allowed to do was expel them from the park. The army "found ways" to punish, sometimes extralegally). Stiff fines and jail sentences made would-be poachers and vandals think twice about their plans.

Quickly the dumps became a tourist attraction. Another institution, the bear-feeding grounds, was born. Tourists gathered in the evening (the bears learned the dumping schedule) within a few yards of the pits to watch one to twenty bears sort through the trash for tidbits. Of course some adventurous souls took to hand-feeding the animals, so that it seemed only a matter of time before a bear would, literally, be fed a hand.

The acting superintendents were reluctant to tamper with what appeared to them to be a harmless situation. In 1893 Anderson commented only that he suspected some bears had been taken by poachers. In 1895, though he felt they had "increased notably," he saw no need to control them; "They are not dangerous to human life. . ." Two years later Acting Superintendent Young reported complaints of bear damage from Norris, Fountain Hotel, Thumb Lunch Station, Lake Hotel, and the soldiers at Canyon, whose store-houses were raided by bears. He suggested that it would be advisable to send "at least twelve" to zoos. The following year he reiterated his sentiment, and was joined in it by at least one newspaper, whose editor objected to the practice of feeding as not only dangerous to the public but to the bears; "They have become too indolent to hunt for themselves." Expressions of concern for the bears, however muted, were rare at this time.

The situation remained much the same throughout the army administration. The number of dump-fed bears increased, a few were killed, others were shipped to zoos, and the feeding grounds were formalized. Feeding by other means than dump was prohibited by Acting Superintendent Pitcher in 1902:

> The interference with, or molestation of bear or other wild game in the Yellowstone Park, by *ANYONE* is absolutely prohibited.
>
> The custom of feeding the bear, on the part of tourists, hotel employees, or enlisted men, must cease at once, as this practice will sooner or later, surely result in serious injury to some individual.
>
> The bear of the Park, while absolutely wild, are perfectly harmless, but when rendered tame by being fed—in any other way except at the regular garbage piles at the various hotels—lose all fear of human beings and will enter kitchens and camps in search of food, thereby frequently doing considerable damage to property and provisions.
>
> For their own protection and for the protection of tourists throughout the Park, hotel managers are requested to post this circular in a con-

spicuous place, and to promptly notify the Acting Superintendent of the Park of any violation of the above instructions.

Whenever a bear becomes vicious or dangerous at any hotel or station throughout the Park, the fact should at once be reported, and a scout will be specially detailed for the purpose of capturing or killing it.

Later that summer Mr. R. E. Southwick, from Hart, Michigan, was seriously injured while violating the new rule. Again, a tradition was established. For over half a century Americans would come to Yellowstone for the avowed purpose of feeding bears. That it was illegal to do so did not matter to many of them.

Injuries began to increase, but little sympathy was wasted on bear feeders. An injured hotel employee in 1904 "got simply what he deserved," according to the superintendent. Between 1905 and 1915, while visitation ranged between 16,000 and 51,000, bears invaded camps, destroyed storehouses, and were a constant headache for the soldiers. Public reaction varied. In one exchange in *Science* magazine in 1913, a bear enthusiast described the "repelling of an attack on the larder," which to him was much like "a midnight sally to rout the neighbor's cow from one's garden patch," as "great fun." His opponent, who "lost all of our grub at the Canyon," considered the bears an "outrageous nuisance," and recommended that "either 95% of the Yellowstone Park bears be killed off or soldiers must be placed on all-night guard around the chief camping places."

There is a report of a bear-caused human death in Yellowstone in 1907, in F. D. Smith's *Book of a Hundred Bears*, published in 1909. It involves a tourist who attempted to chase some grizzly cubs up a tree. According to the published account, he poked at the cubs with his umbrella and was then fatally mauled by their mother. My confidence in the authenticity of this account is not high; its author was a popular writer who heard the story from one of the park scouts, who may not have been above stringing the writer along with a tall tale. One reason for my uncertainty is that this incident, if it occurred, received little or no official notice, while the next reported fatality was a national news item.

In 1916 Frank Welch, a teamster with the Army Quartermaster Corps, was dragged from camp one night by a grizzly that had been raiding camps for several weeks in the Fishing Bridge-Sylvan Pass area. Welch died later of the injury, and the bear caused a good deal more trouble before it was finally destroyed. What is surprising is that even at this point, after grizzlies

A very early photograph, about 1912, of a bear-feeding grounds in Yellowstone; certain formalities, such as fences and grandstands, had not yet arrived. N.P.S. photo.

were a well-established nuisance around the camps, the death of Frank Welch caused great amazement among experienced bear "authorities" who believed that the killing was completely out of character for grizzlies. There was a widespread feeling that the ferocity of the grizzly bear first met by Lewis and Clark had been "educated" out of the species by a century of hunting. Eighty years later behaviorists would tell us that habituation to humans is not the same as domestication, and that it is never possible, and may never be possible, to predict how any individual grizzly bear will act on the basis of what we know about other grizzly bears.

We are much better able to assess human effects on Yellowstone's bears in this second period of administration, partly because the army kept such good records and partly because there were more tourists around to record their own impressions. The bears became secure enough in the company of humans to enter developments and forage openly in the garbage. They became bold enough to break into buildings. Army protection emboldened them yet further, and army management of "problem" bears was well recorded so that we know how many bears were removed from the population.

We also know that a lot of informal "bear management" was practiced that certainly did no good for bear-human relations. Bears that entered the

The bears were quickly recognized as efficient garbage disposals, and a remarkable degree of familiarity between people, bears, and horses was the result. N.P.S. photo.

permanent camp facilities (where visitors could rent tent-cabins by the night) were sometimes fed meat with broken glass in it, or sponges fried in grease. For a few years a colorful old frontier character and self-promoter named C. J. "Buffalo" Jones held the position of Game Warden in Yellowstone, and he assigned himself the job of punishing troublesome bears. He would snare them and use a block and tackle to suspend them from a tree with their hind feet barely touching the ground, then beat them with a switch. He was finally ordered to quit this practice, shortly before he "resigned" in 1905. One could almost wish that Jones had tried this "punishment" on a grizzly rather than on small black bears. The army made a reasonable effort to prevent cruelty to the bears, and saw to it that those found guilty (usually hotel or camp employees) were punished, but in a day when bears were still regarded as little more than varmints it isn't surprising that so many people were quick to abuse the animals. The bears were, in any event, durable and patient enough to keep coming back no matter how roughly they were treated. The miracle is that more people were not hurt. Yellowstone history is a profound testament to the patience of bears.

It is impossible to know exactly how much the number of bears was reduced by hunting before the army arrived, but visitation was so light, and visitors stuck to a few major areas and trails, so that it seems probable the bears were still quite common in the late 1880s. On the other hand, once the army was there and bear hunting ceased, and only official removals of bears occurred with any regularity, the bears' habits were quickly altered. They steadily increased their use of garbage, more and more bears taking advantage of this growing food source.

Later writers have differed on the number of park bears before the 1930s. Some naturalists and scientists have taken the early accounts and superintendents' reports quite literally, and accept the number of bears counted at the dumps as a true estimate of the park's bear population. Others suspect that the gradually increasing number of bears at the dumps were just a reflection of such things as a gradual loss of wariness after more than a decade of being

Cook and bear at a dump, 1928, showing the bears' extraordinary tolerance for human presence. N.P.S. photo.

OF BEARS AND MEN

hunted, a slow adjustment of a large, widely dispersed population of bears to feeding at a few sites, and a gradual increase in garbage that over the years was able to feed more and more bears. I find the latter interpretation much more convincing. There is no reason to suppose that the park was not supporting a healthy wild population of both species of bears (as was much of the surrounding country, where settlement was light), most of whom had not yet discovered dump feeding. The final proof of that would seem to be that as amounts of garbage increased so did the numbers of bears feeding. Garbage does not spontaneously generate bears the way that people once believed a pile of rags would generate mice. By the 1930s and 1940s, as visitation increased, and as the opportunity for bears to feed on human foods likewise increased, the reported number of bears in the park grew from a few dozen to a few hundred.

If we accept, as I think we should, that Yellowstone supported healthy populations of both black and grizzly bears by the 1890s, there is a lesson there for modern bear-watchers. In the process of researching another book, *Old Yellowstone Days*, I read several hundred accounts of the park, written by visitors, scientists, and park employees, between 1872 and 1916. What is striking about those accounts is that before about 1910 those visitors virtually never reported seeing a black bear from any park road. The only place bears were seen with regularity was near the small park developments and at the dumps. Many modern visitors, traveling through the park looking for bears, assume that because they do not see the bears the bears must not be in the park. Here we have an earlier time in Yellowstone's history when black bears were known to be in the park but simply had not yet learned that it was to their advantage to be near roads.

But they did learn it, and in the last few years of the army administration bear-watching (and bear managing) took a new twist. Traditionally accepted accounts have claimed that in the years between 1917 and 1919 a black bear cub learned to beg near the West Thumb Soldier Station. This bear, who became famous as "Jesse James" and was featured in the Annual Report of the Director of the National Park Service in 1919, was in fact far from being first. My own research into early park visitor accounts, along with Dr. Mary Meagher's examination of soldier station records, reveal that it wasn't that simple. Sometime around 1900 a few black bears were occasionally reported by soldier patrols near well-traveled roads. These first reports do not indicate that the bears were actively "panhandling," and make no mention of visitors looking for bears, but evidently bears and tourists were beginning to understand what they had in common. The first tourist account I have located in which a rather bashful bear approaches tourists along a park road occurred in about 1910. Roadside begging was an extension of the familiarity already bred in the dumps and camps. Bears knew that people meant food, and as road traffic increased to the point that it was worth a bear's time to hang around waiting for handouts, more and more bears learned to do it. Some probably learned by example, some by boldness, and almost immediately they were teaching their cubs to do it. By the 1920s, bears could be seen begging at many points on the park's grand loop road, and many people who visited Yellowstone in the 1950s or 1960s will recall seeing thirty or more roadside bears in the course of their visit. It is these beggars that most people think of even yet when someone mentions the bears of Yellowstone.

Serious study of Yellowstone's bears had progressed little by the time the National Park Service was created in 1916. In 1904 Theodore Roosevelt wrote about his presidential visit to the park the previous year and noted that the bears were fascinating and deserving of some naturalist's attention. In 1906 and 1908 William Wright, a well-known hunter-naturalist and the most reliable popular bear writer of his day (even better than Roosevelt), spent several weeks in the park. He took many flash photographs of the grizzlies that visited various dumps at night, and some of the better pictures appeared in his milestone book *The Grizzly Bear* (1910). Seventy-five years later, after dozens of books about bears have been published, Wright's is still among the most enjoyable and is still remarkably accurate most of the time. It is an important contribution to the literature of Yellowstone's bears.

A more mundane investigation, in 1913, made a priceless suggestion that was ignored. Robert Dole of the U.S. Geological Survey examined sanitary conditions in the park, finding dangerous pollution at every turn. His report upbraided park administrators, since "in Yellowstone Park, where the avowed effort is to keep natural features as nearly as possible in their primeval state, the streams should be kept much cleaner." As an aside, he suggested that garbage should be burned or buried, and that all incinerators and dump operations "should be fenced with barbed wire to keep out the bears." Dole was on the right track, but he was ahead of his time. The dump bears had only begun to entertain America.

Chapter 14

1916-1945/
The Great Yellowstone Bear Show

The creation of the National Park Service in 1916 marked the formal coming of age of an almost venerable idea. By 1916 Yellowstone had been joined by a host of sister parks and monuments. Where in 1872 it stood alone, in 1916 it was part of a thriving system with a well-established policy foundation, and, perhaps more important, an avid and growing public. Among this public, and in the structure of the infant agency, were people who foresaw many changes in the future parks. No features of the parks, especially of Yellowstone, concerned them more than wildlife.

The National Park Service Act of August 25, 1916, contained a dual mandate:

> to conserve the scenery and the natural and historic objects and the wildlife therein and to provide for the enjoyment of the same in such a manner and by such means as will leave them unimpaired for the enjoyment of future generations.

Here, the resource, whether geyser, bear, or aster, was given some preference. It could be enjoyed, but not so much that future enjoyment might be threatened or even diminished. The mandate is an eternal challenge.

The strengthening of national park goals was timely, for there was an increasing restlessness among the aware over many aspects of management. Exotic species of animals, introduced in some parks, had destroyed delicate balances. Yellowstone's primitiveness suffered most from the spread of several species of fish, but it had also been threatened with many other introductions; reindeer, chamois, mountain goat, and a variety of birds were considered and rejected. The notion that man can "improve" the wilderness by adding to it has been slow to die.

93

In Yellowstone, from 1904 to 1945, elk were fed to help them through the winters. Predators were killed (between 1904 and 1935 the total was 121 cougars, 136 wolves, and 4,352 coyotes), to further "protect" the elk, deer, and bison. The most spectacular manipulation of the park's animal populations occurred under water. Starting before 1900, under the administration of earlier versions of the present U.S. Fish and Wildlife Service, a massive stocking and stream "improvement" effort took place, with the expressed goal of making Yellowstone an angler's paradise. Many barren waters were stocked, and many native fish were outcompeted by newcomers. Native stocks were hopelessly mixed. A giant hatchery program was developed that, at its peak in the 1940s, was producing over 30,000,000 eyed cutthroat trout eggs a year for shipping to other areas.

As late as 1912 the superintendent of Sequoia National Park recommended the complete elimination of bears from that park. At the same time, and later, a complaining hotel guest could cause the death of noisy woodpeckers in Yosemite National Park.

The scope of the manipulation now seems almost incredible. In the 1920s, when it was widely learned that white pelicans were an alternate host for the parasite that infects many trout in Yellowstone Lake, there was active enthusiasm for an egg-stomping campaign at the pelican nesting sites on the Molly Islands. The campaign was further fueled by an awareness of how many fish those pelicans ate and therefore kept visiting anglers from catching. The campaign was nipped in the bud by public outcry, but it illustrates the mood of many managers. In these cases, and in others, it was clear the visitor came first.

Why was this so? A big reason was that the new Park Service had the opposite "people problem" it has now: There weren't enough visitors. The first two directors of the Park Service, Stephen Mather and Horace Albright, were superb publicists. They realized the only way they could get adequate funding from Congress to support and enlarge the National Park System was by broadening public interest. They were fabulously successful. Yellowstone visitation went from 25,000 in 1914 to 260,000 in 1929. More people, more camps, more garbage, and more bear problems.

The scientific community had begun to respond to growing threats to wildlife even as the Park Service was being born. An article in *Science* (appropriately entitled "Animal Life as an Asset of National Parks") in 1916 stated that the "first necessity in adapting the parks for recreative purposes is to preserve natural conditions." The article urged that professional naturalists be assigned to the parks to make careful studies of conditions, so that managers would act on the basis of fact rather than supposition. The same recommendation was made by other distinguished specialists. In 1921 the American Association for the Advancement of Science resolved to oppose all introductions of exotics (plants too) in parks. They were supported by the Ecological Society of America. By 1927, when Milton Skinner's *The Predatory and Fur-Bearing Animals of the Yellowstone National Park* was published, research was widely regarded as essential to park management.

A good beginning was made in 1930 when a National Park Service "Branch of Research and Education" was established to direct both the gathering and dissemination of knowledge. It initiated the *Fauna Series,* books which dealt with wildlife problems in the parks (*Fauna No. 4,* by Murie, at last established that Yellowstone's long-persecuted predators were of only marginal influence on ungulate numbers), and between 1932 and 1940 there were twenty-five biologists working in the Park Service (Civilian Conservation Corps funding made this possible). World War II put this to an end, and recovery was slow, but that is ahead of our story of the bears.

The Old Faithful feeding grounds in the 1920s. N.P.S. photo.

The challenge of the Park Service Act, to preserve yet enjoy, had been recognized immediately. As one writer put it, "ice and fire were expected to consort together without change of complexion." For the bears, the 1920s were just an expansion of earlier situations, but more bears in dumps prompted officials to announce dramatic population increases. Based on dump estimates, grizzly numbers were said to have gone from 40 in 1920 to 260 in 1933 (keep in mind also that until recently bears were partly or completely unprotected *around* the park, and bears that made seasonal migrations in to the park to the dumps were often killed when they left. We are not certain what effects this killing had on the entire population). As late as 1929 the superintendent commented "the bear population of Yellowstone seems to have reached a point where they are somewhat of a nuisance."

In 1931 bear damage cases totalled 209, and in 1932 they hit an all-time peak of 451. Partly in response to these alarming totals and the growing number of human injuries, the Branch of Research and Education suggested that dump feeding be reconsidered. Not only were dumps unhealthy for bears and a violation of park principles, they were no longer necessary for the park:

> The bear show has been one of the greatest assets of the national parks. However, it has served its greatest purpose in the period when bringing the people to an appreciation of the wonderful things to be seen and done in the parks was of prime importance. Now that the popularity of their values is established and their place secure, it may be necessary to modify the old practices in the interests of the welfare of both people and bears.

The idea was to have wild animals in a wild setting, independent of man's influence. "The sight of one bear under natural conditions is more stimulating than close association with dozens of bears," the report concluded.

Some Park Service officials disagreed, but in some ways the park had already begun to respond to the problem. Live-trapping techniques, for removing bears to isolated parts of the park or to zoos, were refined. Public viewing at dumps was restricted after 1931 to Old Faithful and Canyon, and after 1935 to Canyon. In 1937 it was reported that there was not enough parking space for the 500 to 600 cars that appeared every evening near the feeding grounds, and that as many as 70 grizzlies could be viewed on a good night.

Management was still ineffective. It has been noted that years of high bear damages were usually followed by increased bear removals, so that really

Bear damage to a car top, Fishing Bridge, 1932. N.P.S. photo.

Hundreds of people gathered every night at the Canyon feeding grounds in the 1930s. N.P.S. photo.

little more was accomplished than temporary easing of the nuisance. Starting in 1938, food at the Canyon dump was reduced to disperse some of the grizzlies to other, non-visible dumps in the park. In 1942 greatly reduced visitation due to the war allowed the park to not reopen the Canyon public feeding grounds. Dumping (and bear-feeding), combined with incineration, continued at several sites out of public view. That year eighty-three bears were killed in the park by officials; fifty-five blacks and twenty-eight grizzlies. No doubt some were drawn into developed areas by shortages at the dumps, but there also seemed to have been a shortage of favored natural foods that year. A "ten-year average" of thirty-three bears killed (total, both species) was estimated for 1931 to 1941. The problem was getting worse, and would erupt anew at the end of the war.

Also in 1942, Miss Martha Hansen, 45, of Twin Falls, Idaho, was mauled in the Old Faithful Campground on the night of August 22. She died on August 27, and two years later President Roosevelt approved payment of $1,894.95 to her family (the species of bear responsible, a "large brown bear" by description, is in doubt). The superintendent noted "this is the first relief bill of record due to an injury to a park visitor by a bear." Congress openly criticized the Park Service for failing to solve the bear problem. The Park Service responded that it could not solve any problems until Congress gave it adequate funding to do so.

Bear study progressed only slightly between 1916 and 1940 in Yellowstone. In 1925 Skinner's *Bears in Yellowstone* appeared, a rambling narrative of his many years of experience with park bears. Pleasant enough reading, it contributed little of use to management, since it was not a systematic or disciplined study.

As much concern as bears were, their importance to wildlife experts could not compare with that of the Yellowstone elk, whose population, it was believed, was dreadfully out of kilter with its environment. Thus serious research projects, such as William Rush's in the 1920s and Murie's coyote study in the 1930s, were aimed at understanding that problem. Research was needed, yes, but only so much could be afforded.

At last, in 1944, Olaus Murie undertook an honest-to-goodness field research project for the bears. He learned much about their food habits, and determined that the bears, which administrators seemed to feel were so numerous because of the dump food, could survive quite nicely on natural foods. He further stated that driving bears away from food was no answer so long as the food remained available. He encouraged experimenting with

A black bear trapped for shipment to a zoo, 1922. N.P.S. photo.

bearproofing, especially the use of electricity, and made many useful comments about bear behavior in campgrounds.

And here a great opportunity passed. With substantial scientific evidence to support it, the Park Service might have capitalized on the reprieve of the war years with a massive sanitation campaign, so that when the visitors returned bear feeding would be much less common. They might have, that is, had they not been financially paralyzed by war shortages. As it was, the service could not even brace itself adequately for the hordes, who, after all, were the heart of the problem. Again and again, the issue came back to the public, and the overwhelming need to make them understand that it was unhealthy, unnatural, illegal . . . that it was *wrong* to do the one thing they most wanted to do in Yellowstone—feed the bears.

Chapter 15

1946-1967/
Crisis and Response

A recreation boom occurred at the close of World War II. The national parks, still struggling along on paltry old budgets, responded by falling apart. Everywhere, visitor services and facilities were neglected in the most serious crisis the service had ever faced. Finally, in 1954-1955, a bold new program, Mission 66, was inaugurated, to upgrade park facilities and find ways to respond to increasing (1,000,000 in 1948; 2,000,000 in 1965) numbers of visitors. "To conserve the scenery and the natural and historic objects. . . ." The challenge grew imponderable.

Bear research did not resume. Yellowstone was the subject of continued study (one project ran from 1948 to 1957) concerning elk, which had become its major wildlife problem, but the service spent little on other projects. As in earlier years, park naturalists and rangers gathered what information they could, but this was fragmented progress at best. It was not until 1959 that independent researchers, providing their own funding, began to study Yellowstone's grizzly bears (they eventually received some help from the Park Service).

In 1960 a new set of bear management guidelines went into effect, generally aimed at doing more efficiently what had been done in the past; avoid having too many black bears along the road, stop roadside feeding, and educate visitors. The approach was more systematic, involving more training for personnel in bear capturing techniques (drug-firing guns were now being used) and park management, and record-keeping was improved. Despite these things, the basic problem remained: too much food was still available, and management was still a holding action, trying only to keep the problem at a tolerable level.

In 1963 the Advisory Committee to the National Park Service on Research, while making a service-wide study, was "shocked to learn that the

100

research staff (including the chief naturalist and field men in natural history) was limited to ten people and that the Service budget for natural history research was $28,000 — the cost of one campground comfort station."

That same year a far more famous report appeared, one that is still discussed and debated today: "Wildlife Management in the National Parks," prepared by the Secretary's Advisory Board on Wildlife Management. The report, known commonly as the "Leopold Report" after the board's chairman A. Starker Leopold, was a major step toward restoration and preservation of natural ecosystems in the parks. The board recommended that park biotic communities should be maintained in as near a primitive state as practical, keeping always in mind that human use would prevent achievement of perfect primitiveness. The report has led to occasional criticisms of the Park Service as having an unrealistic goal, but those criticisms are largely unfounded; the report, and the host of subsequent management reports and guidelines used in various parks, are in general quite realistic about what can and can't be achieved in restoration of primitive conditions. Indeed, the Leopold Report itself recommended various kinds of manipulation of the natural setting, when necessary to protect the various elements of that setting, and stressed that the *appearance* of primitiveness was just as much the goal as the actuality:

> If the goal cannot be fully achieved it can be approached. A reasonable illusion of primitive America could be recreated.

In recent years the most interesting discussions of this mission have involved the extent to which the parks are to preserve some particular state of primitiveness: the alternatives include the condition of a park the day it was established, or when it was first visited by Europeans, or by simply letting nature do what it wants. The tendency in Yellowstone has been to recognize that it is more or less impossible to exactly re-create any past state of nature, and that there is much more to be learned and enjoyed by letting the natural system function as it will. This is an inordinately involved issue, one I explore in some depth in another book, *Mountain Time*. For the purposes of the present book, it is enough to say that bear management has offered us an interesting case study in the challenges of natural area management; some of the issues that were probably not even guessed at by the writers of the Leopold Report will be considered in later chapters.

Of more immediate interest was another recommendation of the report, one echoed by the committee on research mentioned earlier: the Park Service needed to do a lot more ecological homework. Furthermore, the Leopold

A 1961 photograph of an all-too-common sight in those days: a grizzly bear making itself at home in a park campground, in this case at Old Faithful. N.P.S. photo.

Report urged that this "mission-oriented research" (that is, research aimed at solving specific resource management issues) should be conducted by the Park Service; it was not believed that independent researchers or researchers from other agencies would necessarily have an appreciation for the Park Service's unusual mission of preservation. The issue of independent researchers and their supposed lack of appreciation of park goals is part of the next chapter; Leopold and his fellow board members were prescient in anticipating problems.

So by the mid-1960s a general goal had congealed, to study the natural resource issues and at the same time attempt to restore conditions to as primitive a state as possible. In Yellowstone that meant many things. When Jack Anderson became superintendent in 1967, he faced a raft of resource issues that were either already hot or showed signs of getting that way. The park's fish populations were in awful condition, the great trout population of Yellowstone Lake having become totally collapsed by excessive harvest. Elk management was constantly a political and ecological problem; the public was outraged over Park Service efforts to keep the herd down to what was at that time considered a "healthy" size by killing or trapping thousands of elk (the meat went to Indian reservations, the live animals were used to restock elk ranges elsewhere in the country). The park was about to embark on a natural fire policy that would reverse an eighty-year program that had suppressed all wildfires and had thereby had untold effects on the dynamics of the natural ecosystem. The centennial of Yellowstone was approaching (1972), and the park would host an international conference of park managers and would be in a world-wide spotlight. The resource, what with the elk problems, the wrecked fishery, and the bears living on garbage and roadside handouts, was not a showcase item. Visitation was climbing, and the roads, developments, and backcountry were showing the wear. Anderson's mission was to do some serious housecleaning, aimed at the restorations recommended by the Leopold Report. People may never stop arguing over whether or not he did it right.

But as far as the bears were concerned, Anderson's deliberations had an additional element. It was apparent, after the 1967 grizzly-caused deaths of two girls in Glacier National Park, that bears were a spectacularly sensitive subject. A bear mauling was Big News. It was, actually, Big News because it was so rare; there were only two bear-caused deaths to that time in Yellowstone's history. It was much rarer than drowning, or even death by lightning, if one considered nationwide figures. It was better family media material than chainsaw murder and much more terrifying, especially to urban folks, than death by automobile. Forty-thousand car deaths a year caused nowhere near the sensationalism that one or two maulings did. It was clear, in the excitement and aftermath of the grizzly-caused deaths in Glacier, that 1) people preferred reading about grizzly maulings to almost any other form of death, and 2) it was unwise to be "in charge" of a grizzly that killed someone.

Meanwhile there was already underway a landmark study of the Yellowstone grizzly, a study that would have great importance, not only for the information it gained but for the controversy that grew out of it.

Chapter 16

1967-1975/
The Grizzly Controversy

 In the summer of 1959 a small team of scientific investigators, led by Dr. John Craighead, initiated an ecological study of the Yellowstone grizzly bear. Dr. Craighead was part of the Montana Cooperative Wildlife Research Unit, a professor of bioecology at Montana State University, and an employee of the U.S. Fish and Wildlife Service. Funding for the study, which lasted more than ten years, came from many sources: The National Geographic Society, the Boone and Crockett Club, the New York Zoological Society, the National Science Foundation, the U.S. Fish and Wildlife Service (then called the Bureau of Sport Fisheries and Wildlife), the Philco-Ford Foundation, the National Park Service, the Atomic Energy Commission, and the Environmental Research Institute. The funding totalled, at last, over one million dollars.

The goals of the study were ambitious:

1. to study the population dynamics of grizzlies, determining population density, sex and age composition, breeding age, reproductive capacity, mortality rate, and population turnover.

2. to determine home ranges, daily and seasonal movements and relate these to food habits, family composition and population density.

3. to determine carrying capacity and habitat requirements and relate these to food abundance, population density or structure and hibernation sites.

4. to investigate the role of the grizzly as a predator and the effect, if any, it may have on regulating the population of elk and other large prey species within a national park.

The last goal was deleted from the study as of the 1964 project report, but the others stuck. It was a project of enormous promise.

Working primarily with grizzlies that frequented the park's several dumps, the Craighead team launched their study. They pioneered radiotracking techniques, field aging techniques, and effective systems for ear-tagging bears for field identification (using variously colored plastic streamers). Once techniques were proven, they tracked bears to dens, recorded age-sex ratios and mortality rates, determined ranges, observed social behavior, and gathered tremendous amounts of information. Theirs was the first major study of grizzly bears, and it remains one of the most exhaustive. Practically every bear study, whether of black, grizzly, or polar bears, that has followed has been indebted to the Craigheads, about whom other bear biologists have said, "They taught us how."

Over the course of eleven years they marked more than 260 animals. In eight years they made "48 instrumentations of 23 different bears," attaching radio-collars to them and accumulating over 1,000 tracking days of data. Because of their scientific work and their related work in filming and popular writing, John Craighead and his brother Frank, at that time a professor of ecology at S.U.N.Y., Albany, became internationally known as grizzly bear authorities. Now and then throughout their study, however, it was evident that all was not well between the Craigheads and the National Park Service. There were occasional misunderstandings and the sort of personality conflicts one would expect, but there was, from the very beginning, potential for more.

As I've already suggested, the Park Service had never taken its scientific responsibilities in Yellowstone as seriously as some wished it would. Bear research had been virtually nonexistent before the Craigheads began their work, and it seems that little thought was given to the terms of the research agreement that was set up between the team and the service. In its earliest terms, the cooperative agreement between the Montana Cooperative Wildlife Research Unit, as represented by John Craighead, and the Park Service had specified that one result of the study was to be a set of management suggestions prepared by the scientists for the use of the Park Service. According to the 1962 version of the agreement, these were called a "management plan." The provision for this management plan was deleted from agreements between the team and the Park Service after 1964, probably because the Park Service was growing more sensitive about its own responsibilities toward resource management. The Leopold Report of 1963 had specified that management-oriented research should be conducted by Park Service scien-

In the early days of their study, the Craigheads and the Park Service usually got along reasonably well; the team's work yielded much information and experience of use to managers. N.P.S. photo.

tists, and perhaps park administrators felt they were giving away too much authority to the Craigheads.

Legally, they might have been. Researchers who work in parks are routinely—almost invariably—encouraged to advise managers on management, and the managers would be foolish not to take advantage of such expertise, but directing independent researchers to actually formulate policy was another thing. At the time that the "management plan" provision was removed from the agreement, there was no apparent dissatisfaction from any party, but it would eventually become clear that sufficient understanding of just what the scientists were to give the park had not been achieved. Their role in relation to management was never adequately clarified.

The Park Service benefited from this study in many ways even before its results were widely published. The Craighead team taught a number of park personnel how to trap and handle bears, and often assisted in the routine handling of problem bears. If their presence in the park was to become something of a problem for the Park Service eventually, it was also quite an advantage at times.

The uproar over improving the Park Service's commitment to the park's ecological integrity was showing real effects by the late 1960s. By the time Jack Anderson became superintendent there was widespread sentiment against any unnatural food sources for bears, and pressure was mounting to close the dumps. The dumps had been the center of focus for the Craighead study, of course, and the Craigheads were far more knowledgable about the park's bears than the park's own managers, and so it came about that the Craigheads put together a report in 1967 entitled "Management of Bears in Yellowstone National Park." It was not a polished, final report with full presentation and interpretation of data (which they were still gathering); it was instead a sort of interim document, designed to advise the Park Service on the basis of the great amount of information that had been gathered to that point.

This report was to become the subject of intense debate and magnificent confusion over the next four or five years, so it is useful to take a look at some of its major points. Already, by 1967 and 1968, an adversary relationship was underway, but here at the beginning, before the controversy got too hot, we can get a look at some of the issues that underlay the later bitterness and hostility. I'll summarize a few of the Craighead's points, and follow each one with the park service's response. However much you may have read about this controversy, some of this may be new to you; a great many of the journalists who followed this story never bothered to sort out the scientific and philosophical problems from the more colorful "personality" sort of news that is so much more fun to write.

> 1. The Craigheads were quick to point out that this report was not really a research report. Their sense of urgency led them to present their summary and suggestions before all the data was worked up, indeed before the study was even completed: "...though unorthodox, this procedure will permit administrators and wildlife managers to make immediate use of the information presented."

The Park Service, which now had biologists of their own in place in the park, and which had the report reviewed as well by scientists in Washington, was publicly uncomfortable with management recommendations that were not supported by scientific data. They became even more uncomfortable with them when they saw to what extent the Craigheads differed from them in just how to manage the park. They must also have been uncomfortable for at least two other reasons: one, that they had specifically deleted from their working agreement with the Craigheads the provision for the report the Craigheads had produced; and two, that they had not made clear the terms of that agreement long before.

2. The Craigheads had learned that Yellowstone Park's grizzlies were not truly "park" bears. They wandered over an area of some 5 million acres, of which the park was only half. The Craigheads recommended that a single unified management program be established for the grizzlies throughout the Yellowstone area, with full cooperation between the various state and federal agencies that would be involved.

Curiously, the earliest I can find this recommendation in the record it was made by a Park Service official, Gordon Fredine, in 1960. But in 1967 the Park Service paid little attention to this recommendation. Eventually, over the course of the next fifteen years, just such interagency cooperation would become political reality.

3. The Craigheads were concerned about the welfare of the grizzly population. They were convinced that the dumps added enough to the nutritional budget of the bears to be an important part of their survival. They estimated that the average size of the population, based on their dump censuses, was 174 animals, and they believed that the population should continue to receive some nutritional supplement if its longterm welfare was to be assured. At the heart of their discussion was a zoning plan for the park, one which would limit access to various key wildlife habitats in the park as researchers and administrators saw fit, thus allowing managers to "manipulate and control animal populations with optimum efficiency."

The Park Service doubted that the grizzlies needed the dumps. In fact it seems that Glen Cole and Jack Anderson were confident the bears did not need them, and that they believed the Craigheads were underestimating the park's ability to feed bears naturally. After all, they reasoned, Yellowstone had been feeding grizzly bears adequately for many years before whites arrived. In this case they were disagreeing with the Craigheads' scientific conclusions. They went on to disagree with the Craig-

Craighead Team members weighing and otherwise measuring a grizzly bear. N.P.S. photo.

heads on philosophical grounds as well, saying that what the Leopold Report was suggesting was a natural population, not an artificially manipulated one. The new direction in the Park Service was toward returning parks to as near a natural state as possible, and the Craighead proposal seemed unnecessarily manipulative.

This difference was largely lost on those reporting the controversy, by the way. Most journalists zeroed in on a later step in the Craighead-Park Service disagreement, the debate over whether the dumps should be closed quickly or slowly, and were unaware that in the first place the Craigheads didn't think the dumps should be closed at all.

4. In fact, the Craigheads recommended that if the dumps were to be closed that the Park Service should bolster grizzly bears' food with surplus elk and bison. They believed that the dumps kept the grizzlies concen-

trated in a few isolated areas during peak visitor seasons, thus decreasing the chances of human-bear encounters, and they encouraged the Park Service to find ways to continue that arrangement for the benefit of both bears and people. If the Park Service didn't feel comfortable providing carcasses, the Craigheads recommended that at least some dumps be left open.

Here again a philosophical and scientific gap—some would say chasm—had appeared between the two sides. By 1967 Glen Cole was beginning to suspect that the notion of "surplus" animals was a fallacy of some sort. The elk management controversy, having simmered for so many years, had become a hot national issue, and the Park Service was compelled to reconsider some sixty years or more of preconceptions upon which the concept of surplus elk had been based. It was not an atmosphere in which a proposal to kill elk to feed bears was likely to be received hospitably, and within a few years additional historical research by Cole and other park biologists would convince them that the "surplus" concept was out of place entirely in Yellowstone. Whether or not the dumps kept the bears and people apart was a tough question, one the Park Service wasn't prepared to answer completely, not having access to the data gathered by the Craigheads. But even had that data been available, hindsight tells us that neither the Park Service nor the Craigheads could have conclusively won that argument. Almost twenty years later there is still disagreement over just what a dump does to bears, whether it conditions them to lose their fear of all humans even if they see very few humans at the dump. One would think that the Craigheads' judgment on this question should have been the best in the world, but Cole and other Park Service people disagreed. Yellowstone was like many other parks with dumps, and those parks had a wide experience with bears. It was hard to convince Park Service people, even the most scientific, that a dump was a good thing for bears *or* people.

5. As I have said, the Craigheads suggested that if the dumps must be closed it be done gradually, so that the bears could adjust to finding other food sources after several decades of partial dependence on garbage. They were worried not only about bear nutrition but about a sudden dispersal of bears to developed areas in and outside of the park.

The Park Service was inclined to disagree, but accepted the recommendation. At first, in 1968 and 1969, the amounts of food were reduced rather than eliminated. I can save you some suspense on this one and tell you that it never has become clear which approach would have worked better. The Craighead study eventually published most of its data, but none proved that a slow closure was preferable. The Park Service decided on abrupt closure in 1970, not liking the way the slow closure was going, and though the abrupt closure did indeed disperse bears there is no way of knowing now if it did so more or less than gradual closure would have.

6. The Craigheads encouraged a far more systematic bear management program. Record keeping was lax, bear management was not as high a priority as it needed to be, and personnel needed more training.

There were probably some Park Service people offended by this kind of talk, but it was in good part true. Some rangers had a longer experience with bears than the Craigheads, but most didn't. The Park Service as an agency does not have a good record for caring for its administrative paperwork, and it took several years for the park to develop first-class records regarding bear management. This record-keeping problem would later come back to haunt the park. At the peak of the controversy journalists would point out the park bear-management records were incomplete, implying that records were intentionally lost or altered. What was much more likely (and I base this on my experience as park archivist for several years in the mid-1970s) was that some personnel just didn't care about keeping records in the first place and did a lousy job.

7. The Craigheads urged the Park Service to improve visitor education so that people knew what to do and what not to do around bears.

The Park Service would certainly have agreed. The problem faced by all researchers and managers is in good part public ignorance of the resource's needs. The challenge is a formidable one, though, and has never adequately been addressed by the Park Service. Indeed, I doubt that the agency alone could ever perform the public relations miracle of explaining to 2½ million people annually what a wild bear is for.

8. The Craigheads suggested that the black bears should be "managed to provide maximum visitor viewing with a minimum of incidents." Based on past records, the Craigheads estimated that an annual control kill of about twenty-eight bears should be appropriate to keep the roadside black

bears visible but not too troublesome. At the same time, they recommended that the no-bear-feeding rule be vigilantly enforced.

Here was a case of total philosophical disagreement. Park Service administrators had a goal of wildness for the black bears; they disapproved of roadside begging as a betrayal of the principles of the National Park Service Act. If roadside feeding was stopped and the bears redistributed in the backcountry, control kills should drop to almost zero. Probably most appalling to the Park Service was the Craigheads' suggestion that black bears not be fed along the road and yet remain visible for public viewing. Earlier generations of Park Service officials had expressed that same idea, that somehow the bears would stay there even if you didn't let people feed them. By the 1960s it was clear to managers that either you had bear-feeding along roads or you didn't. If you didn't you didn't have bears along the roads at all. They wouldn't stay unless fed.

9. The Craigheads urged that additional research be done, both by them and by others, to refine our understanding of the ecological relationships of park wildlife.

In principle the Park Service agreed, though obviously they would prefer to have the most important research projects, those that would bear directly on management decisions, done by Park Service scientists rather than by independent ones. Research was on the increase in the late 1960s, including a black bear study initiated in 1965 at the suggestion of the Craigheads. But very soon the Craigheads' research would itself become an object of controversy.

So there they were, already drawing the lines that would harden rapidly by 1970. The Craigheads had the scientific expertise, and they believed that their data, though largely unpublished, supported their recommendations. The Park Service not only wanted to see the data, they energetically disagreed with some directions the Craigheads wanted to go no matter how much data the Craigheads had. It is ironic that with so many major differences between them, so many philosophical gaps between their goals for the park, the controversy should center almost totally upon one topic—the dumps.

The Craighead study had revealed many things about the behavior and movements of grizzly bears that used dumps. From their study they certainly could have made many sound judgements over what will happen to the bears when the dump food is no longer available. The Park Service, however, concluded that for the Craigheads to go an additional step and suggest that one schedule of closure would cause less potential for bear-human conflict than another was to display excessive optimism in the usefulness of the data gathered during their study.

Past experiences in the Park Service dumps varied. The case of the 1941 closure of the Canyon dump, mentioned earlier, has been used to prove that bears disperse quickly into developments and camps when denied garbage. Record high numbers of both grizzly and black bears were killed the year after the dump was closed, and without question some portion of these were bears looking for another source of easy food. But the comparison is not that simple. The 1942 dispersal was accelerated by an apparent shortage of

A "bear-jam" a few miles east of Mammoth Hot Springs in the 1960s, in this case with photogenic triplets. N.P.S. photo.

natural foods that year, which no doubt kept the bears on the move. Furthermore, visitation was way down, so there was less human food available at any source, in or outside the park. World War II personnel shortages may also have complicated the situation, though we don't know how many personnel killed more bears that year because it was simpler than chasing them out of campgrounds. In any event, the situation was not similar enough to the planned dump closures of the late 1960s for comparisons to be especially trustworthy.

There were few other examples to go by. One was in Glacier National Park, where in the 1960s the Many Glacier dump had been closed with no apparent ill effects on bears or people, but grizzly ecology is different in Glacier; the comparison is not a very safe one. There was only one known example of a gradual reduction of garbage at a dump, and it too was in Glacier, where the slow closure resulted in an apparent increase in bear problems.

More than relying on any precedents, the Park Service objected to gradual dump closure in principle because it would give just that many more generations of cubs the opportunity to learn to like human foods and because it would concentrate the bears during periods of increasing garbage shortage, thus increasing the risk of bear-caused deaths among bears. These objections were essentially conjectural, but the Park Service found them more persuasive than the Craigheads' opposing conjectures.

One popular misconception that cropped up here at the beginning, and still reappears now and then, is that the Craigheads believed that the bears would starve to death without the dumps. Journalists jumped on this oversimplification, conjuring up images of faint (or bloodthirsty) grizzly bears wandering across some ecological desert in search of a little nourishment. The Craighead study had amply demonstrated that the park produced a great variety of natural foods, that indeed the bears found food to support themselves for two months in the spring before garbage showed up at the dump and again in the fall for two months after the garbage supply disappeared. The Craigheads were concerned that the loss of this nicely located food source would disperse bears in search of other easy food sources, thus causing more bear mortalities and possible human injuries. They were further concerned that in the long run the natural food supply of the park was not sufficient to maintain the population at its present level, and that eventually the population could decline dangerously, but that is a different proposition from hungry bears. It is also a proposition still being discussed in the 1980s, and, as we'll see later, one with substance.

Between 1967 and 1971 the availability of Craighead data on the dumps became an issue itself. Anderson wanted to see the data that would support the Craigheads' recommendation. Letters were exchanged, some fairly impatient, about this data, and soon it became a hopelessly confused part of the public controversy. Journalists knew only that the Craigheads were the ones with all the data, and that the Craigheads believed their data supported their recommendation that the dumps be closed gradually. The Park Service complained that the data was not forthcoming. The Craigheads were, however, publishing some of their findings, and sending various publications along to the park. Somewhere in here, the data in question, specifically the material that might support gradual dump closure, became mixed up in the public mind with *all* data. The result was that the Craigheads and their growing band of supporters would say that the Park Service *was* receiving Craighead data and was ignoring it. They were, indeed, receiving Craighead data, but none of it was useful in proving that the dumps should be closed slowly. As long as the disagreement over the closure of the dumps went on, it went on without that key data materializing.

Even without the data, however, the Craigheads were in the better position. Who knew better than they how to project the most likely behavior of this population of bears? Certainly nobody in the Park Service knew, and in fact there was no one in the world with their scientific credentials as grizzly bear authorities. Anderson and his staff, partly because they had a different philosophical goal for the park, and partly because they were not impressed with the Craighead argument, were skeptical about a slow closure of the dumps. They were put in the uneasy position of disagreeing with world authorities, and that position cost them dearly in the growing controversy over bear management. The philosophical differences between Anderson and Craigheads were totally lost in the controversy, and the issue of data availability was soon buried under additional layers of debate over new interpretations of the data that did surface.

I must say that the Park Service contributed its fair share to this initial confusion over data. I confine my discussion of the controversy in this book to material drawn from sources I can document: correspondence, publications, reports, and so on. That way, whatever else I may add to the dialogue at least I'm not adding to the misquotations that seemed to plague the story. But here I want to make an exception, and say that when I arrived to work in Yellowstone as a ranger-naturalist in 1972 it was widely thought among Park Service employees that the Craigheads had never submitted any data

Grizzly bears at the Trout Creek dump shared the garbage with other animals, including ravens. This particular bear, photographed in 1967, is wearing one of the Craighead Team's ear streamers for field identification. N.P.S. photo.

to the Park Service throughout the study. That is simply not true. I'm sure the public heard this same distortion often from Park Service people. The Craigheads had published numerous annual reports. They had produced a few articles and monographs. I know from my review of correspondence in the park archives that at least some of this material was received by the superintendent's office.

I also realize that I've devoted a lot of words to the very first stage of this controversy. I'll speed up soon enough; without this foundation, the later events are impossible to understand.

The largest remaining dump in the park was at Trout Creek, several miles southwest of Canyon Village. In 1968 the Park Service began to separate the garbage there, dumping only edible material. They also reduced the amount of edible material in an apparent attempt to follow the Craighead suggestion of phasing out the dumps. The reductions in garbage were accompanied by an increase in bear problems, which led park managers to conclude that an abrupt closure of the dumps would at least get the problems over quickly.

The Craigheads objected that the Park Service had reduced the garbage too quickly.

In the meantime the Craighead team was proceeding with the wrapup of its study. In January of 1969 John Craighead reported that the project was 95% complete, and that the "study should be continued on a reduced basis as the principal objectives have been realized." There was at this time considerable discussion between Craighead and Anderson over just what work should continue in the park, centering around the issue of color-marked wildlife. The Park Service wanted what they called "conspicuous" markings, such as ear tags and streamers, removed from the various elk and bears that had been tagged over the years. Anderson felt that he was getting too many complaints from photographers and other visitors who wanted to see naturally occurring animals. Craighead pointed out that very few visitors ever saw grizzly bears, that very few elk had been marked or radio-collared, and that the marked grizzly bears could be of great value to Park Service managers for years to come in monitoring bear movements. Both remained firm in their positions, but of course Anderson had the power to rule in the matter. Looking back, Anderson's conviction that the tags would be unappealing has always puzzled me. He was especially concerned that the park be a showplace of natural area management during the many celebrations and conferences associated with the park's centennial in 1972, but it has always seemed to me that a tagged or collared grizzly bear is just so much proof of management doing a good job by relying on scientific research for direction. Obviously, Anderson saw it differently, and this comes down to an esthetic judgment over what a park should look like. As it turned out, Yellowstone's grizzlies had a great many more collars to wear in the future, whatever happened in 1972.

Most important in John Craighead's communications to Anderson in the spring of 1969, I think, was a tone of restrained triumph that a monumental research project had been completed. In April, Craighead sent Anderson a letter summarizing the most important achievements of the project and listing forthcoming scientific reports that would result from the work. It's too bad, for all concerned, that the Craigheads and the park never got to bask in the glory of this achievement together.

The disagreement over the dump-closing schedule was a topic of a meeting of the secretary of the interior's Natural Sciences Advisory Committee in Yellowstone in the fall of 1969. The committee reviewed the available literature on dumps, and listened to all viewpoints. The Craigheads presented their recommendations in a two-hour session that included charts and graphs of data they had gathered. In a move that must have seemed odd to many at the time, and that signalled just how bad things had already gotten in the disagreement, the Craigheads refused to make their presentation until all Park Service personnel left the room.

The secretary's committee was composed of A. Starker Leopold (Chairman), Stanley Cain, Charles Olmsted, and Sigurd Olson. Olson was ill at the time of this meeting and did not attend. Their report first summarized the goals of bear management:

1. to maintain populations of grizzly and black bears at levels that are sustainable under natural conditions as part of the native fauna of the park.

2. to plan the development and use of the Park so as to minimize conflicts and unpleasant or dangerous incidents with bears.

3. to encourage bears to lead their natural lives with minimum of interference.

Though the committee made a number of recommendations involving research and management, it did not specifically side either way on the dump-closing issue. They agreed that the dumps must be closed, but also believed that there was no way of knowing whether one schedule of dump closing would cause more or fewer bear problems than another. They were, in short, unpersuaded by the Craigheads' presentation:

Unfortunately, prognosticating how garbage fed grizzlies will respond to deprivation depends on judgement rather than data.

The Committee's report left Anderson free to proceed as he saw fit with the dump closures. Committee members had not energetically supported rapid closure, but they had agreed with his opinion that Craighead data could not be applied to predicting grizzly behavior when the dumps were closed. In October of 1969 the Rabbit Creek dump near Old Faithful was closed and covered over, not to be opened the following year. In March of 1970 the committee met again, in Portland, Oregon, to review progress in bear management. After a briefing on the closure of Rabbit Creek and the closure of the Trout Creek dump, scheduled for the next fall, the committee approved the program:

We feel that you are implementing the program in the manner and spirit of the mutually agreed plan.

Trout Creek was the big one. All the other sizeable dumps in the park had been closed, leaving only Trout Creek and a few outlying dumps that would continue to cause problems near the park for the better park of the 1970s (the last, at Cooke City, was finally closed in 1978). At Trout Creek, where so many famous grizzly bear photographs were taken (you can recognize them because the bears seem to be standing on dirt rather than in grass or weeds), hosted as many as 100 grizzly bears some days.

In the fall of 1970 Trout Creek was closed. The grizzlies, after eighty years of garbage, were on their own. Concurrently, the Park Service had intensified its public education program, was removing black bears from the roadsides, and was bear-proofing garbage cans throughout the park. Guidelines (based in good part on recommendations from the 1967 Craighead report) were established for dealing with bears that repeatedly foraged for garbage in developments: a bear that was trapped and relocated, and then returned to a development within two years could, if managers saw fit, be removed

At feeding time, many grizzlies would gather at the Trout Creek dump. This dump was not reopened after 1970, and the dispersal and redistribution of bears that had used it is still a subject of debates over how much the bears needed garbage. N.P.S. photo.

from the population either by being killed or by being shipped off to a zoo. Many bears, as it turned out, were given more than two chances, but Park Service personnel were familiar with the concept of the "incorrigible" bear, one that will return again and again and will teach its cubs to do the same. Managers were committed to removing such animals from the population.

The Trout Creek cleanup was necessary for more than esthetic reasons. The environmental movement resulted in a host of garbage-related regulations, among them Executive Order 11507, "Prevention, Control, and Abatement of Air and Water Pollution at Federal Facilities." Trout Creek dump sat astride Trout Creek, and was a violation of both air and water standards. Dumps are inherently ugly, but this one was now a violation of federal law.

While the Park Service was making all these changes, their meaning was being interpreted in many ways. Specifically, they were being called a bad idea, and Anderson and his staff were being called worse. By 1969 Frank Craighead, who would always be more vocal and bitter in his comments than his brother John, had gone public with his opposition to the park's dump closures. His accusations went beyond disagreements over science and philosophy. They even went beyond suggesting the park was incompetent. In an article in the *Jackson Hole Guide* (Wyoming), Craighead described a "deteriorating situation," and accused the Park Service of "ill-conceived procedures."

> The number of bears that have been killed has not been accurately reported. It has been stated that the objective is to immobilize grizzlies in campgrounds when the instructions have been to shoot to kill any grizzly seen. Bears that are shot and wounded, then later killed, have been described as bears that have been killed in fights with other bears.

The Park Service denied these charges, and none of them have ever been proven, but here was another layer being added to the controversy, one that had nothing to do with science *or* philosophy. Claims like these were made frequently for the next few years. Most came from uninformed sources (all national parks have running feuds with at least some of their neighbors about something, and all live in a rumor-mill atmosphere) such as the famous "barstool biologists" who happily pronounce on any subject, but some continued to come from people of greater public respect, like Frank Craighead. Many were absurd, like the claims that big pits had been dug in secret places in the park and filled with the bodies of hundreds of bears. Some were more substantial, like accusations of unreported bear deaths. There was talk of a "coverup" of bear killings now and then until the late 1970s. I can't tell you exactly what happened. I don't think anyone can. If Frank Craighead had proof that bears were killed secretly or with distorted record-keeping, he hasn't produced it yet. Not one person has come forth since 1969 with even one solid piece of evidence, such as the skull of one of these clandestinely killed bears, or an admission from one guilty ranger, or a photograph of such a killing or such a carcass. Frankly I don't think the Park Service could have successfully carried out such a secret program; there are too many people in the park at any time willing to blow the whistle, either openly or through friends. No such evidence has surfaced formally, though occasionally there is informal hearsay.

If you want a thorough, angry, and remarkably one-sided account of just how badly the Park Service was accused of behaving, then you must read Frank Craighead's book *Track of the Grizzly*, published in 1979 (you ought to read it anyway, for its fascinating account of the scientific adventure of bear study). In this book you will discover, among other things, that dishonesty was not merely rife in the Park Service, it was well-nigh required. From his perspective, the Park Service was on a mission not only to destroy the bears, but his reputation as well. Whatever he may be right or wrong about in the book, he reveals an embarrassing inability to admit that some of these people, in the Park Service and on various involved committees, may simply have disagreed with his science.

I can't overemphasize how quickly this controversy became almost viciously emotional, and how ripe it was for publicity. Accusations flew, and were published, but proof never appeared. This isn't to say that the Park Service was guiltless of Craighead claims, but it is to suggest that the rule of "innocent until proven guilty" did not apply to the government. Perhaps the situation was best summed up by Wyoming Game and Fish Department biologist Larry Roop, who said that reading the Craighead account of the controversy was "comparable to reading only one side of a divorce case."

But it was just this kind of uncertainty, all of these unproven and suspected things, that made the controversy such a complicated mess. It reached the point where it didn't really matter what the Park Service said it was doing; a certain percentage of their audience was conditioned to disbelieve them. This kind of atmosphere, however hard it may have been on the bears, the Park Service, and the Craigheads, was just heaven for newspaper readers and journalists, and very quickly the noise was being heard in some important political offices. And, by the time the politicians got involved, whatever hope there had ever been for calm, rational discourse was gone.

A few stereotypes developed. The Craigheads became the beleaguered independent scientists whose work was being quashed by faceless bureaucrats. Glen Cole became a scientist-puppet whose job was to produce reports that would support the dump closures. Anderson became a sort of tyrant figure, who, for reasons that never became clear, had suddenly become committed to the destruction of Yellowstone's bear population (the destruction of the bears by park personnel—by lifelong professional conservationists—was puzzling; nobody was able to explain why the Park Service would want to do such a thing). The media, as is their wont, became the heroic exposers of all this evil and injustice.

And, as a result, the bears became pawns.

Government bureaucracies do not welcome uninvited media events. The Park Service, however right or wrong it was on any given issue, did a terrible job with public relations through the controversy; it did not really improve at getting its story out to the public until the 1980s. Cole and other park scientists published their findings in routine ways, either in technical journals or in Park Service reports, where the public doesn't see them. Anderson and his staff weathered a terrible beating in the press, and frustrated their opponents by simply going ahead with their plans despite all the public uproar and publicity. The Craigheads, who proved to be excellent and appealing publicists, grew ever more certain that the dump closures would hurt the bears. Anderson remained confident he was on the right track, and with the backing now of the Natural Sciences Advisory Committee he moved ahead.

Cooperation between the Park Service and the Craighead team ended in 1971, in yet one more action that increased the heat of the controversy. The main study was over, but the Craigheads wanted to monitor the dispersal of the bears, which would require continuation of the techniques they had developed over the eleven years of their study. By this time there is no doubt that Anderson didn't want them around anymore, and his attitude was probably shared in both the Park Service and the Bureau of Sport Fisheries and Wildlife, judging from the terms of the new agreement that the Craigheads were offered. It was a memo of understanding between the Washington office of the National Park Service and John Craighead's employer, the Bureau of Sport Fisheries and Wildlife, and it contained two unusual stipulations.

3. All oral and written statements, including, but not limited to, progress reports, popular and scientific articles and other publications, talks, and press releases prepared by the Montana Cooperative Wildlife Research Unit concerning grizzly bear research within Yellowstone National Park shall be submitted to the Director, Bureau of Sport Fisheries and Wildlife for approval prior to publication or otherwise disseminated to the public.

4. The Bureau recognizes the National Park Service as having the responsibility and authority for all management activities within Yellowstone National Park, and the Bureau will obtain the concurrence of the Director, National Park Service, prior to making any expressions relating to the management of grizzly bears within said national park.

The Craigheads said this was a restriction of academic freedom, and would not accept the arrangement. In retrospect, No. 3 seems quite reasonable, since supervisory review is a routine matter for scientists. No. 4, on the other hand, is a bit unorthodox, to say the least. Independent researchers are commonly consulted as advisors on management. A free flow of suggestion and opinion is a matter of course under these circumstances. It seems plain that one or both of the parties to the agreement believed that the Craighead team was being too outspoken.

The restriction on public statements is not a pretty one, but it is not as absolute a limitation as it might appear. The Craighead team could continue its work, and could continue to publish material of a scientific nature with only routine supervisory control. What the team could not do was publish statements about management. In principle, and according to the earlier study agreements, the team was not responsible for management actions anyway. In fact, the team worked closely with Park Service personnel, and had a very clear and obvious interest in how management was conducted. It is safe to say that many other scientists in the same situation would not accept such an agreement. On the other hand, John Craighead's supervisor, the Director of the Bureau of Sport Fisheries and Wildlife, agreed with the restriction and signed the agreement. John Craighead did not, and so the study ended.

Immediately there was reaction in the popular press. It was said the Craigheads had been railroaded out of the park, that they had been denied the right to do research, and that the park was violating academic freedom. The Craighead field headquarters in the park, an old building loaned to them by the hotel company, was torn down as part of the pre-centennial cleanup. This was seen as proof that the Park Service wanted to obliterate all trace of Craighead work. There was surely no denying that the Park Service did not grieve the ending of the study.

The conclusion of the Craighead study was generally distorted by the time it reached the public. The impression given by most popular articles was that the Craighead study had been cut short, ended prematurely before its work was done. As John Craighead himself reported, the study was essentially complete by 1970. What was cut short was Craighead efforts to monitor the dispersal of the dump bears. They had been seeking to extend the original study to gather this very important new information, but they had not been kept from finishing the original study.

That said, it was still a great misfortune that the study ended when it did. There existed right then in Yellowstone the expertise and technical equipment to monitor the dispersal of at least some of the bears and to observe just how the change in food habits affected them. This information would have been priceless for managers in other areas, and it would have gone a long way toward settling some of the disputes that were then in progress in Yellowstone.

Unfortunately, the disagreement between the Park Service and the Craigheads had gone too far for even the remotest kind of cooperation. Craighead-marked bears had both color identifying tags (these were the ones Anderson objected to) and small inconspicuous ear tags that also identified the bear for record-keeping purposes. As the Park Service handled and moved bears after the dumps were closed, they removed the color tags and either left the small ear tags on or replaced them with their own, tagging as well bears not marked by the Craigheads. Of course park personnel could have used as much information on the past history of the Craighead-marked bears as they could get, but when Anderson requested such information the Craigheads refused to send it. The Craigheads probably saw refusal as a matter of holding on to valuable scientific information. Anderson probably saw it as spite. Whatever it was, it kept park personnel from acting as intelligently as they might have about individual bears because they had no way of knowing the past history of those bears.

Bear control was a hot topic in 1970 and 1971, as the Park Service stepped up efforts to remove problem bears and as agencies on lands surrounding the park became more active in dealing with their grizzlies. In 1970 Yellowstone Park personnel killed twelve grizzlies and sent eight others to zoos. Twenty-four more bears were known to have died, either from management actions or from illegal kills, in the three surrounding states, for a total of forty-four known bear deaths in one year, the highest known total in history. The next year the park killed eight and sent one to a zoo, but the surrounding states brought the total to forty-four. Eighty-eight grizzly deaths in two years, in a population that the Craigheads reported had averaged only 174 animals up to 1967, was alarming, to say the least. But by 1972 Glen Cole and his staff had developed their own set of interpretations of the bear population's status, and they were dramatically unlike those offered by the Craigheads. Again, I'll summarize some of the most important ones, Craigheads first, then Cole:

Population size

The big question, after a couple years of high mortalities, was how many grizzlies are left, and are there enough to maintain the population? The Craigheads were certain that the population was now in serious trouble, and that the fact that many bears seemed to be dispersing beyond the park boundaries, where they were even more likely to be killed, was also a serious ongoing problem. In short, they believed that by 1971 too many bears had been killed already and that the Park Service must stop.

Cole postulated the existence of a large number of grizzly bears in the Yellowstone area that the Craigheads had not counted. He suggested that they were being optimistic in assuming that all the bears in the whole area used the dumps and were therefore counted by them. The Craigheads, in their 1967 report, had specified that "almost all" of the grizzlies did indeed use the dumps and get counted. Cole pointed out that a black bear study done in the late 1960s in Yellowstone had shown, first, that there were two distinct populations of black bears—beggar bears and backcountry bears—and, second, that practically none of the grizzly bears that were incidentally observed by the researchers had Craighead tags. Only one of twenty-seven grizzlies observed by these researchers had a Craighead tag, when the Craigheads assumed they had marked a much larger proportion of the population than 1/27. On the basis of this difference, and on incidental observations by Cole and his staff, Cole suspected that there were 50 to 100 more bears in the Yellowstone population than the Craigheads reported. He believed, then, that this larger population could stand the strain of the increased control removals.

Injury rates

The Craigheads compared their data on human injuries by grizzlies from 1959 to the 1968-1971 period, and found that in the earlier period the average was 1.67 per year and in the latter it was 3.33. This they blamed on the dispersal of bears into developments after the dumps were closed.

Cole responded that the Craigheads did not have complete records of injuries (I must say that as a historian who has used the park's records extensively, I am more impressed with Cole's ability to sort out historical records than I am with the Craigheads'). He further objected to lumping data from 1968 and 1969 in with later years, because those two years were a transitional period with limited supplies of garbage and some unsanitized developments. His injury figures, which I found convincing enough to use in the appendices of this book, showed an average injury rate in the 1960s of 4.4 per year, with an average injury rate of .7 for the period 1970-1973.

Population future

The Craigheads predicted the continued decline of the population and much more trouble in developed areas if management was not revised.

Cole thought the high kill totals of 1970 and 1971 were only temporary and that in a very short time the control kills would drop to practically nothing. He further suspected that when the bears were redistributed in the wild that more cubs would survive to adulthood, basing that suspicion on the high cub mortality (30 to 50%) reported among dump populations compared with lower cub mortality among wild populations. He further suspected that the sows might begin reproducing at an earlier age, on the average, once away from the social pressures of the dumps. This, he suggested, explained the smaller average litter size reported among park grizzlies in 1971. In the 1960s the average litter size had been 2.2 cubs; in 1971 it dropped to 1.9. He concluded that there were not fewer bear cubs, only more families of smaller average size.

What was already happening by 1971 was that, as the Craigheads criticized the Park Service for unreliable scientific hypothesizing, the Park Service pointed out that Craighead data was no longer fully applicable, and had never been complete. Cole based his position on observations of grizzly bears made by a variety of his staff, most of whom did not have the Craigheads' experience or skill at recognizing individual bears. On the other hand, there were some very skilled observers on the park staff, and Cole was rigorous and unyielding in his sifting of reports of supposed grizzly sightings. The Craigheads based their position on their knowledge of a grizzly population under the influence of several dump food sources. Once divorced from the dumps, the bears would use their range in different ways than when they could concentrate so much attention on one dump. This change in bear habits, and the persistent Park Service suggestion that the Craigheads were underestimating the size of the population, left a cloud of uncertainty over the data gathered by the Craighead study. It was a landmark study, yes, but did it still tell us what we needed to know about the bears?

In time, some of the suggestions of both sides would prove true. The bear population, as it would turn out, did not behave as either side predicted it would, but took a sort of middle course, which may or may not tell us something about the nature of opposing positions in a controversy. That is a bit ahead of the story, though.

Bitter words continued to pass between the contestants in 1971. Anderson wrote to John Craighead to object to statements the brothers were making about park management, and to complain that the Craigheads still weren't coming across with the data on the tagged bears that the Park Service needed to help with the relocations of problem bears:

> Here we find preliminary data from park management operations presented in a less than objective or in an inaccurate manner to force your point of view on the National Park Service. You can continue to do this if you wish, but I do not think it should be under a cooperative agreement for scientific studies. We will always welcome recommendations with supporting data, but the latter has not been forthcoming. I find that criticisms are a poor substitute for information where management decisions must be made.

Craighead responded by accusing Glen Cole and Anderson of violating previous agreements. He said that Cole had "simply taken over" parts of the Craighead study, and that both Cole and Anderson had ignored Craighead data and, in fact, had said they didn't believe the data when they saw it. In reading over this correspondence I am struck by how often these people aren't really talking to each other. They're talking past each other. They make good points, but they were too far apart to really communicate.

Also, they have firmed up their misunderstanding over data. When Anderson says he needs more data, the Craigheads claim they've sent him lots and that he's ignored it. He doesn't bother to specify which data, and they don't bother to ask. To Anderson, Craighead reports on the dispersal of dump bears and the high number of killed bears didn't tell him anything he didn't know. I gather from Craighead reports and from popular articles that the high mortalities of 1970 and 1971 were widely seen as proof that fast dump closure was not the right way to handle the situation. That's not what those high death totals prove. They only prove that a lot of bears died when the dumps were closed fast; it's still just as possible to argue that closing the dumps slowly would have killed even more bears. That's the position Anderson took.

Actually the confusion over dead bears was considerably more complicated than most participants were making it out to be. There were many unanswered questions about that grizzly bear population, some of which were almost totally conjectural but which still should have made careful thinkers cautious about pronouncing on dumps.

For example, for many years in Yellowstone the grizzly bears had been deprived of their full share of three of their most important natural food items: elk, bison, and trout. Elk and bison management had kept the populations of those animals very low for decades, and heavy fishing pressure had collapsed the Yellowstone Lake trout population by the 1960s, so that bears no longer had access to a lot of animal protein that had been available in primitive times. Had these factors reduced the bear population, and to what extent had the dumps replaced the losses? Then, as the Park Service allowed the elk, bison, and trout to recover their prehistoric abundance, how well would that replace the loss of the dumps?

Or consider this one. Record-keeping, of things like injury rates, bear mortalities, and so on, greatly improved in the 1970s (partly as the Park Service developed self-defense mechanisms to anticipated criticism). How meaningful was it to compare injury rates in different periods of the park's history when in one of those periods the people responsible for keeping the records were demonstrably uninterested and in another period they were almost obsessively careful about it?

Or this. Critics of the park's bear controls in 1970 and 1971 point to the greatly increased number of control actions—trappings or killings of bears— as proof that the bears had all dispersed from the dumps and moved directly into trouble. What we have here is a dangerous oversimplification. I don't think there's any doubt that dispersal occurred, but the question we have to ask is, to what extent did it cause the deaths of the bears? After 1970, rangers who for years had casually watched bears in and near campgrounds were suddenly ordered to take action any time they saw a bear. Right there is immediate certainty that more control actions will occur. Keep in mind that grizzlies appeared regularly in the campgrounds even before the dumps were closed, including bears that also used the dumps. After 1970, rangers were under orders to take care of any bear in a campground. This means that, whatever the dispersal may be contributing to the problem, there will be a great many more bear actions than in the past. What with bear management practices altered so totally after 1970, it's hard to know to what extent the increase in bear killing was necessitated by dispersal from the dumps. It may just have been necessitated by a new park policy that required more bear management activity. That doesn't let the Park Service and various other agencies off the hook for killing those bears, but it does place the role of dump-food deprivation in a different light.

These are subtle matters, not susceptible to conclusive analysis. But they are also important, because they reveal how many factors park managers had to consider. They deal in unaccountable variables, and conjecture, and they remove the bear management story just a little further from scientific controversy. It got removed in a big way in 1972, when Yellowstone suffered its first bear-caused human death in thirty years.

In 1971 Yellowstone celebrated an entire year without a single grizzly-caused injury, but the celebration was short. The next summer a young man named Harry Walker, from Alabama, was fatally mauled near Old Faithful by a grizzly bear. A large book could be written about this one incident (I'm surprised someone hasn't, considering the success of the book *Night of the Grizzlies,* about the two Glacier Park deaths in 1967). The following information is drawn from park records and the court proceedings. Mr. Walker and a friend were camped in the woods not far from Old Faithful. It was an illegal camp, not near the Park Service campground. Late at night they returned from a visit to the Old Faithful development and met a grizzly bear that had found food left lying on the ground in the campsite. The bear killed Walker and his friend escaped. Walker's parents sued the government on the grounds that he had not been adequately warned of the danger, and they won an award of $87,417.67 in damages. The Park Service appealed the case and the decision was reversed. The Walkers attempted to recover damages through congressional action, as the Hansens had done in 1944, but were unable to do so.

Walker and his friend had entered the park as hitchhikers, and so they had not received the warning literature normally given to people entering the park. They were informed by an acquaintance at Old Faithful that they were camped illegally. Being from another part of the country, they apparently had no experience with camping in bear country.

The Walker case was mostly a trial of park management. Dr. Frank Craighead testified for the plaintiff, reviewing his past criticisms of park management (as early as 1970, John Craighead had predicted that a human fatality would occur from the Park Service's program). To read the Park Service's reports of this episode, Walker and his friend were clearly negligent in several ways. To read Frank Craighead's account, they did absolutely nothing wrong. What really was at issue was park bear management; Harry Walker was an opportunity to again take the case to the public, and the tragedy of his death seemed like a minor element in the story of the court case.

But Walker was like many other Yellowstone visitors. In many other places they could behave just as he did and run no risk at all. The implications of court cases like this one go far beyond personal tragedy. At stake is just how far the parks will be allowed to have a natural setting. People stumble into hot springs, and fall off of cliffs. Other people object to too many railings and boardwalks around hot springs, and barriers that obstruct their view from cliffs. There is some small portion of the visiting public that would like to remove all danger from the parks; more than one scientist has recommended that all grizzlies be removed from Yellowstone. What makes me uncomfortable about each of these court cases, no matter how justified the suit might be, is that they create park policy in a judicial vacuum sometimes thousands of miles from the park. A judge with no interest in, or experience with, wilderness and national parks, can have an inordinate effect on park management, if only as managers try to anticipate where they must be most careful to avoid lawsuits. That may be good legal behavior, but it doesn't seem the best way to run a wilderness. That the Park Service technically "won" the Walker case couldn't have been much comfort to them.

A second court case, in 1973, was a little more lighthearted in its entertainment value. Late that year the Fund for Animals, a Washington, D.C.-based protectionist group, filed a lawsuit against the secretary of the interior, the director of the Park Service, and the park superintendent because no environmental impact statement had been prepared prior to closing the dumps and changing the bear management program. The case was nearly farcical. The Park Service, which had been working on an E.I.S. anyway, was nettled because it seemed to them that closing the dumps was solving, not creating, an environmental problem, and because there never should have been dumps in the first place. In any case, when it became known that an E.I.S. was in progress, and that a review of the park's bear management program was being prepared by the National Academy of Sciences, the Fund for Animals agreed to a dismissal of their suit, agreeing also to retract some remarkably inaccurate statements they'd made in a press release about the Park Service and its management.

The most important event of 1973 was the formation of an Interagency Grizzly Bear Study Team, consisting of research biologists from the Park Service, the Forest Service, the U.S. Fish and Wildlife Service, and representatives of the states of Wyoming, Montana, and Idaho. The purpose was simple: to learn about this "new" grizzly bear population that was now more or less dispersed from the dumps. Two objectives were to learn more about:

1. The status and trend of the grizzly bear population.
2. The use of habitats by bears and the relationship of land management to the welfare of the bear population.

Here at last was an agency-crossing effort that the Craigheads had espoused since at least 1967 (though they were concerned more with management than research, and weren't sure this study was all that necessary considering all the data they had already gathered), and it got off to a rocky start. Anderson, burned by his last encounter with grizzly bear research, placed severe restrictions on the team of researchers, disallowing even radiocollaring. But by 1974 the team was at work, and was quickly establishing not only the need for additional research but their ability to do it. Richard Knight, head of the team, had his work cut out for him; the entire conservation community was waiting to see what the team would find, and was probably also waiting for the slightest opportunity to criticize those findings. Knight eventually proved to be as durable as the Craigheads, and, as we'll see later, he produced just as impressive a study, but it was a slow start.

It was a start that got a considerable boost in 1974 from the National Academy of Sciences. In 1973, the secretary of the interior, responding to the towering national controversy over grizzly management, asked the Academy to "study and evaluate data on the population of the grizzly bears in Yellowstone National Park and to make recommendations concerning the scientific and technical implications of that data." The chosen committee was chaired by a distinguished ecological scholar, Ian McTaggart Cowan.

The Committee on the Yellowstone Grizzlies, whose report appeared in 1974, reviewed a small mountain of reports and publications from the Craigheads and the Park Service. Among the most important new ones was a computer analysis of the bear population made by the Craigheads using data gathered during their study. It projected possible future bear populations depending upon management actions, and it predicted a dire future for the grizzly if the number of bears killed annually did not stay low.

It's worth interrupting the narrative here to mention that at the moment this new computer report appeared, the entire controversy took on a new complexion, though I don't think many people realized it at the time. Perhaps because of continued criticisms from Glen Cole, the Craigheads had become more tolerant of the idea that perhaps they had not counted all the grizzly bears. According to this new report, they estimated that their dump censuses counted about 77% of the grizzly bears in the Yellowstone area. This is significant because up to this time there was at least one participant in the debate—the Craighead team—who was working from solid facts, that is, from the actual number of bears they had seen in the field. The day they moved into the computer modelling arena, where their expertise was no greater than (in fact less impressive than) the expertise of many other scientists, the whole discussion moved to a new, more conjectural plane. The Craigheads postulated the 177-bear average of their counts from 1959 to 1970 was 77.3% of the total population, which, during that period, would have been 229 animals. Cole, on the other hand, estimated that the Craighead census efficiency was only about 50%, and that there were between 319 and 364 bears in and near the park. From here on out, debates centered over how to best estimate the number of hypothetical bears, an exercise at which the Craigheads proved no more convincing than anyone else.

The committee found fault with much of the Park Service's program. They stated that Cole's research program was "inadequate to provide the data essential for devising sound management policies for the grizzly bears of the Yellowstone ecosystem." They objected to restrictions placed on the Interagency Study Team, saying that "it is not possible to determine new biological parameters without re-establishing a recognizably marked element of known size in the population." They agreed, in general, with the Craigheads that "it is most probable that the grizzly population was substantially reduced" from 1968 to 1973, but they also said that "there is no convincing evidence that the grizzly bears in Yellowstone are in immediate danger of extinction."

Their reaction to Craighead work was almost as interesting as their criticism of the Park Service. Though they essentially agreed with the new Craighead population estimate (the committee used 234 as a best estimate), they criticized the Craighead computer model as too rigid. They were inclined to agree with Cole that some "compensatory processes," such as increased cub survival once the population was dispersed, had to be figured into new population projections. On the other hand, the committee admitted that they had no way of knowing yet if such processes had occurred. And yet on the other hand they were inclined to believe that the processes were going to permit the population to recover. Something for everyone, though not in every sentence.

Their recommendations for the Interagency Study Team were especially timely, and included, as already mentioned, the right to mark bears, as well as increased involvement by independent researchers and a clearer separation of the team, physically and fiscally, from Yellowstone research offices. They further recommended that the team not be headed up by an employee of the National Park Service, but by "a neutral individual acceptable to all cooperating agencies."

For the bears, the committee emphasized reducing all known bear deaths in what was now being widely called the Yellowstone Ecosystem to ten or less a year. There was special concern about the number of bears killed outside the park as "nuisances," bears that caused stock or other property damage. One of the strongest messages the committee sent to all participants through this report was that it was imperative to keep the number of bears killed each year as low as possible.

The response by the various parties to the committee's report was probably predictable. The press, and various supporters of the Craigheads, went right to the many specific criticisms of the Park Service and made them into headlines. The Park Service went right to the line about the bear population being in no immediate danger of extinction and felt vindicated. They were both right. Or wrong.

Being an agency with formal responsibilities in a matter of this sort, the Park Service responded specifically to the report. Cole, in a memorandum to the research files, analyzed various committee calculations, showing to his own satisfaction that their population estimates did not hold up as well as his. The Park Service refused to consider having a "neutral individual" head up the Interagency Study Team on the grounds that it would "pre-empt agency management responsibilities," and further pointed out that Knight was recruited directly from the academic community to head the team. The suggestion that a Park Service head of the team would somehow be tainted must seem especially annoying to the Park Service now that Knight has frequently proven himself to be an independent, tough scientist, and now that push has come to shove and all the meaningful funding for the Interagency Study Team comes from the Park Service. In those first years many agencies were willing to chip in, but in the long haul the Park Service is paying the bills.

There is an extraordinary footnote to the committee's work. In 1975, Cole and Cowan communicated further, comparing notes on the committee's population calculations, and Cowan reversed his earlier position, agreeing with Cole that the Craigheads seriously underestimated the uncensused portion of the population. Cowan concluded that "we will now be estimating that the total population averaged 301 grizzlies over the 1959-70 period." This, though it amounted to a more or less complete vindication of Cole's earlier estimates, and though it gave the Park Service additional reason to believe their management program was on the right track, didn't get much publicity. In fact, most later writers, especially in the popular press, are unaware of it.

The Interagency Study Team responded to the committee's report in many ways. Team budgeting was separated from park budgeting, and the team's headquarters were removed from the park offices to Bozeman, Montana. The team got into the radiotracking business, at first with bears that were trapped outside the park but eventually with bears throughout the Yellowstone Ecosystem.

I have often wondered if, when the committee recommended increased involvement by "independent researchers" they were actually naive enough to think the Craigheads would be invited back in just then. If they were, they were to be disappointed. But if "independent researchers" meant an influx of personnel from the academic community, then the Interagency Study Team was just what the committee was after. About a dozen graduate projects, resulting in theses or dissertations, have resulted from the team's cooperation with nearby universities (the Craighead project resulted in one such thesis in the same length of time).

The report of the Committee on the Yellowstone Grizzlies is something of a milestone in the story of the controversy. Obviously, the report settled very little. It may have, for at least a short time anyway, reduced the level of hysteria about the condition of the grizzly population. After 1971 the number of bears killed in the Yellowstone ecosystem dropped quickly. In 1972 the total was twenty-four, with nine killed by the Park Service control program. In 1973 the total was eighteen, and in 1974 it was sixteen. In 1975 it was three, and there was talk in the Park Service of a problem solved and a bear population that had now adjusted to its new wild lifestyle. There was a lot of truth to that, but the problem was only evolving. It may never be

Black bears trapped in developed areas are usually hauled by truck to an isolated portion of the park; only grizzlies get flown to distant backcountry sites because of costs and the grizzly's greater determination to find its way back to a good source of food. N.P.S. photo.

fully solved as long as people and bears want to use Yellowstone. Since 1975 we've learned a lot about what will be required to at least keep the problem under control.

Before turning to that, though, we must catch up on the black bear. For most Yellowstone visitors in the 1970s, the only evidence of the bear management program was the disappearance of black bears from the roadsides. The black bear story was rarely an issue in the controversy, though since the early 1980s blacks are getting a little more attention as the debate goes on. Their divorce from roadside feeding proceeded swiftly. All campgrounds were equipped with bear-proof garbage cans by 1970, and by 1971 all but two of the cabin complexes were also "sanitized." This meant that every day the Park Service was emptying 2,000 bear-proof garbage cans. Roadside beggar bears were chased from the road, or trapped and transplanted. Incorrigible ones were destroyed or removed from the park. At the same time, the ancient regulations against bear-feeding were suddenly, and strictly, enforced. Visitors who for decades had enjoyed a holiday at the Yellowstone zoo suddenly faced fines for their efforts. By 1975 it was possible to spend two or three days driving the park roads and not see a single beggar bear.

Many visitors were disappointed, just as some had been when the last public feeding ground had been closed in 1941. Most people, when the situation is explained to them, will grudgingly admit that it is better for the bears. For some, a trip to the park was not worth the trouble without bears to feed. For others, it seemed the Park Service was somehow failing them because it could not make bears easier to see. Very few people are old enough to recall the days before roadside begging became common, when Yellowstone's bears were rarely seen except at a few dumps. Even the oldest "old-timers" know of nothing in Yellowstone but beggar bears. The change in black bear distribution was accomplished much more easily than a corresponding change in visitor attitudes about bear feeding. Park visitors may never stop asking rangers "where are the bears?"

Yellowstone's bear controversies are a marvel. To those not involved it must seem incredible that professional scientists and managers, all of whom were committed to protecting the natural resource, could make such a mess of their communications and reduce normal administrative process to such confusion. To those who were involved, the mess is old news. If they could have figured out a way to avoid it, they probably would have. The controversies were ugly; they degenerated into quarrels. The controversies were destructive; they enabled people who don't care about bears, and who wanted to develop some grizzly bear habitat outside the park, to point out that the researchers couldn't even agree on the status of the animal, so why should they worry? The controversies may have had one small benefit though, one that surely could have been achieved in a less painful way. They did at least alert many people to the problems faced by the bears of Yellowstone. As we will see, the bears, especially the grizzlies, will need all the friends they can get.

Chapter 17

Grizzly Bear Recovery

The controversy over grizzly bear management did not end in 1975, but, following the report of the National Academy of Sciences committee, management did enter a new phase. The committee, by formally delineating the full scope of the problem of protecting the bear, helped to focus attention on the future. Though there was certainly plenty of reason to debate the events of the early 1970s, there was something more important to be done, and that was to concentrate on making sure that the grizzly bear, whatever its exact status, had the necessary help to survive. To provide that help, scientists, managers, and a broad assortment of conservationists would have to spend less and less time reevaluating statistics from the past and more and more time learning about the needs of the bear in the present. Eventually enough could be learned about the bears without garbage to make some meaningful comparisons to the old days of the dumps, but in the meantime there were other things to do.

What changed, then, was a divided management structure that left each agency more or less independent in managing the grizzlies that were at any given time under its jurisdiction. Piecemeal, as I'll show in a moment, the necessary bureaucratic equipment was developed to do what a few foresightful people had been urging for years: manage the bear's domain in and around Yellowstone on an ecosystem basis, not on a fragmented, boundary-segmented basis. What changed at the same time was that the park's various critics and supporters, both individuals and organizations, devoted more and more energy to seeing to it that this boundary-crossing effort was taken seriously. It became widely apparent by 1975 that the future of the bear depended largely on giving it room not only in the park but in the rest of its remaining territory near the park. Though bureaucratic boundaries will never completely disappear, after 1975 there was less talk among thoughtful people of individual bears as "Gallatin Forest bears" or "Yellowstone Park bears." They were all bears of the Yellowstone Ecosystem, and they needed the whole place to survive. It was up to the government agencies involved to see to it that they got what they needed.

The Park Service provided an important piece of the machinery back in 1973 when it initiated its bear monitoring program. The monitoring system provided a coordinated, centralized clearinghouse for all bear sightings, black, grizzly, and unknown in the park. With this system it has been much easier to know what bears (and people) are up to at any time in the park. For example, the system allows managers to alert a ranger that a series of sightings over the past few days seems to suggest that a grizzly bear sow with cubs may be heading for certain meadows (or trails) in his area, and that he might want to keep hikers in that area alerted. This is not a scientific program, mind you; its goal is management. But it has yielded considerable information that complements what the scientists are learning, and it has given managers a much better grip on potential problems than they had before. But it was only a small part of what was needed and what eventually would be created in an attempt to have what is almost universally called a "recovered" population of grizzly bears.

Recovery became the appropriate term for the management process in 1975 when the grizzly bear in the Yellowstone Ecosystem was officially classified as "threatened" under the terms of the Endangered Species Act. Once an animal has been formally classified as "threatened," which is not as grave a classification as "endangered," its future gets a new look by a whole lot of people.

This classification came at a time when there were still a good many people in the Park Service convinced that the grizzly bear population was in no danger, and when there were critics who were expecting the last grizzly bear to vanish any minute. Like anything else the government might have done right then (or any other time, come to think of it), the classification was criticized from many quarters.

The advantage it gave the grizzly bear was that once so classified, an animal has certain legal rights. Perhaps most important of these is that the animal's habitat needs will be clearly defined, and a "recovery plan" will be developed. The classification as "threatened" compelled agency managers in and around Yellowstone to determine the critical habitat necessary to the recovery and support of a healthy grizzly bear population. The agencies must do more than determine the critical habitat; they must make sure it remains useful habitat.

For the most part this seemed of little concern inside Yellowstone Park, at least as far as formal development goes. After all, practically all of the park was wilderness, with less than 1% actually developed. However, thanks to the research of the Interagency Study Team, we know that even the park is not measuring up as it should as habitat. First, there are a couple of troubling developments called Fishing Bridge and Grant Village. Fishing Bridge is a complex of stores, campgrounds, and similar services just east of the outlet of Yellowstone Lake. It is one of Yellowstone's most popular developments, built early in this century. Grant Village is a modern sort of resort-type development along the west shore of the Lake, built mostly in the 1970s and 1980s. The park's master plan, in its 1973 form, said that when the Grant Village complex was complete it could serve to replace Fishing Bridge, the latter known to be in a glorious natural setting that deserved better than a trailer park on it. In the early 1980s, as the Grant Village complex neared completion, the Park Service began to show real interest in actually removing the Fishing Bridge development. They phased out the cabins over the course of a few years, but ran into intense public and political opposition to doing any more.

At the request of the director of the National Park Service, in 1984 Yellowstone's staff put together a detailed report on the ecological effects of the Fishing Bridge development. The development, which includes a 308-site Park Service campground and a 353-site concessioner operated trailer park, sits astride the peninsula between the Yellowstone River and Pelican Creek. The report described this area as "a crossroads of energy forms and life forms that is unique in Yellowstone Park." This has many implications, but for grizzly bears the results are plain. Grizzlies have few better habitats in Yellowstone than the Fishing Bridge area, and even when there are no human food sources there, the bears want to live there. As a result of human presence and the bears' natural interest, the report estimated that since 1966 Fishing Bridge has cost the bear population at least nine adult females, with an additional loss of at least nine female cubs that those females were prevented from pro-ducing. As we will see later, that number of bears could have significantly altered the present population status of the bears in Yellowstone. The report also demonstrated that Fishing Bridge has experienced a strongly dispropor-tionate number of human injuries by grizzly bears; between 1968 and 1983,

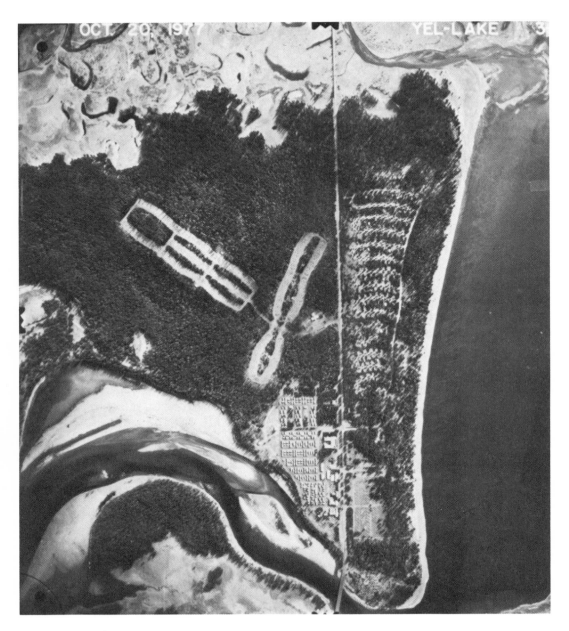

An aerial view of the Fishing Bridge development in the late 1970s. Since this picture was taken, the cabins on the bottom have been removed. The outlet of Pelican Creek is on top (east), and the outlet of Yellowstone Lake is beneath the campground. The site has generated controversy as the Park Service has tried to remove the development as being a major "population sink" for grizzlies. The campgrounds are at the heart of a major ecological crossroads, one the bears naturally tend to use heavily. N.P.S. photo.

62.5% of all injuries that occurred either in a development or within one mile of a development occurred at Fishing Bridge.

Working for the Park Service as a consulting researcher, I helped write that report. As the information came in from various researchers and technicians, we could see again and again that back in 1973 the park planners had been right; this was a singular place, with exceptional value to grizzly bears. The final report made it quite clear that, had the Fishing Bridge development never been built back in the early days, it would certainly never be allowed now. It is a frightening grizzly population sink.

But, as the Craigheads learned long ago in a different sort of controversy, just having a great deal of scientific information doesn't necessarily prove you'll get your way. Various citizens' groups, including a national recreational vehicle group called the Good Sam Club (Fishing Bridge is the only campground in the park with full-service hookups for campers) and business groups in Cody, Wyoming, have applied pressure on the appropriate politicians so that it remains unclear if the park will be able to remove Fishing Bridge. Just knowing it needs to be done is not enough, and the park is now being glowered at from several directions. Defenders of the grizzly bear point out that, back when Grant Village was being built, the U.S. Fish and Wildlife Service only agreed that it would not have adverse effects on the grizzly bear because the Park Service promised to remove the Fishing Bridge development. Now both developments are there, and both are having their effects. The last sentence of the report sums it up:

> If Fishing Bridge alone were able to seriously affect the grizzly bear in Yellowstone, Fishing Bridge operating in concert with Grant Village has a potential cumulative effect that is disastrous.

The problem is bigger than a misplaced development. The problem is increased pressure on grizzly bear habitat throughout the park. As the Interagency Study Team gathered data on the movements of the free-ranging bears of Yellowstone it gradually became clear that those movements, even miles from any development, were significantly affected by human presence. By the early 1980s, for example, it was apparent that the entire lower Pelican Valley, one of the richest bear habitats in the park, was largely deserted by the bears once summer came and hikers and fishermen moved in. Scientists use polite terms like "avoidance behavior," but practically speaking we are just squeezing bears off their range.

Again the Park Service took steps to mitigate the damage, and again the public outcry was great. A group of "Grizzly Bear Management Areas" was established in Yellowstone's backcountry. They totalled about 20% of the park, and each was designed to protect the bear. Some, such as those around trout spawning streams, were closed to visitors for a few weeks a year. Some were restricted so that hikers could not travel except on established trails. And some were essentially closed to the public. In each case the Park Service, basing the decisions on what they knew about bear use of the area, limited human use only as much, and as long, as seemed absolutely necessary, and it was made clear that the closures were experimental, with an eye toward seeing how the bears responded to these sanctuaries. No major visitor attractions were affected during the tourist season. Less than 1% of park visitors would even be potentially affected by the closures.

But all that was lost by the time it got to the public. *Newsweek*, for example, ran an incredibly inaccurate article under the title "Whose Park Is It, Anyway?" in which a variety of outfitters and local businessmen were quoted on grizzly bear ecology. They brought in the Craigheads' opinions (misrepresenting at least one of them), though the brothers have not studied Yellowstone's bears for fifteen years. They even misquoted me (one knows one has become fully part of the problem when one is misquoted in *Newsweek*). But not a word did we hear from the Interagency Study Team, the only current scientific authorities on Yellowstone's grizzlies. The *Newsweek* article hopelessly confused the proposed Fishing Bridge closure with the backcountry closures, treating them like part of one simple plan. The average *Newsweek* reader must have been indignant that these Park Service people were being so dumb and keeping him out of the park.

But the *Newsweek* article was typical, if revealing: the loudest shouts come from the small minority most immediately affected, whether it be the recreational vehicle owners at Fishing Bridge or the outfitters who make a living guiding tourists in the backcountry. Small groups like those traditionally are the best organized, while the grizzly bear must depend for defense on conservation groups that, no matter how loud they may be, are often lacking in political clout when it comes to a specific case. The Park Service is still — much more quietly — doing what it can to limit access to certain key bear habitat in the park, but there is little fanfare. Ironically, the park critics who backed the Craigheads when they wanted to set up a zoning system to better manage Yellowstone's backcountry were silent when the park got around to trying the idea out.

The disillusioning thing about all this debate, at least for the newcomer, is the great extent to which right and wrong aren't as important as more powerful or less powerful. Opponents of the Park Service felt this way back during the dump debates. In that case the Park Service had the necessary political backing to do what they thought was right. Now, when there is widespread agreement among the scientific authorities (something that rarely happens) that the Fishing Bridge development is a dreadful drain on the bear population, the political power is insufficient to get rid of it. The reality of bear politics is hard on idealism.

It may yet happen that the Fishing Bridge development will go. In 1985, the new director of the National Park Service, William Mott, expressed his interest in seeing it removed, and it is still an active management goal. Officially it is still going to happen, but no one will say how soon. The bears can't wait too long.

The rhetoric of these debates is worth consideration here. The first refuge of those who oppose any restriction or new management of human use in the park is to point to the founding legislation of Yellowstone where it says that the park is "for the benefit and enjoyment of the people." It doesn't, they proudly announce, say anything about *bears*! It surely doesn't, but a century of subsequent legislation, the laws that really defined the park after the founding legislation created it, have a great deal to say about bears. Most specifically, the National Park Service Act of 1916 required the Park Service to conserve the wildlife and to allow people to enjoy it "in such a manner and by such means as will leave them unimpaired for the enjoyment of future generations." That's pretty clear; our enjoyment of the bears depends upon the bears being protected from impairment.

National parks are, by legal definition, different from most other places of public recreation. Because of the dual mandate that also requires the Park Service to keep the park unimpaired, public use of the parks must be more gentle. Otherwise the most piggish definition of "benefit and enjoyment" would probably prevail. Obviously, neither the public enjoyment nor the preservation of the natural setting will be perfect; visitors cannot eat park elk, and park elk cannot graze where there are hotels. Those kinds of compromises are implicit and explicit throughout park legislation. But we aren't talking about compromise this time. We're talking about a bear population that is threatened, and that may go down the tubes if we don't strike some new balances between human use and natural protection.

But park resource management problems are nothing compared to what the grizzly faces in the lands beyond park boundaries. Out there, there isn't

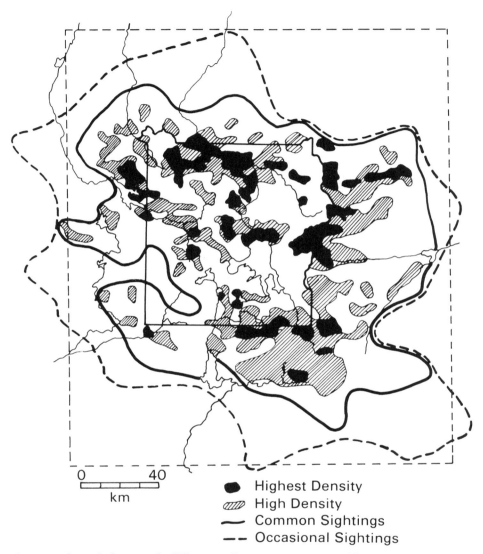

■ Highest Density
▨ High Density
— Common Sightings
-- Occasional Sightings

Densities of grizzly bears in the Yellowstone Ecosystem, 1973-1984. The solid innermost line is the park boundary, and the outer dotted line is a general boundary of what most managers consider grizzly bear range. Most of the highest density areas—those in black—in the park coincide with areas of preferred grizzly bear vegetation, high concentrations of elk and bison, or both. Courtesy of Interagency Grizzly Bear Study Team.

even a National Park Service Act to lean on. There is instead the far more complicated legislation, and infinitely more political arena, of the national forests.

Yellowstone is almost completely surrounded by national forests, those marvelous "lands of many uses" where no one user is ever satisfied that he has truly gotten his fair share. The problem is that half of the Yellowstone grizzly bear's habitat is out here too, and grizzly bears long ago proved that they are not adept at sharing their range with humans. To a great degree, since the fireworks of the early 1970s, when the park was constantly at the center of attention, people concerned about the bear have shifted more and more of their attention to these surrounding wildlands, because it is here, rather than in the park, that the most habitat is in immediate danger.

The national forests are managed by a "multiple use" system, whereby a balance is sought between recreation, logging, mining, wildlife protection, and so on. Because of the extraordinary character of the region around Yellowstone, much of which is no less scenically grand and ecologically diverse than the park, alot of it has already received substantial legislative protection. Most of the Shoshone National Forest, east of Yellowstone, is already classified as wilderness or is proposed for wilderness. A large portion of the Gallatin National Forest, which is both north and west of Yellowstone, is also wilderness. So is some of the Bridger-Teton National Forest to the south of the park. But in all cases there are perilous gaps, and sometimes huge regions, where the grizzly must compete with a wide variety of human uses.

The Forest Service has the same legislative obligations as the Park Service when it comes to grizzly bears. Though they may welcome many uses on their land, the Endangered Species Act requires them to protect the bear's habitat. That process is not going uniformly well. Rick Reese has summarized the many threats posed by developments in his book *Greater Yellowstone: The National Park and Adjacent Wildlands*:

> The impacts of these threats taken one at a time could be mitigated, but taken collectively, and in the absence of some immediate protective measures, their cumulative effect threatens to disrupt this system of wild lands to such a degree that an irreversible degradation of the biological and geological communities of the Greater Yellowstone Ecosystem and Yellowstone National Park seems inescapable.

That is the gloom that hangs over the grizzly bear. If I had a hundred pages to spare I could list all the threats specifically (as Rick has in his book, which takes the pressure off of me to do it again). They run the full range of national forest and private land uses: oil and mineral development with their accompanying disruptions for roadbuilding and exploration; increased recreational pressure, including ski resorts, second home building, hiking, hunting, backpacking, snowmobiling, and the like (we are all part of the problem, however holy we may feel about our environmental awareness); logging; geothermal energy development (this one, geologists suspect, could end up killing the park's geysers as well as the bears, because no one knows if the subterranean "plumbing" of the geothermal areas near the park is hooked up

The modern bear-proof garbage can defeats the efforts of practically all bears. N.P.S. photo.

with the geyser basins); and, if I may generalize even more, the creeping chamber of commercism that infects all beautiful land. I don't have a hundred pages to elaborate on these threats, but I don't need them, because, as Rick partly suggested in that quotation, the danger is a cumulative one.

In the past, and to far too great an extent now, each little intrusion on grizzly bear habitat has been justified through narrow vision. ("The bears can get along without these four acres along this stream where I built my summer cabin—heck, there's five million acres out there for them.") By piecework, nickel and dime, we have been whittling away the grizzly bear's habitat for a century in the Yellowstone area. We are still at it. The message we're getting from the bear, through the Interagency Study Team, is that we must stop. Not soon, but now. There is a proposal—and I am sure it will become reality—for a reactivated gold mine near the north entrance of Yellowstone. It will occupy "only" a few dozen acres, some of which was already damaged by previous mining development. Its environmental impact statement cannot say what effects it will have on grizzly bears; it may take little of their habitat, but it will generate an infusion of labor to the area, and increase such things as poaching, joy-killing, road-kills, and recreation in that area. The environmental impact statement doesn't bother to address the cumulative impact of those new elements in the grizzly bear's Yellowstone range when combined with Ski Yellowstone, a proposed development near Hebgen Lake on the west side of the park that would plop a whole new resort down in what is known grizzly bear habitat (so far with the blessing of Gallatin National Forest), or with the Gallatin National Forest's plans to increase annual logging levels from 13.2 million board feet to more than 20 million board feet (with local logging companies lobbying for 35 million board feet), or with any of dozens of other big and small threats.

To their credit, the national forests around the park are responding with some sympathy to the needs of the bear, and not only because they are legally required to; some of the new appointments in management in these forests are themselves known grizzly bear defenders (Steve Mealey, whose study of Yellowstone grizzly bear feeding habits in 1974 and 1975 was the first M.S. thesis to come out of the Interagency Study Team work, was appointed supervisor of the Shoshone National Forest in 1983). But the bureaucratic momentum to try to do everything with the same resource is tremendous, and conservationists and scientists frequently complain that the forests (to say nothing of the private lands near the park) are still not living up to the bargain.

What has emerged in the past decade, and what the national forests and a host of special interests are trying to come to terms with, is a very old idea, really, but one that has never before been presented with the vigor and force it now has: that the entire Yellowstone region, perhaps ten million, perhaps twelve million acres, needs some unified, long-range management direction that will keep preservation of the area's unique natural characteristics foremost at all times. There is now an organization, The Greater Yellowstone Coalition, in Bozeman, Montana, working to promote that goal. In 1985 there were congressional hearings in Washington on the future of the area; the various land managers involved more or less defended their part in the system, with most disapproving of any sort of umbrella administration, while various conservationists urged just such oversight. As far as the lands outside the park go, especially in relation to the grizzly bear, Yellowstone Superintendent Robert Barbee pretty much summed up the current hopes of bear defenders:

> We are not the first, however, to suggest that merely because multiple use is the guiding principle of the national forests does not mean that it must be applied uniformly throughout the national forest system. Some forests may be best managed for timber harvest, or grazing, or recreation, even to the exclusion of some other types of use. That possibility, or option, seems perfectly applicable to forests in the greater Yellowstone ecosystem. Considering the area's extraordinary values, we believe that the entire Yellowstone area may be best managed, not by trying to do many things satisfactorily, but by concentrating on doing one thing especially well. That one thing is protecting the integrity of the natural systems which are the area's single most important resource.

The occasion for those words was the publication of the draft management plan for the Gallatin National Forest in the spring of 1985. All the national forests are in the process of producing long-range plans, and so far there is plenty to worry about in the plans for the forests that neighbor Yellowstone. Getting the national forests to act a little more like national parks is asking a lot of them. I happen to think they should. A lot of my neighbors here just north of Yellowstone happen to think they should act even more like national forests than they already do, that too much attention is being paid to protecting a couple hundred grizzly bears when loggers' jobs are at stake. Life is not simple.

Whatever may become of the debates over management of bears in the park, the future of the bear will be decided on these lands beyond the park's boundaries. It will in all likelihood be decided in the next few years. It will be a cumulative effect, again, of many decisions, which, while it will ease the conscience of any individual involved, will not diminish the blame we must all share if the bear disappears. The bear may last for decades yet even if things don't go its way in the decisions over managing the Yellowstone area, but one way or another its fate will probably be decided soon.

The structure of bear research and management has evolved in healthy directions since the formation of the Interagency Study Team, and in that we find one of the comforting signs that it is possible for a variety of agencies to communicate effectively now and then.

A moratorium was placed on all grizzly bear hunting in the areas around Yellowstone in 1974. On July 28, 1975, the grizzly bear in the lower forty-eight states was declared threatened under the terms of the Endangered Species Act, and the wheels were slowly set in motion for the preparation of a recovery plan for all six identified areas still occupied by grizzly bears. All six were in Montana, Wyoming, and/or Idaho, though in 1979 a hunter surprised himself and the world by killing a female grizzly bear in southwestern Colorado; if more bears are discovered there (and the chances are slim), that area will be added to the recovery plan as well.

The formalization of modern bear management and the development of the recovery plan is a complicated bureaucratic process that has involved numerous state and federal agencies. Starting in 1974, the Park Service in Yellowstone prepared a draft environmental impact statement for their ongoing management plan, to cover not only research and park management, but cooperation between various involved agencies in efforts to keep bear mortality down. The document moved slowly through writing, public review (with ample criticism), extensive revision (thanks to the ample criticism), and, finally, publication of the completed statement in 1982.

In 1979, work began on the actual Grizzly Bear Recovery Plan, the primary guiding document that was the responsibility of the U.S. Fish and Wildlife Service. The Fish and Wildlife Service has responsibility for monitoring other agencies' management of endangered species. The first draft of the plan was completed in 1981, and the final draft was approved in 1982. The plan provides "a biologically sound program that will result in the recovery of the species and its habitat to a level that will no longer require protection under the Endangered Species Act." There is in this something of turning back the clock; if the Yellowstone population is, indeed, in trouble (as many now believe, and as we will consider in the next chapter), then the responsibility of government is to see to it not only that it doesn't get into worse trouble but that it gets out of trouble entirely. As we will see, there is still considerable difference of opinion over just what constitutes trouble.

Since 1983 all grizzly bear recovery efforts in the lower forty-eight have been coordinated by the Interagency Grizzly Bear Committee. The committee was established as part of an agreement between the Departments of Interior and Agriculture and the governors of Montana, Idaho, Washington, and Wyoming. It is composed of representatives from the various agencies, both state and federal, for whom grizzlies are a concern. Their goals include not only oversight of research projects like the Interagency Study Team but also a variety of law enforcement and public education efforts.

In 1979 the Forest Service published its "Guidelines for Management involving Grizzly Bears in the Greater Yellowstone Area," a careful and thorough document prepared by Steve Mealey, who at that point was a wildlife biologist for the Shoshone National Forest. This document dovetails in function with the general recovery plan and the park's E.I.S. It is the "Guidelines" that provides the specifics of bear management in and around Yellowstone. It established five different "management situations," that is, five ways that land in the Yellowstone area could be defined:

> Management Situation 1: areas containing grizzly bear population centers, key to the survival of the species, with seasonal or year-long grizzly activity, under natural, free-ranging conditions.

> Management Situation 2: areas lacking in grizzly population centers, with some useful habitat and occasional presence of grizzlies possible. Such areas are considered unnecessary for grizzly bear recovery, but may be included in Management Situation 1 as information is gained on the population.

> Management Situation 3: areas where grizzlies are present infrequently but are possible.

> Management Situation 4: areas of great potential suitability that do not have grizzlies but are needed for the recovery of the species.

> Management Situation 5: areas without grizzlies, or only rarely with grizzlies, that are thought unsuitable for bears and are unnecessary for recovery.

Of the five, only Management Situation 1 currently holds an unqualified welcome sign to grizzly bears. In Management Situation 2, bear use is to be taken into account when decisions are made, but bears do not get preference over all other uses. In Situation 3, bears get no breaks, and will be "discouraged" from staying around. Situation 4 areas are not lost to the bears, and, depending upon what research reveals, may become grizzly areas. Situation 5 is probably so inhospitable that grizzlies won't be an issue.

The park itself is designated Situation 1, as are large portions of the surrounding wilderness. In some areas near the park, already-established uses have eliminated what was once obviously Situation 1-quality habitat, so that, for instance, a Situation 1 boundary line may abruptly swerve around a small community. The assumption there, apparently, is that a good many of the developments already existing in the Yellowstone area—practically all of them, in fact—can stay without endangering the grizzly as long as we're careful about what's left.

So the rules are in place, the players know their responsibilities, and there is little question that the administrative machinery and scientific knowhow exist to save the bear. Whether or not it all works depends on the public, and our willingness to share a little more than we have elsewhere.

Chapter 18

Counting on Bears

 In the past twenty-five years, many scientists have taken a shot at estimating the number of bears in the park. We've already seen the huge difference between the Craighead estimates and those reached by Cole and the National Academy of Sciences.

Those estimates, though, were for the population prior to the great disruptions of the dump closures. When the Craigheads, in 1974, published their estimate that there had been an average of 229 bears during their study, they also estimated how many had survived the increased control kills of the dump-closing years. Their conclusion was that by 1974 there couldn't be more than about 136 grizzlies left in the Yellowstone ecosystem, and that the number was declining. The National Academy of Sciences, of course, using Craighead data but incorporating Cole's suggested portion of bears missed by the Craighead count, estimated that the pre-dump-closure population was 301 but did not make an estimate on what it might be in 1974, only that it was depressed but probably recovering. Cole was more confident than that, and in 1975, based on the first findings of the Interagency Study Team (which did not make so bold as to agree with him) and additional observations by park staff, estimated that the population might be recovered from whatever depression in numbers was caused by the high number of removals in 1970-1972. He estimated the population at 250-320, an estimate he stuck with in subsequent years.

The Interagency Study Team was understandably reluctant to jump in with any attempt to reinterpret other people's data and somehow combine it with what they had gathered to that point, so their first try was merely a careful generalization about possibilities: in 1975 Knight and his team allowed that there were probably somewhere between 237 and 540 grizzly bears in the Yellowstone ecosystem. In 1980 Knight and his associates were willing to suggest that there were probably 300-350 grizzly bears. In 1981, stressing that they were making a "point estimate" and not a final calculation, Knight and his team used their accumulated data to estimate 247 bears in the population. This estimate, like the next one, was based on only that portion of the population that they had observed and handled, which made it difficult to know how accurate it was because their "sample size" was relatively small. Though they typically observed or handled 100 to 130 grizzly bears in a summer's study, they had no way of being certain exactly what proportion of the population those bears represented. Population estimates were conducted by extrapolating from a known part of the population to calculate the rest. Thus, estimating (based on how many sows were seen each year with cubs, and knowing that in any given year about one-third of the sows would have new cubs) that there were at least 30 adult sows in the population, and knowing that the adult sex ratio was 62 males to 38 females, they were able to estimate about 49 adult males. Then, also based on observations during the study (they knew that the ratio of subadults to adults was 68 to 32), they added the known adult males and females for a total of 79, plugged it into the formula, and arrived at about 168 subadults. This gave them a total of 247 grizzly bears. Repeated calculations of this sort, year after year, tend to even out the discrepancies of years when observation conditions are not good or when the sows have a smaller than average or larger than average "crop" of cubs. But the accuracy of the calculations always depends on the success at determining just how many sows with cubs there are in a given year. It is not a perfect method, but with a dispersed and hard-to-observe population of animals, it is a respected and established one. Knight and his team did not overstate its reliability, but they used it as they could for general "ballpark" estimates.

Then, in 1982, in the team's annual report for the 1981 field season, came a new estimate that stirred up a great deal of excitement: 197. As usual, the team did not want this taken too literally:

> We wish to emphasize that this is a point estimate based on some small sample sizes, and we are unable to assess its accuracy at this time.

It was also more of a minimum estimate than a mean estimate, so that it probably reflected what the population was at least, rather than at most. But after all the optimistic high numbers it was a shock, and it started a whole new round of uproar, some of which we'll get to in a moment.

By 1984 the team had ten years of information on the new population that was divorced from the big dumps. They were in a position to make some comparisons, and those comparisons reveal many things about the early stages of the controversy.

The biggest news, to most people's minds, was that this population of approximately 200 bears (a minimum estimate) was gradually declining, largely because the number of female grizzlies being killed was too large. Again, the scientists counseled caution in reading these calculations. In a report in *Ecology*, Knight and L. L. Eberhardt summarized their calculations this way:

> Clearly the population will decline into the future if our estimates of certain essential parameters are correct. The simulations suggest that extirpation is not likely over a 30-year period, but there is, of course, no way to be sure that present conditions will persist for 30 years. Most likely they will not, in view of the virtual certainty of greatly increased human use of essential parts of the Yellowstone Ecosystem. Nor do we have any way to predict the impact of reduced population size on its viability.

I want to come back to population viability at reduced size in a little while, but it's possible to do some scorekeeping here that many controversy-watchers might find useful.

First, as soon as the figure of 197 bears was made public, and then again when the projected decline of the population was announced, the first reaction of many people was that the Craigheads had been right all along. Let's look at what they might have been right about.

In 1974, the Craigheads estimated there were about 136 grizzlies left in the ecosystem. This was not a minimum estimate. Now, ten years later, the Interagency Study Team reports a minimum population of about 200. The Craigheads were convinced the population was declining, as is the team. If the Craigheads were right, how did the population "decline" from 136 to 200? If indeed the population *has* been declining since the early 1970s, then it must have been considerably larger than 200 back then. If that was the case, then Cole may have been right about its size but utterly wrong about the direction it was going in. It was apparently going down, though as of 1986 it still has a long way to go to reach 136. Knight and his colleagues suspect that there were indeed a lot more than 136 bears in 1974, though they are as usual reluctant to push any one number too hard. Stephen Herrero, a Canadian scientist, has suggested that the population may actually have re-

Interagency Study Team leader Richard Knight and Team member Bonnie Blanchard prepare a grizzly for radio-collaring and release. N.P.S. photo.

covered in the mid-1970s and *then* gone into a decline not directly related to the high management kills of 1970-1973.

It isn't always fruitful in a situation like this to look back and try to figure out who "won" each argument, partly because as the science progresses it often makes earlier hypotheses irrelevant by introducing new variables. There are some new variables in this story, but there is also some point in looking back. The Craigheads and Cole were both quite confident about their projections and calculations. It would serve us to see how they hold up.

As far as the population's size, it appears that the Craighead estimate of 1974 was much too low. Knight's 1982 estimate of 197 was a minimum estimate, meaning there were at least that many bears then. We can't tell how many more there may be in the total population, but at this point it's at least clear that much of Cole's assurance that the population was all right in 1974 was justified. Of course he was estimating 319-364 bears in the population then; for those numbers to be proven right, it will have to be established that either 1) Knight has missed a lot of bears in his estimates or 2) the population has declined since 1974.

Knight has repeatedly said that he is not relying too heavily on the completeness or accuracy of his estimate, and he has also projected that the population is declining, and so there is still some chance that Cole's estimates were very close to being right. Time, and the continual refinement of population estimates, will probably tell us more. At least it looks now as if Cole's estimate of the bear population was closer to being right than the Craighead estimate. That would be no surprise to Cole, however; his viewpoint was repeatedly reinforced by the evaluations of independent population specialists in the 1970s.

On the other hand, it's always hard to fault a conservative estimate like the Craigheads made. Their estimate may have been too low, and perhaps it generated unnecessary alarms, but with an animal as slow to reproduce as the grizzly bear, it's hard to play it too safe. And, as we will see, some of Cole's other projections have not stood up as well.

The Craigheads were worried that the closing of the dumps would reduce the nutritional budget of the bears, which could have serious consequences for the grizzly population in terms of average litter size and the health of individual bears. Cole was confident that though litter size would perhaps drop it would be because more younger sows would give birth to smaller average litters. The data gathered by the Interagency Study Team gives this round, with one reservation, to the Craigheads. The average litter size during the Craighead study was 2.24. The average litter size during the team's study was 1.9. As already suggested in the first part of this book, grizzly sows had their first litter almost a year later, on the average, after the dumps were closed than before. Furthermore, the average size of adult bears decreased significantly after the dumps were closed.

Those look like pretty clear cases of the Craigheads making much more accurate projections than Cole did, and they may be, but nothing ever seems to be that simple. Since the Craighead study ended, there have been several studies of bears influenced by dumps, and they generally indicate that dump bears are in better physical condition than non-dump bears because of all that easy food. Even in Yellowstone Knight was able to study some bears that fed in the smaller outlying dumps the first few years of his study and then reverted to natural foods after those dumps were closed; those bears got smaller when they lost the dump foods. Again, it looks like the Craigheads had it right. But Yellowstone doesn't give us a constant laboratory to work with, and in the 1970s, a formidable variable was introduced that to some unknown extent makes the obvious differences in the bears since the dump closures less impressive. Yellowstone experienced a drying trend in the 1970s; Professor Harold Picton of Montana State University published a paper in *Nature* in 1978 that offered an alternative hypotheses for the decline in litter size, at least:

> The decrease in litter sizes observed since the closure of garbage dumps seems to be largely a consequence of unfavourable weather during the periods of the final fattening of the mother, winter sleep, birth, lactation, and early spring foraging.

Picton's paper was based only on the first five years of the post-dump period, but it added a note of caution to conversations about litter size that has never gone away, and was reinforced by another paper, by Picton and Knight, 1983. This one, with several more years of population data, reinforced the other one, observing that climate conditions were favorable for grizzly reproduction in the 1960s (during the Craighead study), but that "Climate may have imposed a downward trend upon the carrying capacity since the middle 1970s."

Further complications of the theoretical exercises involved in figuring out how the bears are doing were suggested by Dale McCullough, a populations specialist at the University of California, in 1983. McCullough, in a paper presented at a bear biology symposium that year, pointed out that the average litter size since the dumps closed does not necessarily mean much:

> The percent of adult females with litters, a more reliable predictor, has proven impossible to obtain in recent research. Thus the conclusion that reproductive rates have declined based on low mean litter sizes may be misleading because it might be offset by a higher percent of females with litters.

McCullough's point is that, unlike the dump days, when the Craigheads could easily determine average litter size because so many bears were visible at dumps, Knight is working with a much less visible population, and his sample may not be complete enough to accurately portray average numbers of females with young. As we will see in a moment, the "completeness" of current counts (or, more precisely, the degree of *in*completeness) could have a greater effect on estimates of population trend.

McCullough offered a second, even more intriguing thought. He pointed out that a higher average litter size is not necessarily a sign of a healthy population. Indeed, many animal populations exhibit what is called a "density dependent response" to population numbers, so that when a range approaches its ecological carrying capacity the average litter size will decrease. The sizeable hunting mortality of the 1960s, when total grizzly mortality was more than nineteen per year, may have kept that grizzly population at a level where there was sufficient "room" for consistently large litters. Now, or since the early 1970s anyway, with a great deal more concern about bear mortality, it is difficult to be sure exactly what the lower average litter size means. As McCullough put it:

> A recent concern is an apparently high adult mortality in the eco-system. If in fact adult mortality is high, the reduced adult density should be reflected in high mean litter sizes. Therefore, an increase in mean litter size, rather than being cause for optimism, may be cause for concern, and decline cause for optimism . . . In conclusion, litter sizes can be interpreted as a good, bad, or indifferent sign about the status of the population. In the face of uncertainty we are forced to be prudent, and interpret low mean litter size as a bad sign.

But there is more to current uncertainty than these ruminations on varying litter size. Members of the Interagency Study Team, speaking informally in 1986, have suggested that a smaller average grizzly bear may just be a logical consequence of changing that bear's habits. Not only does it not get as much free food, it has to do different things than it used to in order to get food at all. Look at the pictures of those bears at the dumps; they were lovely big butterballs, perfectly adapted to preying on leftover Salisbury steaks and stale boysenberry pie. A bear in Yellowstone today probably spends more of its time chasing down less passive types of food. Whatever the available nutrients, the resulting bear is likely to be leaner and lighter than a bear that does not have to do as much chasing.

Climate changes, uncertainty about census efficiency, density dependent responses, alterations in bear behavioral needs . . . These are the sorts of factors that have made most scientists cautious about pronouncing confidently about the exact status of the bear population. As time has passed, in fact, the scientific community in general has become less confident about such pronouncements. Things don't look anywhere near as simple now as they did to the participants in the early stages of the controversy.

But this cautiousness is often not shared by the public. Subtle factors of this sort are rarely brought to the attention of the average person who just happens to be interested in grizzly bears; managers and scientists don't get the word out beyond their own circles, and journalists, at least in the case of the Yellowstone bear story, have most of the time proven incapable of dealing with such complexity. Whether because a simpler story is easier to write, or because many journalists just don't do enough homework, this kind of issue is usually simplified for public consumption. An article in the January 1986 issue of *Outside* magazine, for example, simply ignored all these complexities (one of a host of errors in the article) in an apparent attempt to sensationalize an incredibly involved scientific issue and place all possible emphasis on the worst-case scenario—a rapidly declining bear population—that does no justice to the real situation. If I can make only one point in this chapter it is that the Yellowstone situation is too ecologically complex to be fully revealed to the casual glance. The extent to which the scientists themselves disagree seems sufficient proof of that.

One of the most interesting things about what became known as "the numbers game" was that it was largely played inside computers. As I suggested earlier, that put the discussion on a different level than it had been back before 1973, when the Craigheads were talking only about bears they had actually seen and handled. Since their 1974 computer population simulation was published, Craighead data has been evaluated and reevaluated numerous times by other computer specialists, some with considerably more stature in that field than the Craigheads. That original Craighead data has been used to prove almost as many things as have the Holy Scriptures, and the disagreements are huge. Some computer specialists have taken the same essential data, introduced some different but arguably valid variables, and proved that the grizzly bear population needn't have declined at all during the dump closures. The data, and the Craigheads' use of it, have been picked apart again and again, to the point where any cautious observer would think twice about trusting any computer simulation or projection too much. Which is what Knight has been telling us to do for years: here is the best we have right now, but don't count on it being perfect, or even good. It's just the best we have. Luckily, as Knight's study continues, the best we have has gradually been getting better.

In a sense, though, all this arguing over just how many bears there are, or just how quickly they reproduce, or how big they grow or how long they live, is missing the important point. If, as the Park Service tells us, the goal of management in Yellowstone is to have a population in balance with its setting, then the question becomes "How many bears is enough?"

There have been two popular ways to answer this question. The first is the approach taken in the Recovery Plan, where, based upon Cowan's 1975 reevaluation of the Craighead computer analysis, we are told that a "recovered" population in the Yellowstone ecosystem will be about 301 bears. The planners immediately acknowledge that, if it should prove true that the garbage was sustaining the population at an unnaturally high number before 1970, then it may become necessary to redefine a recovered population at some lower number. But until we know more, we'd best stick with those early estimates just to be safe.

That is the Recovery Plan approach, and it is the formal, operational goal of grizzly bear recovery now. It appears that there is a growing sentiment that Yellowstone may not ever be able to reach 301 bears no matter how good the natural food situation gets, but so far it hasn't been incorporated into the plan. If the weight of scientific evidence continues to lean that way, I am sure it will be incorporated eventually. There's no hurry, and I for one don't mind the thought of managers being compelled to get the Yellowstone Ecosystem into good enough shape to produce more bears.

But then there is another approach that has addressed the issue of grizzly bear recovery from its gloomier end. Several population specialists have, in the past few years, attempted to calculate just how small the population dare get before it cannot recover and will be extirpated. They define a "minimum viable population" as one that has at least a 95% chance of lasting for 100 years. Like the computer projections of population and population future, these calculation do not agree. They do not even approximately agree. They range from 50 to 125. But even at that great a variation, they give us some general range that we can at least know we had better stay above.

The concept of minimum viable population is one with many ramifications. It depends not only on the bear's biology, but upon our effects on the bear's behavior. There is a population of brown bears, less than 100 of them, that have been living in a few hundred square miles in and around Italy's Abruzzo National Park for centuries. They are surrounded by populated country, and they are extremely shy. As Steve Herrero, one of the scientists who has studied them, has put it, "Thousands of years of coexistence between Europeans and brown bears have left behind a race of bears that excel at avoiding people."

We have been doing the same thing, subtly, with the grizzly bears in our national parks. Yes, they are safe from hunting in the park, but for generations the most aggressive ones, the ones most likely to attack humans or go after human food, have been the ones most likely to be removed from the population and given no opportunity to contribute to the gene pool. The tendency to remove aggressive bears is probably increasing as human pressures around Yellowstone increase; aggressive bears are the ones most likely to be shot by sheepherders near the park, or hit by cars near developments, to say nothing of being killed by managers for attacks on humans.

On the other hand, grizzlies in Yellowstone have had two kinds of opportunities to become accustomed to humans and thus to increase the likelihood of someone getting hurt. The first opportunity was food, which bears learned to associate with humans, and for which bears would endure a great many discomforts and overcome many obstacles. In most of the Yellowstone ecosystem now, bears don't get the chances to get food that they used to. There is still the occasional fool who intentionally baits in bears, but they usually don't get away with it long.

The second opportunity is simply human presence. Bears, after seeing so many humans nearby, become used to them. They may become less likely to run away. Biologist Dale McCullough, writing in the *Wildlife Society Bulletin* in 1982, pointed out that getting rid of human food does not automatically solve all bear problems:

> Availability of food and positive conditioning are only part of the problem. Even elimination of human-related foods (assuming this is practical) may not solve the problem of habituation. Restricting negative condition and favoring habituation by frequent, innocuous contacts between people and bears (typical of park situations) can create problem bears without any reinforcement by food per se.

What McCullough was suggesting is that not long ago, in fact back when the Park Service began to clean up its act and divorce bears from human foods, it was widely assumed (even it if wasn't consciously thought) that once the garbage was gone, all problems would be gone. But it doesn't work that way. The bears, once divorced from garbage and made "wild" in some ecological sense, still encounter people. There is no portion of Yellowstone so isolated that a bear living there is unlikely to encounter humans. One difference between the grizzly bears of the dump days and the grizzly bears of today is that the modern bear is much more likely to encounter people, not only because the bear is free-ranging but because there are a lot more people. Backpacking increased several hundred percent in Yellowstone in the 1970s.

What all this means for bear-human encounters is difficult to say for sure. I know that some hunters and some game managers think they've got a sure-fire answer, one they're quick to offer in Yellowstone every few years. They announce, smugly, that a hunting season in the Yellowstone area would teach those bears who's boss around here. The idea that hunting will make animals wary of people is an old one, and it is often true. But the reasons it works are more complicated than most hunters suspect. There seems to be an assumption that if you shoot a few bears now and then the rest will somehow learn (whether they heard any of the shots, or saw any of the dead bears) to avoid humans. Behaviorists suspect that the process by which bears become wary from hunting is a "selecting process"; that is, a process whereby over the course of many generations of bears the most aggressive individuals are regularly culled from the population. An open hunting season offers no assurance that the aggressive bears will be the ones killed. If shooting bears was to be adopted as a way of making bears more cautious, it would have to be applied discretely to individual bears that are judged to show signs of being too aggressive. It would also have to be applied only outside the park, because a host of laws and conservation groups would hardly allow hunting inside the park.

But even at that there is a great deal of looseness in the principles of shooting as a way of conditioning bears to avoid humans. For one thing, as I have already suggested, it could be argued that for many years now managers, poachers, sheepherders, and other people who legally or illegally kill grizzlies in and around Yellowstone have been selecting out the most aggressive animals. Do we have any way of knowing that hunting would operate in a more efficient manner? No, we don't. More important, the mortality level that already exists is too high; until it drops dramatically, the possibility for sport hunting is a theoretical one anyway. But most important of all, the confidence of hunters aside, there is still a great deal we don't know about how grizzly bears react to human presence or human aggression.

A study in Glacier Park indicated that bears with no connection to human foods who regularly encountered humans became habituated to them in an interesting way. After seeing enough people on the trails, these grizzlies became much less apt to charge people than were bears who only encountered an occasional person. More charges occurred on lightly used trails than on heavily used ones. What does this tell the manager who thinks that bears who are used to seeing humans are more dangerous because they've "lost their fear?"

As always, the issue is complex, and quite often it will come down to the imponderable and irreducible single element of temperament: both the individual bear's and the individual human's. Several research projects are currently underway to help us better understand how bears react to humans. A research project under the Interagency Study Team has actually gone out and created "encounters" with bears in order to radiotrack disturbed bears (fainthearted researchers need not apply) to see the extent of disruption of their routine. Other researchers are experimenting with rubber bullets to see if bears can be conditioned by some combination of pain and human voice noise to avoid humans (this is a tough one, considering how much pain grizzly bears have shown they are willing to endure in order to get what they want).

Steve Herrero, mentioned earlier, has written a simply superb book called *Bear Attacks, Their Causes and Avoidance.* In it he considers not only the science of these habituation problems, but the philosophical implications:

> If we want to have both grizzly bears that regularly flee from people and also have high levels of human recreational use but no hunting, then we might try to mimic some of the effects of hunting. Repellents might be applied to bears when they first experience people. The question is, do we want to condition grizzly bears to avoid people? Is this to be the grizzly's fate in its last sanctuaries in the contiguous United States? If we were successful we might drive grizzlies away from important habitat, causing possible population decline. Since the grizzly is classified as a threatened species in the lower forty-eight states under the terms of the Endangered Species Act, it is questionable whether using deterrents that decreased grizzly populations would be legal. A combination of research to tell us what is possible and a lot of soul-searching to help us decide what is desirable will be needed to resolve these issues.

We have a lot to learn yet about bears and people. Never before have we been trying so hard to learn it, but then never before has it mattered so much. If we decide we are going to do something to the Yellowstone grizzlies to change their behavior, we're going to have to do it very carefully.

Keeping bears and people from hurting each other is a subject that seems, even more than most bear-related subjects, to bring the easy-answer experts out of the woodwork. All ya gotta do is open up the dumps again, that'll take care of it. All ya gotta do is shoot a few of them now and then, that'll keep 'em in line. Heck, back in the sixties we hunted grizzlies in all the states next to the park, and everything was okay. As I've said before, easy answers ignore complicated realities. Maybe hunting did make the bears more cautious back in the 1960s. Indeed, maybe the dumps had nothing to do with it at all; maybe those bears were hunted often enough when they left the park that they were less likely to bother people. But then, of course, there were hardly any people using the backcountry back then, and there are several times as many now; we have no way of knowing that it wasn't simply a lack

Over the course of the 1970s and 1980s, the Park Service's campaign to educate the public to the risks—for both bears and people—of bear-feeding gradually took hold, so that interest in bear-feeding has shown signs of declining. N.P.S. photo.

of people to attack that accounted for the low number of backcountry attacks in the 1960s. Or consider the arguments of the more articulate proponents of dumpfeeding, such as Frank Craighead. He said that the dumps segregated humans from bears, and he also said that grizzlies did not associate the food they got in dumps with humans. Park Service managers and biologists had a lot of trouble with that statement, and one of the reasons was that as soon as the dumps were closed, at least by Craighead accounts, the bears immediately went looking for other sources of human food; that suggests that the bears *were* associating the dumps with humans.

This easy answer syndrome is one of the most puzzling—or perhaps comforting—elements of the bear controversy. The hunting magazines run editorials pronouncing upon the efficacy of hunting the grizzlies. The protectionist magazines run editorials against such "slaughter" of wildlife. Everyone has a pet theory. It is probably just as well they're all out there, each making its respective racket, because the resulting din is at least democratic and kind of balances itself out, leaving managers and scientists securely in the middle and inclined to take a middle course. What it comes down to is that several agencies are in the business of trying to manage the grizzly bear at the same time that they are trying to learn just what kind of management the grizzly bear most needs.

Just how much we have to learn has been tragically demonstrated a few times in recent years. In late June of 1983 a young man named Roger William May was dragged from his tent at Rainbow Point Campground near Hebgen Lake (west of Yellowstone Park) and killed by a grizzly bear. It happened in the middle of the night; the campground is a short distance west of the park boundary. The bear that did it, #15 on the Interagency Study Team's roster of study subjects, was captured near the site shortly after and destroyed. Though there were some garbage problems nearby, there was no really obvious reason why May was singled out. Bear #15 had been livetrapped by the team a total of nineteen times over the previous ten years, but that did not make him an extraordinary bear. C.B.S. News hopped on a suggestion that Serny-lan, the drug used to tranquilize trapped bears, could have caused hallucinations or somehow made the bear go crazy, but biologists doubted there was anything to the idea. Wyoming biologist Larry Roop said "it has as much credibility as saying people who take nitroglycerine for heart disease are going to fall dead in the streets when their chests explode." But it was good for some exciting headlines.

Then, in July of 1984, a young Swiss woman, Brigitta Fredenhagen, was killed while camped alone on upper Astringent Creek some miles east of Canyon Village in the park. She was dragged from her tent, apparently after going to sleep, and was killed and partially eaten. The board of inquiry could find no significant shortcomings in her way of keeping camp; she had "apparently received and followed all safety recommendations." This bear was never located and as far as could be known never showed aggression of this sort again. It was judged to be a subadult grizzly bear, two or three years old judging from various measurements taken at the site.

These two incidents would once have been called "unprovoked attacks" but are now seen as evidence of something we still don't fully understand (the old "unprovoked attack" phrase seemed to imply that the attack was the bear's fault). They added a profound urgency to the ruminations I've just reviewed about bear behavior. They also added some sensational flavor to a renewed interest in bear feeding.

Chapter 19

Don't Feed the Bears, Again

The excitement in the early 1980s over the new population estimates and the projected population decline brought about a resurgence in interest in somehow bolstering the bears with some additional food, either in the form of reopened dumps or some other nutrition. Alarm spread once it was known that the Interagency Study Team had reported a smaller-than-expected bear population, and the result was a whole new round of bear-feeding debates. It was covered in the popular press, though it wasn't reported with any especial accuracy; there was just this overwhelming feeling among concerned people that, well, we have to do *something*, don't we, rather than just watch these bears disappear?

They wanted to concentrate the bears away from trouble outside the park. These supporters of supplemental feeding were diverse. They included Frank Craighead, now standing alone among grizzly bear biologists as an advocate of reestablishing bear-feeding, the Wyoming Outfitters Association, the Murie Chapter of the Audubon Society, and Wyoming Senator Alan Simpson. They were not only loud, they were influential.

As usual, loudness and influence did the trick. Early in 1983 a special task force appointed by the Interagency Grizzly Bear Committee met to consider the possibilities and consequences of supplemental feeding. It was a momentous meeting, because the task force included not only representatives of the National Park Service, the U.S. Fish and Wildlife Service, and the Wyoming Game and Fish Department, but right there in the middle of the list, representing the Wildlife-Wildlands Institute of Missoula, Montana, was John Craighead. This made for a rare and promising combination of perspectives, and the report the committee produced made for good reading.

166

The task force recommended unanimously against supplemental feeding, pointing out that if human mortalities were kept low enough the bears could get along in the Yellowstone area just as they had done for thousands of years. They did not rule out the possibility of applying supplemental feeding some time in the future, but they said that supplemental feeding is "not a cure-all and should not become a substitute for proper management of habitat and human activities inside and outside the park." This same sentiment was expressed independently, by the way, at about the same time, by Dr. Charles Jonkel, another leading grizzly bear authority who has concentrated on studying the bears of northern Montana. He wrote that supplemental feeding is "a quick fix approach, not worthy of serious consideration."

Their main concern here was that, even if supplemental feeding worked, and somehow reconcentrated the park's bears at feeding stations, and actually did boost their nutrition enough to help (and none of those things were assured of happening), it missed the point of having a grizzly bear recovery plan. It shortcircuited the process by which the various government agencies were being compelled to give the bear sufficient habitat to care for itself.

The task force found it difficult to envision a supplemental feeding program that would have a good chance of working. Simply reopening the dumps would be of questionable worth, even if it was legal, because the dumps would not provide food in the fall, after the visitors leave; without food in the park in the fall, the bears would certainly wander out to feed on gut-piles and get shot accidentally or on purpose by hunters. Moreover, the elk population was now very large, and the bears had just spent fifteen years getting used to the new possibilities for nutrition; there was serious question if dumps or feeding stations could entice the grizzlies away from all those good gut-piles and other fall opportunities outside the park.

The report had little use for the idea of using "surplus" elk, pointing out that in order to provide sufficient elk to feed the bears the park's northern herd—the largest and most visible—would have to be massively manipulated and reduced by half, something that, even if it made ecological sense would be a political nightmare. The task force then pointed out that the northern herd, if reduced, would provide virtually no springtime carcasses, critical protein for newly emerged bears. Again, these grizzlies had just spent fifteen years getting used to this newly enlarged food source, and many were now denning near areas of known springtime carcass concentrations. Noting all of this, the task force concluded that feeding bears on elk "could create biological problems as acute as those currently under consideration." They didn't mention the political problems, but considering their audience I suppose they didn't have to.

The task force also feared that establishing feeding sites would necessitate closing large portions of the backcountry to protect the bears and the visitors from each other. Indeed, Yellowstone Park Research Administrator John Varley, who was not on the task force, commented to me that it would be virtually impossible to keep people from getting to the bears once the feeding sites were known. That, of course, would make things just that much more convenient for poachers, who were getting up to $10,000 for the various parts of a prime grizzly at the time.

On a more mundane note, the task force also pointed out that the supplemental feeding project, wherever the food came from, would be enormously expensive, and the bill would have to be paid every year.

The task force had some hopeful things to say, too. They observed that the increased number of elk was gradually taking up some of the slack left by the dump closures, as were the increased number of bison. They did not mention the trout, but could have. They also suggested that managers investigate ways to use food as a short-term tool to control bears. If, for example, a known sheep-killer is radiotracked on his way to a sheep herd near the park, managers could drop a road-killed elk or a dead horse in his path and slow him down while the sheep are moved.

Of course the task force didn't need to say most of that. As soon as they'd recommended against supplemental feeding as unnecessary at this stage, they had said all that was really critical.

It was terribly nice, I thought, to see the Park Service and at least one of the Craigheads in formal agreement on something, and it must have been some kind of milestone in the controversy, too.

In a way, the disagreement over supplemental feeding is part of the problem I mentioned earlier, that it has not been clearly decided just how many bears are enough. Those who adhere strictly to the Recovery Plan must consider anything less than 301 insufficient. But there is another perspective, one that I've heard from both inside and outside the Park Service. This perspective does not require a set number for the population. The first question you ask, instead, when told that the population is declining, is "so what?" By asking that question, you are really asking, "what does the decline mean?"

Does it mean that the population is heading toward some new equilibrium with its environment? That's what Knight and Eberhardt were hinting at when I quoted them earlier about being unsure of "the impact of reduced population size on its viability." They were wondering, tentatively, if the decline is headed somewhere besides total disappearance. They assumed it was:

> In the absence of the supplemental food supply provided by the garbage dumps, it seems quite likely that the Yellowstone grizzly population will, if man-caused losses can be reduced sufficiently, stabilize at a new population level.

What that level might be, and whether it would be high enough to assure the bear's survival, they could not say. Bears are so mobile that if their numbers shrank so that Yellowstone Park alone, without the surrounding country, could contain their ranges, even then they would not be safe because they are so inclined to move long distances, and because subadults would always be wandering out looking for a range of their own.

The word from the Interagency Study Team on population trends has not been as simple as saying that the population was probably on a decline. The discussions of climatic influences on grizzly bear numbers are not mere asides; they are central to the issue because they are what determine habitat conditions. In 1983 Knight and Picton, in their evaluation of climatic effects on the bear population, went one step further than saying the climate is affecting the bears. They suggested that, whatever the current population size, it may be the best the bear can do under present climatic conditions:

> Climate correlations such as presented here are indicative of high environmental resistance due to climate. This suggests that the population is near its ecological carrying capacity.

Modern range managers make a distinction between "economic carrying capacity" and "ecological carrying capacity." The former is the intensity of use, say in a cattle pasture, that can be maintained year after year with the highest level of commercial stock production without reducing production potential the following year. The latter is what nature will allow, and nature treats a range in a profoundly different way than does a rancher. In Yellowstone, set aside to preserve wilderness conditions, ecological carrying capacity is the preferred choice of managers.

But what is being suggested by Knight and Picton is that, no matter what the carrying capacity may have been in the 1960s — 229, 301, or whatever — it probably isn't that now. However many bears the Yellowstone ecosystem may have been able to support back then, it can't support as many now. In fact, they suggest, it may be supporting all it can. If, as they estimate, it is now supporting at least 200 bears, then the population is well above any-

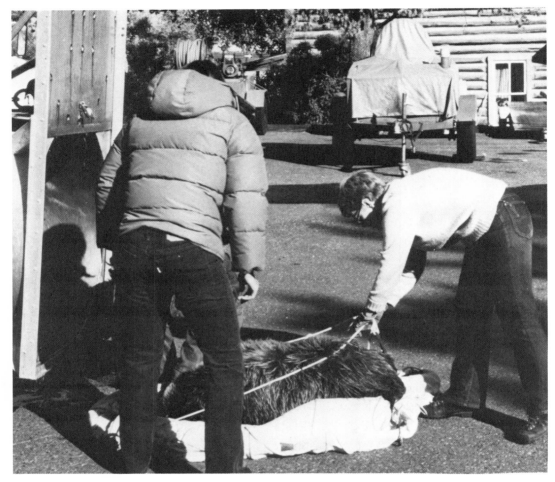

A grizzly, just taken from its transfer trap, being placed in a sling for transport under a helicopter. N.P.S. photo.

body's "danger point" of how many bears the population must have to survive. But a good many people, including quite a few who favor supplemental feeding, seem to be locked in on the notion that there is a certain number of bears that is "right" for the Yellowstone population.

Bears, like most other animals, do not have flat, constant population sizes; they fluctuate with environmental conditions. As Knight and Picton are suggesting, Yellowstone's grizzlies are doing just that, responding to a drying trend in the climate (and doing so at the same time that they have adjusted to a loss of dump foods). If their suggestion that the population is at or near its

A grizzly in transfer trap being airlifted to a backcountry release site in the early 1980s. N.P.S. photo.

carrying capacity turns out to be right, then 200 bears may be all we get. Perhaps 180 is all Yellowstone can support sometimes, perhaps even fewer. Perhaps Knight and his team, who are properly cautious about saying they've got the population just right, have missed several females in their census work, and the population right now is 250 and stable; Knight has assiduously avoided falling into the trap of announcing he's sure he knows how many bears there are. What seems most important is keeping track of the population's trend, and knowing that the number hasn't dropped below some minimum safe figure.

And this brings us back to the beginning of the controversy, when the

Craigheads proposed that the Yellowstone area was simply not good enough bear habitat to keep the population safe, and that the bears needed supplemental food. The question, though hardly ever asked quite this way, has come down to this: can Yellowstone support its bears? Anderson, Cole, other Park Service people, the various interagency committees, and most independent observers have asserted all along that of course it can, it has done so for thousands of years. And that's hard to argue with, in principle. Knight's study also suggests that Yellowstone should have no trouble supporting bears as it always has, even allowing for fluctuations in the population due to climate. The problem, he has pointed out with statistical elegance, isn't bears. Bears know how to make more bears. The problem is people.

The big problem continues to be man-caused mortality. The National Academy of Sciences, back in 1974, had urged managers to keep all grizzly mortalities in the Yellowstone ecosystem to ten or less. Several years managers have been able to do that, but more years they have not. In 1977 the total was fifteen. In 1978, ten. It was down to seven in 1980, but hit fifteen and seventeen the two following years. A tragic proportion of those dead bears have been females, the most critical element of the population these days. Every female is essential, and every female lost is a major disappointment. Knight and Eberhardt, in another recent paper, "Projected Future Abundance of the Yellowstone Grizzly Bear," in the *Journal of Wildlife Management* in 1985, report an "annual mortality of prime-age females of about 8%, or three to four such bears each year." They calculate that if that could be reduced even to 5%, that the population might stabilize rather than decline. Just one or two more females surviving each year—one or two not killed by humans and permitted to go on breeding—and the grizzly bear population could hold its own the way it did back when the dumps were open.

The point is that, Cole's and the Craigheads' arguments aside, there is no rule that says litters must be a certain size, or that bears must mate at a certain age, or that bears must weigh a certain amount. All that is necessary is, whatever those other factors may be, that the bears don't die any faster than new ones can grow up to replace them.

But, bears are not being born fast enough these days. Poachers are killing some. Sheepherders are killing some in grazing allotments in the national forests. Knight has been complaining since 1980 that grizzly bears and sheep are simply not compatible. The national forests are passionately reluctant to eliminate this use from the Yellowstone area entirely, and woolgrowers are pressuring them hard not to. As is so often the case, no one wants to yield, and inevitably in circumstances like that the grizzly bear ends up yielding most. There are also complaints that research itself costs too many bears; there are small losses here, a total of four since 1973. And of course managers on the various lands involved still have to kill "problem bears." One of the hopes of those researching ways to make bears avoid humans is that perhaps some of these bears that are now judged incorrigible can somehow be reconditioned and returned to the population with new attitudes.

So the bears are still out there, and the counts go on. Count the cubs, count the yearlings, count the sows with young at heel. Count the annual mortality, and try to count the suspected but unconfirmed losses. Count on controversy at every turn, count on uncertainty with every new scientific calculation. Count on a level of crackpot opinions. Count on poachers and thrillseekers who bait grizzlies into their backyards with garbage. Count on occasional feuds between the agencies, but also (I hope and expect) count on increasingly refined cooperative efforts to protect the bear. Count on the inevitable human inefficiency to complicate even the best intentions. Count on many concerned individuals (though never quite enough) and organizations to give the managers a push now and then. But don't count on the bear to last forever.

Chapter 20

Now you see them...

In all the excitement over the status of the grizzly bear population there is risk of missing another kind of excitement, over the huge amounts of information we have gained from the Interagency Study Team project. This happened before, you will recall, at the conclusion of the Craighead study. That study ended in such bitterness and controversy that hardly anyone took the time (or felt like taking the time) to celebrate a major scientific achievement. I'd like to avoid letting that happen again.

By 1985, the Interagency Study Team had put in more than a decade of intensive research in one of the longest and most productive bear research projects ever. More than sixty papers, theses, reports, and publications had been produced, and enough data was in hand to complete many other projected reports. According to the 1982 annual report of the team, the research will continue until about 1989, when final evaluations of the study findings should yield great amounts of additional information, but already by 1985 the results were impressive. Between 1975 and 1984, 118 different grizzly bears were radiocollared and monitored for varying lengths of time (a less happy report is that due to high mortality only 31 of that 118 were verifiably alive by 1984). During that same period, a total of 219 different bears were handled by the team in the process of trapping, immobilizing, tagging, or radio-collaring work. A host of other specialized projects was carried out, designed not only to learn about grizzly bears but to refine study techniques.

This is fascinating stuff for any student of natural history. In the first part of this book I have summarized the wealth of information provided by the study, but I find that in my reading of their reports I am just as intrigued by the process of learning as by what is learned. In radiocollaring grizzlies (using collars powered with three-year lithium batteries), they discovered that "perspiration from certain male grizzlies had been noted to corrode nonstainless steel antennas." They discovered, during a two-year study (1975-1976), that time-lapse cameras set near bear attractants in an attempt to establish how many grizzlies used an area were not especially helpful; they only worked well during daylight, and were very expensive to maintain. They discovered—or reinforced the discoveries of others—that any given collection of bear "scat" had certain limitations as evidence of what bears actually ate. Foods that were most efficiently and completely digested by bears were then least well represented in scat collections, so that though bears might be observed eating great amounts of carrion in the spring, the scat collection would not fully reflect the amount. The same would hold true with fish consumption; many of the scats would be left near the spawning streams, vulnerable to being washed away by high water. Berry scats were much softer—and subject to more rapid deterioration—than scats from grasses. Bison often die along stream bottoms in early spring; grizzlies are known to eat large amounts of bison carrion, but high water from spring runoff then carries away not only the scats but also parts of the remaining carcass. Thus many of the bear's favorite foods may show up in unrealistically small amounts in the most conscientious of scat collections. It was only through a combination of scat analysis, site examination, and other techniques that an accurate idea of bear feeding could be obtained.

One of the most surprising findings—at least for those who accept traditional lore about the habits of grizzlies—has been the high percentage of their time that grizzlies spend in heavy cover. I've already reviewed some of those findings in Part I, but there is an implication of this behavior I've not yet discussed much. Grizzly bears, like black bears, are terribly difficult to see in their natural state in Yellowstone. Only in certain seasons, in certain locations, do they ever make it easy for us; they rarely even make it easy for the researchers, who can track them with radiotransmitters.

This trait will no doubt continue to vex people in Yellowstone for years to come. Most visitors to Yellowstone either recall or have heard about the days when black bears were fed by the dozens along roads; some may even know of the old dump-feeding days, when the grizzlies were equally visible. The idea that Yellowstone still has bears even though they are no longer visible is hard to accept. The idea that in a natural state of things Yellowstone may have considerably fewer bears than it did when they were being fed is also hard for some people to accept. The public will no doubt continue to express confusion, doubt, and anger over the shortage of visible bears, and the Park Service will continue to tell them that what can no longer be easily seen is still there. It does not promise to be an easy future. But for those willing to study the scientific record, in all its statistical richness and understated excitement, it never need be a future of ignorance.

The black bear continues to be a footnote in the bear controversy, but I suspect that won't last forever. The black bear has not been studied in Yellowstone since the 1960s, and there is great hesitation about doing so now because any such study would invariably disrupt some grizzly bear activities; it would be very hard to trap just black bears, for instance. But the Park Service is interested in such a study, and it is probably coming, because scientists are growing curious about the smaller bear.

Estimates of black bears in Yellowstone usually ran to several hundred. Cole made an informal estimate of 650 in the early 1970s, and that is the last real attempt to figure out how many there are. There may be fewer than that, though, and a few Park Service critics, including Frank Craighead, have found time to suggest that here, too, the park has a problem.

Tentative hypotheses are offered by several biologists. The redistribution

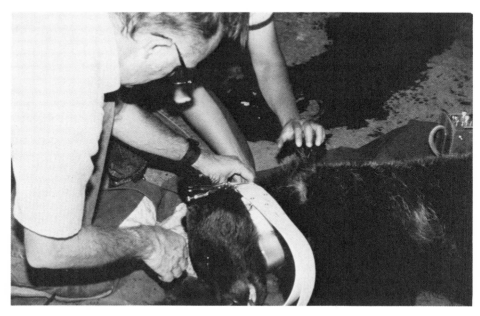

Young grizzly bear being fitted with expandable radio collar that it can "grow into" over more than one season of radiotracking. N.P.S. photo.

of grizzly bears and their return to something more like a natural set of feeding habits may have somehow influenced the black bears. Perhaps the blacks had occupied some niches which the grizzlies are now taking over. Perhaps the dry spell in the 1970s took its toll on them as it did on the grizzlies.

When grizzlies and blacks coexist, blacks become specialists in avoiding grizzlies. Maybe the blacks have stabilized at some new, lower population level. Maybe, critics suggest, the Park Service killed more blacks than were reported and the population has (for some reason not provided by the critics) not recovered. There is a severe shortage of information here. Some people will look to science to fill it, others will happily fill it with conjecture or rumor. What puzzled me when I was working in the park was that people could complain that there were no bears in the park, but as soon as someone left out an ice chest, or a couple of half-eaten hot dogs, a bear would materialize like ants at a picnic. It happened again and again. You couldn't have gotten a bear into that campground any quicker if you'd hired one. That suggested to me that, at the very least, there were enough black bears in Yellowstone to keep a nose aimed at every campground.

I recently lived for five years in Vermont, on the edge of Green Mountain National Forest. It was some of New England's better bear country, with black bears taken by hunters in all directions from my little village. I spent a lot of time out at odd hours, returning from a variety of fishing and social expeditions, down along the creeks just at those gloaming hours when bears are supposed to be active, and I never saw one. They were there; the hunters proved it every fall, and the beekeepers occasionally regretted it. They were just remarkably secretive. Finally, just shortly before I moved from Vermont, a bear ran across the road in broad daylight a couple hundred yards from my house, just as I happened to be driving that way. That bit of personal experience only reinforces the historical lesson Yellowstone offered me: just because you can't see them doesn't mean they aren't there.

But to many people it doesn't even matter if they're there. I gather from my readings and conversations that to some people the loss of bears, especially the loss of the grizzly, from Yellowstone would not matter. What, they would say, was really lost? We couldn't see it, and it surely wasn't good for anything in *today's* world. I wouldn't have written this book if I had any sympathy for an attitude like that. It smacks of the common human arrogance that asks only "What's in it for me?" as if everything can be measured in terms of some abstract market value.

But in a sense they're right, because the loss would be hard to quantify.

The loss of a scientific specimen, a priceless one, would matter only to scientists and naturalists and a few of us who can't get enough information about bears. The vacating of the bear's ecological niche in Yellowstone would be felt subtly throughout the system, but the system would go on without disastrous changes; there do not seem to have been many changes when the grizzly was wiped out of the rest of its range. The disappearance of an animal so seldom seen by the public would not matter that much to the average visitor. It would certainly be felt by anyone who loves to be in grizzly country, but such people are still in a minority.

The loss, at last, would be cultural. Some of the best bear biologists have reflected at length on this subject, which at first appears rather airy. It is not. Every person in the country would lose something if the grizzly disappeared. A superbly restrained expression of this is found, of all places, in the findings of a court case that had nothing directly to do with bears. In the 1974 case *Minnesota Public Interest Research Group v. Butz,* in which the U.S. Forest Service was challenged for not preparing an environmental impact statement before cutting timber in northern Minnesota, a very useful phrase was coined: "existence value." The suit had been brought under the terms of the National Environmental Policy Act (1970), one objective of which was to make the federal government responsible for preparing an E.I.S. for any "proposals for legislation and other major Federal actions significantly affecting the quality of the human environment." In the Minnesota case, the court described such effects in broad terms, so that one does not necessarily have to *personally* experience something to need and appreciate it:

> Existence value refers to that feeling some people have just knowing there remains a true wilderness untouched by human hands, such as the feeling of loss people might feel upon the extinction of the whooping crane even though they had never seen one . . .

On these terms, the existence value of the Yellowstone bears is immeasurable. Unfortunately, our society is not comfortable with quantities it cannot measure, and so is apt to disregard them.

To most Americans, bears and other wildlife are a distant and minor concern. Not one in 10,000 will ever see a grizzly, much less have a chance to learn to appreciate it. As one observer put it, "a reverence for the bear was common among North American Indians . . . In our culture, by way of contrast, we seem not to reverence any animal unless it be the golden calf or the Wall Street bull."

But I don't think that's the last word, especially as far as public concern for the grizzly bear goes. Recent national surveys have shown that when the average American is asked, he or she shows a clear preference for preservation of grizzly bears even if it costs a lot or requires people to give up some land. Though they are unfortunately argumentative, the grizzly bear does have a lot of friends; the controversy has shown that, and it has also shown something else. After the first few years, when concern translated most often into writing fiery articles, some of the conservation groups have put their considerable resources behind the protection of the bears. The National Audubon Society has perhaps committed the most—in time and money—but several others have served both as constructive critics and as supportive backers of the various agencies involved in grizzly recovery. Bears have more friends now than they ever have, and those friends have slowly learned how to make a difference. They can play a crucial role in the future, taking up the slack when the agencies lack the initiative, and jumping on the agencies when a program shows signs of slipping.

American human nature isn't going to change so that suddenly everyone is willing to just hand over the Yellowstone Ecosystem to the grizzly bear. But American attitudes can change, and they have been changing for some time to the benefit of grizzly bears. I'm worried that they will not change fast enough, but there is nothing but our own self-interest to stop us from saving the grizzly. We have the scientific knowledge, and we have the political machinery. All we need is the determination. The most optimistic defenders of the bear would like to reestablish grizzly populations in some parts of its former range in the Rockies. That is an intriguing idea, but first we must concentrate on guaranteeing the survival of existing populations, like the bears of Yellowstone.

Saving the grizzly—you can help

There are lots of ways to get involved in helping to protect the grizzly bear. When you're in grizzly country, hike wisely and use the land gently. That goes beyond vacation visits, of course; if you care about grizzly bears, don't build your second home in, or invest in developments in, or otherwise tamper with, grizzly bear habitat.

Animal protection is a political process even more than it is a biological one these days. The legal machinery exists to do everything necessary to preserve the bears in Yellowstone, but legal machinery needs energy to run; the best-planned bureaucracy won't move without sufficient public enthusiasm. The federal lands in the Yellowstone area, including the park and the several surrounding forests, all have their mission very precisely defined as far as grizzly bear preservation, but they have other missions as well, and other interest groups who insist on being satisfied. It is sometimes true that the best-motivated agency administrators must wait for a push from their friends before they can get something done.

Of course there are a host of ways to push. One can join any of dozens of organizations; some will dress up in bear suits and hold demonstrations in park developments, others will apply their lobbying skills to increasing appropriations. You have to decide for yourself how you can best contribute, and what kind of contribution will do the most good.

There are already a number of professionally-run organizations working for grizzly preservation. The Greater Yellowstone Coalition is an influential umbrella group representing dozens of more specialized interests, all of which have some stake in seeing the area in and around Yellowstone managed in a way that will respect its ecological and cultural integrity. Its address is Box 1874, Bozeman, Montana, 59771. Though most of the major conservation groups will devote some attention to the grizzly bear in the future, the National Audubon Society has distinguished itself in bear protection recently by putting its money where a lot of people's mouths were; the society has offered substantial rewards for information leading to the apprehension of poachers. Its address is 950 Third Avenue, New York, New York, 10022. A specialized group devoted to education and research regarding bears has recently appeared. It is The Great Bear Foundation, Post Office Box 2699, Missoula, Montana, 59806. The foundation, operating through consultation, publication, and public education, has been working to promote protection of all the remaining grizzly bear populations in the lower forty-eight states.

Whether you join already existing groups or simply start your own letter-writing campaign, make sure you know what you're talking about. There are about ten grizzly bear "experts" for every grizzly bear. There is something about bears that makes some people reckless. This is not a battle that will be won by emotion, or by sensational journalism (all too common in bear news already), or by misdirected crusades. Do your homework, know the facts (read the science itself, rather than the journalists' summaries), and then, if you think you can help, go ahead.

PART III

The Bears of Yellowstone/
An American Romance

Chapter 21

The Bear as Person

 Outside of the primates, it is unlikely there is another animal that can match the bear in complexity of image. Most others, in fact, are quite simple in their popular stereotypes: dogs are faithful, cats are fickle, owls are wise, rats are dirty, and mules are stubborn. In literature the portrayals of bears have been diverse. As a member of Frank Baum's terrifying trio of "lions and tigers and bears," as a ranger-hatted friend of forest children ("Only YOU . . ."), as a mythic spectre in Faulkner's "The Bear," as a kindly *Jungle Book* giant, as a stitched and clumsy little fellow named Pooh, and as a host of animated hucksters, the bear has done it all. Bears are silly and magnificent, untouchably wild and hopelessly tame, shameful cowards and bold heroes. The bear is the most confusing of our animal ideas, and that may be its biggest problem. It has the unfortunate capacity to seem human. Bears stand comfortably (one scientist noted "the bipedal habit which . . . seems to be behind much of the anthropomorphic adoration, respect, and fear—"). They work hard, but not if they can avoid it. They play, loaf, and give all the outward signs of humanity, including theft, malice, and humor (they are called "the clowns of the forest," and "the happy hooligans"). Moreover, they have attractive qualities as animals—they are roly-poly, loveable, easy to please, and rare enough to be novel.

To the average Yellowstone visitor they represent some combination of the above characters, and probably others. All of this seems alot to expect of an animal, even one so charming as a bear, but the sight of one never fails to make the day successful. I have often been confronted by families who "haven't seen a thing here in the park." Usually I find that they have seen deer, elk, moose, bison, and so on, "but we haven't seen any *bears*!"

It is not hard to understand the preference. The bear's ability to interest

183

N.P.S. photo.

people has been amply demonstrated by authors who have found its flexible character so useful. The visitor watching a magnificent bull elk graze in a mountain meadow, even if that visitor has never seen an elk before, will get restless quickly. He's seen horses do the same thing, back home, for hours. The bear is a different matter; it turns over rocks, climbs trees, eats candy wrappers (and elk), hibernates, mauls people . . . now there's an animal a man can appreciate! It may do none of those things while he watches it, but his knowing that it might makes the difference.

It might have been better to entitle this final part of the book "Bear Appreciation," for that is the subject. We have examined the ecology of bears, and we've seen where they fit in the park's management program, but we have not faced the personal side of the story—What is in it for me, as a park visitor, when I want to enjoy the bears? The assortment of lore, legend, and advice that follows will not provide a simple answer to that question, but it will shed some light on the possibilities.

There is one element in bear lore that is almost universal, and that is humor. Practically every bear story told around a campfire has comic relief. The bear manages to be funny by its very appearance. Its activities with men are so rarely harmful that they approach slapstick, but under many circumstances, even unpleasant ones, laughter is a nervous release. Losing lunch to a bear is funny. Being treed by a bear is funny. Being chased, as in a cartoon, with whirring legs and melodramatic music, is even funnier. But being caught by a bear is not funny at all. We can laugh at the situations as long as we respect the realities.

For years a popular yarn on the campfire circuit has involved the way to tell a grizzly bear from a black bear: sneak up behind it and kick it, then climb a tree. If it climbs up after you, it's a black. If it knocks the tree down, it's a grizzly. A more recent variation is to kick it and then simply stand there. If, two seconds later, you are still alive, it wasn't a grizzly. A popular joke a few years ago concerned a hiker who was treed by a grizzly. The bear fumed, roared, and clawed at the tree, but the hiker was safely out of reach. After a few minutes the bear left, but just as the hiker was about to climb down he saw the bear returning with a second bear. Together, the two bears shook the tree, but were unable to loosen the hiker's hold. They gave up and left, and again he started to climb down. This time he saw *three* bears coming down the trail, and they shook the tree so that it waved and swayed, but the hiker held fast. When they finally left, he was sure he would be safe, because he could not imagine there was yet a fourth bear nearby to help them. Just as he began to climb down, he looked down the trail and saw the bears returning, carrying a beaver.

In that story, when you read of the bears coming down the trail, odds are that your mind saw upright, pot-bellied, short-legged Yogi-type bears. They were probably grinning. We carry many images with us, and apply them subconsciously to fit what we hear. The bears of Yellowstone, as described in Parts I and II, deserve the best, most honest image we can give them. They are even more enjoyable and stimulating in real life than they are in caricature.

Chapter 22

Famous Yellowstone Bears

 Individual bears rarely become famous as characters or individuals. They may become well known anonymously, by mauling a hiker or being photographed by hundreds of visitors, but only once in a while does a singular, identifiable character emerge. Often, as we will see later, an individual bear gets well known locally. Countless Yellowstone bears have been named and admired by park personnel and visitors. Before begging was stopped, black bears often returned to the same roadside area each year ("Lucy's back at her station"), and others made themselves reputations in campgrounds. It doesn't take long, and names are convenient and quickly applied.

I recall a small black bear that frequented the Mammoth Hot Springs area in the mid-1970s. Because this bear had a long patch of blonde hair on its back, it became known as "Streaker" (an unusual public performer then in fashion had something to do with the inspiration). The name became more appropriate when Streaker learned to recognize ranger patrol cars. At some point in his life Streaker must have been driven from the road by an impatient ranger, for he "streaked" for cover at the sight of the car.

In the 1960s and later, when many bears were trapped and transplanted, they were often known by their numbers, referring to the identification number they were given for radiotracking purposes. In 1977 one ranger in my acquaintance expressed concern when he was assigned to a backcountry patrol in an area where Number Nine had just been released. Number Nine was a boar grizzly of over 700 pounds.

Naming seems unavoidable. Some criticized the park for using numbers, as if this somehow depersonalized the process of dealing with bears. In view of the bears that had both numbers (official) and names (unofficial), the criticism

186

seems silly. Further, rangers and biologists long ago proved how relative all words are. Fifty-four quickly becomes "Ol' Fifty-four," which can have all the sentimental weight of "Mergatroyde."

But a few bears, real or fictitious, have made the big time. Ernest Thompson Seton produced two storybook characters based on Yellowstone originals. The first was Wahb, a minor but lasting contribution to children's literature. Wahb's story, *The Biography of a Grizzly,* first appeared in 1899. In the book, Wahb was born in the mountains east of the park and grew into an enormous and dreaded giant who fought a lifelong battle with ranchers. He died peacefully in Death Gulch near Wahb Springs (see pp. 200–203 for more on Death Gulch). *The Biography* has gone through countless printings, and Walt Disney based a feature movie on the story, altering only the ending so that it was adequately happily-ever-after. For half a century Wahb reigned as Yellowstone's most famous bear. Seton, who was criticized for anthropomorphism, would have been amazed at Wahb's successor, for where is there a more manlike bear than Yogi?

Seton also produced Johnny Bear, an insecure little black bear who appeared in *Lives of the Hunted* and *Wild Animals at Home.* Johnny was a fairly wimpy little character, and lacked the quality to endure.

Perhaps the first *real* Yellowstone bear to become famous was Jesse James, the famous begging bear of the late 1910s. His exploits appeared in national publications, and were even featured in the 1919 Report of the Director of the National Park Service. Jesse was a fleeting celebrity, however, as his identity was lost as more and more bears (and Jesse was by no means the first) joined him along park roads. In 1925, an identical character, "Spud," was written up in *American Forests* magazine. Once beggars were common, it was impossible for one to be more famous than the rest.

In 1931 Naturalist Dorr Yeager captured a newly born black bear by taking it from a den under a building at Old Faithful. His story of raising "Barney" at Park Headquarters was published, but Barney was not destined to have lasting fame.

It was not until the late 1950s, in fact, that Yellowstone inspired another nationally-known bear character. At that time Hanna Barbera produced a refreshing new television cartoon series, "The Huckleberry Hound Show." The fame of one of the featured characters on that show eventually eclipsed not only Huck's but also that of the New York Yankee catcher for whom Yogi was named.

Yogi Bear was stereotypical. He embodied known habits of black bears,

" ' AIN'T HE AN AWFUL SIZE, THOUGH ? ' "

"Wabb," the hero of Seton's epic animal story Biography of a Grizzly.

"Barney," the black bear cub raised by park naturalist Dorr Yeager, in 1931. N.P.S. photo.

especially their fondness for human food ("Pickanic baskets") and their seeming clownishness. He was a roaring success (soon given his own program), the most famous bear ever, and all right there in Jellystone Park.

Yogi has made life miserable for countless rangers. "Hey Mr. Ranger sir, where can we see Yogi?" He has also caused consternation among all who wished to have Yellowstone's bears treated as wild animals. Yogi was weekly reinforcement of the worst misconceptions visitors had about Yellowstone's bears. Rangers are paid to answer the same question again and again ("What time does Old Faithful go off?" "Does it always rain here?" "Where's the bathroom?"), so their burden would not have been reduced had Yogi not been created. But solving the beggar problem was a little different. The cartoon generated immense sympathy for the hero, who was, after all, just guilty of a little good-natured tomfoolery. The ranger in the cartoon was not quite mean, but he was not really a nice man, either. Rangers have frequently encountered hostility from visitors who insisted on seeing and feeding bears.

It is not fair, however, to blame Yogi's creators for this problem. Yogi is now as valid a part of our culture as Mother Goose or Aesop. There is

"Yogi." Hanna Barbera photo.

nothing wrong with talking animals in fiction, and Yogi is good wholesome entertainment. It is not Yogi's fault that some people are unable to distinguish between an animated creation and a wild animal.

If Yogi is blameless, some other recent portrayals of bears are not. Fictionalized accounts of wild animals, using live bears, have been popular in movies and television for years, and many do great damage to the image of wild animals. Some turn bears into gigantic buffoons, with all the aggressive tendencies of an easy chair. Others are nothing less than monster movies. The more savage the monster, of course, the bigger the box-office success of the film. None of these films have involved Yellowstone, or any other national park, because Park Service officials would not allow it. The recent movie "Grizzly" took place in Georgia (yes, Georgia) for that reason. The impression made by one film monster with almost supernatural ferocity is a deep one, especially on young minds. In some people it may never be erased. Public perspective on wildlife is poor enough without this kind of encouragement.

Chapter 23

Hunting Yellowstone's Bears

Though I love a good hunting story, I have an aversion to the blood-and-gore tales so popular in bear literature—"The enraged drooling beast, eyes red with pain and fury, roared as it stood over the helpless hunter." It is well established that bears are peaceable enough if we let them alone. And so, lest this chapter be seen as pandering, a brief apologia is offered for a discussion of hunting bears in Yellowstone.

Hunting, as has been explained, was an acceptable form of recreation in Yellowstone prior to 1883. Most popular writing about bears has been done by hunters or ex-hunters. Before the many research projects of the last twenty years were undertaken, we owed practically everything we knew about bears to hunters. They produced some sensitive and lasting natural history, and some very fine writing. Visitors sometimes assume that because hunting is illegal in national parks, park personnel must disapprove of hunting elsewhere. This is a mistaken impression. Hunting has been shown to be incompatible with park goals. On the other hand, park goals apply to very few other places. In most places hunting is a legitimate and reasonable use of the land.

Not all of the accounts that follow are truly hunting tales. One concerns the destruction, by odd but practical means, of a dangerous grizzly, and another tells of a hunting trip that strained all definitions of good sportsmanship.

It is the opinion of some authorities that the well-armed bear hunter is the least safe person in bear country; that hikers, bird-watchers, fishermen, and ranchers will sustain far fewer injuries per encounter than hunters. One well-known naturalist is convinced that the bear can sense an aggressive attitude. Scientists won't go that far, but it is clear that the non-hunter usually enters the wilderness in greater humility, with more willingness to fit into the picture without disturbance. Perhaps therein is part of the justification for hunting stories. There is something to be said for a little sensational drama of this kind. Violence between man and bear, as it occurs in a few wild parts of the country, is the closest most of us will ever come to the realization that humans, like all other animals, can be a prey species.

In 1870, two years before the park was established, A. Bart Henderson was one of several prospectors working in and around what is now the northeast corner of Yellowstone. He differed from the others in that he kept a diary, full of references to game. Most daily entries were only a few lines long, but bear encounters were frequently mentioned. On July 4 he noted "I killed several deer and three bear." On the sixth he "killed a large bear near camp." On the ninth, in an unusual burst of verbosity, he came close to telling a story.

> Dad & muself left camp to prospect. Met an old she bear & three cubs. After a severe fight killed the whole outfit, while a short distance further on we was attacked by an old boar bear. We soon killed him. He proved to be the largest ever killed in the mountains, weighing 960 pounds.
>
> We returned to camp, after killing five bear & doing no prospecting. Home & James returned from Rock Mountain — rough country, no gold.

Such perfunctory calm about what must have been an enormous animal is admirable (we are not told how the bear was weighed), but leaves all too much to the imagination. On the next day he reported killing six more. On the eleventh his entry, which today would be worth a cover story in a major outdoor magazine, was brief:

> Clear and beautiful. All hands out prospecting. Found 3 cents to the pan today. I was chased by an old she bear today. Clime a tree & killed her under the tree.

The *important* news, "3 cents to the pan," came first. Henderson's understatement is magnificent. On July 28, it was

> clear and warm. Remained in camp to prospect — no gold. Killed several elk, buffalo and deer. Buffalo bull run thru camp while all hands were in bed. Home had wounded him. Located trail & killed a bear.

One wonders if Home wounded him earlier, or while he was running through camp. Another question remains; some have read accounts like these as proof that Yellowstone's bears (and, indeed, all grizzlies) were initially very aggressive with humans. Quite a few of Henderson's encounters were obviously had while hunting—at least two involved "she bears," who may have felt cubs were threatened—so it is difficult to generalize. We can only regret he did not elaborate.

The same year, in September, other Yellowstone adventurers encountered a grizzly with more lighthearted results. Walter Trumbull, a member of the Washburn-Langford-Doane expedition, reported on the hunt that took place south of Yellowstone Lake.

> Some of the party who had gone a short distance ahead to find out the best course to take the next day, soon returned and reported a grizzly and her two cubs about a quarter mile from camp. Six of the party decorated themselves as walking armories, and at once started in pursuit. Each individual was sandwiched between two revolvers and a knife, was supported around the middle by a belt of cartridges, and carried in his hand a needle carbine. Each one was particularly anxious to be the first to catch the bear, and an exciting foot race ensued until the party got within 300 yards of the place where the bear was supposed to be concealed. The foremost man then suddenly got out of breath, and, in fact, they all got out of breath. It was an epidemic. A halt was made, and the brute loudly dared to come out and show itself, while a spirited discussion took place as to what was best to do with the cubs. The location was a mountain side, thickly timbered with tall straight pines having no limbs within thirty feet of the ground. It was decided to advance more cautiously to avoid frightening the animal, and every tree which there was any chance of climbing was watched with religious care, in order to intercept her should she attempt to take refuge in its branches. An hour was passed in search for the sneaking beast, which had evidently taken to flight. Then this formidable war party returned to camp, having a big disgust at the cowardly conduct of the bear, but, as the darkie said, "not having it bad." Just before getting in sight of camp, the six invincibles discharged their firearms simultaneously, in order to show those remaining behind just how they would have slaughtered the bear, but more particularly how they did not. This was called the "Bear Camp."

Nathaniel Langford mentioned the incident in his diary, explaining that "we traced her into a dense thicket, which, owing to the darkness, we did not care to penetrate, for not one of us felt we had lost that particular bear."

An incident of the sort that gave the grizzly its great reputation for strength was reported by Superintendent Norris in 1879.

Philetus Norris, second superintendent of Yellowstone, who reported on grizzly hunting in 1879. N.P.S. photo.

A fine young horse, somewhat lamed by scalding in the fire holes, having been left near Obsidian Canyon, was killed by a grizzly that in devouring the carcass and fragments of game killed in the vicinity, continued to haunt the place. In trailing him in the snow nearly knee deep some weeks afterwards, I killed two large antlered elks, but a few yards apart, and, it being nearly night, I only removed their entrails and camped along near them, confident that bruin would visit them before morning. I then found that he had dragged the elk so near together as to leave only a space for a lair of boughs and grass between them, which he was intently finishing, when I, at a distance of 100 yards, opened fire with a Winchester rifle with fourteen ordinary bullets in the chamber and a dynamite shell — being all that I dared to use at once in the barrel. This I first gave him high in the shoulder, the shell there exploding and severing the main artery beneath the backbone. He fell, but instantly arose with a fearful snort or howl of pain and rage, but got four additional ordinary .44 caliber bullets in the shoulder, and nearly as many falls before discovering me, and then charged. Hastily inserting another dynamite shell, I, at a distance of about 50 yards, as he came in, sent it through his throat into his chest, where it exploded and nearly obliterated his lungs, again felling him; and as he arose, broke his back with the seventh shot. Either one of these would have stiffened any other animal, and surely have proved fatal to him; but deeming delays then dangerous, I peppered him lively. Finding Stephens across Beaver Lake, we returned with our saddle and pack animals, and after killing a pair of wood martens that were preying upon the carcasses, we dressed the animals, packing all possible of them 26 miles to our blockhouse at the Mammoth Hot Springs. We there found the hide of the bear just as spread out, without stretching, to be 8¾ feet long from tip of snout to roots of tail, and 6 feet 7 inches at its widest place; and from his blubber brought in, Stephens tried out 35 gallons of grease or oil. Its extraordinary size is the only reason for at all mentioning the animal in this report.

He later reported about the grizzly's temperament:

> Although, save in defense of . . . carcasses or of its young, this bear seldom provokes attack upon man, it invariably resists one, and if wounded usually charges furiously, either to its own death or that of its foe, and not infrequently both. Indeed, it may be truly said to be the mountaineers most dreaded foe.

Early hunters differed on this matter of ferocity, some saying the animal usually fled when shot, others saying it attacked. Overall it must have been unpredictable, as it is now.

Bears were rarely removed from the park by administrators until after 1900, and then only as ordered by the acting superintendent. Once a bear was labelled a troublemaker, shooting was the customary means of destroying it. Occasionally the circumstances called for different tactics (A. Bart Henderson likely would have called them more "severe").

The enormous grizzly that killed Frank Welch in 1916 was finally destroyed by order of the acting superintendent with a little help from Major Fries of the Army Corps of Engineers. (The Corps was in charge of park road work at that time, and had work camps along the roads. Welch worked in one of these.) Major Fries provided a nearby camp, which had also been visited by that bear, with "fifteen sticks of 40 percent dynamite." A generous bait of garbage drew the great bear over the dynamite, and according to one observer the explosion "raised that bear up maybe four or five feet . . . broke every bone in his body."

One last hunting episode should be included here, though it is a disappointing tale. In 1920 Saxton Pope and Arthur Young received permission from the Department of the Interior to kill four Yellowstone grizzlies for the San Francisco Museum of the California Academy of Sciences. In the agreement they made it clear they were going to use bow and arrow (the sportsmanship of hunting grizzly with bow is still debated—most bowhunters who go after grizzly or brown bear are backed up by a rifleman—but clearly Pope and Young were incapable of consistent clean kills). Their avowed purpose, aside from collecting the specimens, was to see if it could be done. They found a group of four (sow with three young—probably two-year-olds) and commenced firing. Their first arrows hit the sow and a cub. The two bears immediately attacked one another, perhaps, since they had not seen an enemy, assuming their nearest neighbor was the cause of their pain. Pope's second arrow missed them, then both put arrows in the sow, who finally saw the hunters and charged. The bowhunter's guide, Ned Frost, then shot her with a rifle, which stopped her long enough for the hunters to put two more arrows in her and kill her. The cubs, one wounded, escaped. Pope described this, and killing of several other bears, in page after embarrassing and gruesome page, in his book *Hunting with the Bow and Arrow*. The superintendent's report on the whole affair was outspoken, and not concerning poor sportsmanship:

> The party proceeded to the Grand Canyon, where they established their headquarters. Soon three grizzlies were killed, and the party was notified that only one more bear could be killed.
>
> As there were difficulties in finding another suitable specimen, permission was requested to kill a large grizzly seen near the Canyon gar-

bage dump. This permission I refused on the ground I felt that this would spoil the amusement the tourists were then taking in seeing the bears.

Nevertheless, the party stationed themselves on the trail used by the grizzlies in going to the garbage, and there killed four more bears. After this killing, no bears, black or grizzly, appeared for nearly ten days, thus causing disappointment to thousands of tourists. Not only were seven bears killed, but four cubs were left motherless and one other was believed to have been wounded.

Pope's account is triumphant, even gloating. They had, indeed, killed grizzlies with the bow and arrow, but had they not been backed by a rifleman the very first bear they shot probably would have done them in. The episode, whatever good it did their fame, was terrible sportsmanship, and, if the superintendent was right, a violation of their agreement.

Chapter 24

Making Themselves at Home

Yellowstone Park, in spite of its vast wilderness, is in some respects not typical bear habitat. Bears are very adaptable animals, and they have made some surprising adjustments to living in the park.

Black bears were, of course, long willing to enter developed areas, such as campgrounds and residential areas, but some time, probably after 1900, they discovered the convenience and comfort to be had by denning under buildings. Bears reportedly burrowed under or broke through walls of buildings (hotels and stores, most often) in what had become a well-established habit by 1920. In 1925, Ranger Joseph Douglas reported:

> On or about December 18 an old black bear and brown cub holed up for the winter under the Lake Hotel. For several days previously the old bear had been seen taking quantities of green willow branches into the prospective den. Later she was seen scraping into the den quantities of snow. Since the date mentioned the winter keeper has been feeding the bears about twice weekly, the animals showing their heads at the den entrance in quest of the table scraps. This is thought to be the first time a bear has thus "registered for the winter" at the Yellowstone Lake Hotel.

At least some of the chosen buildings were vacant in the winter, and food was usually not an incentive. A dry and ready-made den was probably a welcome change for a bear.

A few years later it occurred to the rangers to take advantage of what was actually an excellent opportunity to learn about bears. The case of Barney, mentioned earlier, was such as effort, but produced little of value. During the winter of 1931-1932 Ranger Curtis Skinner managed to devote some time to studying one family at Old Faithful. In October, Skinner arranged a den-site under the "old government mess house" by digging a hole through the foundation wall and preparing a den-shaped enclosure inside. He kept it baited, and though several bears fed at the bait none chose to den there. Skinner knew of bears under at least four other buildings in the Old Faithful area, so he had no trouble finding other subjects. He chose an apparent family group (cubs could be heard crying from rooms above the den) under the Haynes store. In February a hole was cut through the floor and he was able to observe the family. He twice succeeded in removing the cubs and weighing them. It turned out that there was also a second adult under the floor (it was a spacious area). This lone bear "appeared to be causing the mother some trouble and during the observation the two older bears engaged in noisy combat."

Skinner's findings were in some ways at variance with traditional bear lore. He learned, for example, that bears do not sink into a deep coma-like sleep. His account is instructive, even with all the additional information we now have:

> At various times during the winter, I had the opportunity to look in upon four different dens containing adult black bear. I found none of them asleep, although they were decidedly lethargic and reluctant to move even when molested.

For all its shortcomings (Skinner was absent in early winter, so he did not make observations then), this was one of the earliest attempts to seriously and systematically study any aspect of bear life.

As building standards improved, and as bears were no longer drawn into developed areas by food, basement-denning disappeared. There were other unusual accommodations available to bears, though, and not just for sleeping.

Bears make use of Yellowstone's thermal areas in all seasons. Like many animals, they are probably drawn to the heat during cold spells. The snow is less deep in the geyser basins in the winter, and often there are patches of bare ground and even green plants. Also like other animals, bears occasionally are victims of thermal accidents. The carcass of one black bear was found in Prismatic Lake (now Grand Prismatic Spring) in 1908, apparently the result of such an accident. Large animals, like bears, bison, and men, do break through the thin crust around large hot springs once in a while. Another bear, reported on in 1940, had a more pleasant experience:

On the afternoon of August 29th, we were stalking a Black Bear on the Mammoth Terraces in order to get a picture. Bruin was very accommodating and suddenly decided to take a bath. He ambled over to the base of Angel Terrace, looked around for a moment, and then climbed up the terraces to one of the pools. After testing it for temperature, Bruin crawled in, carefully dipped up the water with his paws, and went about his bath.

The pool is about four feet long, three feet wide, and eighteen inches deep. The temperature of the water was about 90°F. Judging by the bear's action in locating the pool and by his activity afterwards, taking a bath in the warm water of the Hot Springs was evidently not a new experience for him.

Equally common has been the practice of sleeping in naturally heated dens. Bears sleeping in extinct hot springs openings, or thermally heated dens of other kinds, have been discovered at Mammoth Hot Springs, Norris, and in the Old Faithful area. The ones in Mammoth have been both at the Hot Springs themselves and down along the Gardner River, about a mile away. Runoff from the Hot Springs disappears back into the ground nearby and reappears down along the river. Its temperature by the time it reaches the river (it may be reheated in transit) is about 140°F, quite enough to warm a number of den-size crevices.

Near Norris four caves were discovered in 1951 that had very similar shapes and were apparently intentionally dug (presumably by grizzlies, since black bears dig much less) in the thermally heated ground. None had active springs in them, but all were warmed a few degrees by heat transferred from warmer ground below. The investigator, Merrill Beal, reported:

> I would hesitate to call these caves steam heated, for such a condition would probably make for a very uncomfortable winter hibernating spot. However, since the ground temperatures are considerably higher than normal and remain quite constant, hibernation in one of these dens might be likened to sleeping in an electric blanket, and it is likely that the bears using the caves derive a certain amount of additional comfort as a result of this influence by hydrothermal activity.

One of Yellowstone's most bizarre bear stories involves the peculiar little thermal area named Death Gulch. The gulch is actually a shallow basin in a small draw on the upper Cache Creek drainage. Because of the location of the thermal activity, the basin is occasionally filled with unbreathable gases from a hot spring. The area of heaviest concentration of the gas is rarely more

N.P.S. photo.

than 15 feet deep and 100 feet across, but early investigators found that this was a large enough area to kill wildlife, including grizzly bears. Death apparently occurred by asphyxiation rather than by poisoning. It was this spring which inspired Seton to end his tale of Wahb by having the aging bear vol-

Dead grizzlies in Death Gulch, 1897.

untarily enter the gulch and peacefully fall asleep. Dr. T. A. Jaggar reported on an 1897 visit to the gulch:

> Climbing through this trough, a frightfully wierd and dismal place, utterly without life, and occupied only by a tiny streamlet and an appalling odor, we at length discovered some brown furry masses lying scattered about the floor of the ravine about a quarter of a mile from the point where we had left Cache Creek. Approaching cautiously, it became quickly evident that we had before us a large group of recumbent bears; the one nearest to us was lying with his nose between his paws, facing us, and so exactly like a huge dog asleep that it did not seem possible that it was the sleep of death... One huge grizzly was so recent

a victim that his tracks were still visible in the white earthy slopes, lead-ing down to the spot where he had met his death. In no case were any marks of violence seen, and there can be no question that death was occasioned by the gas.

The scientists were discrete about the duration of their visits. It appeared to them that the gas trap was only truly potent on certain windless days, and that a predominance of bears was probably the result of the circumstances; there was no vegetation to interest many other animals, and once one had succumbed its rotting would invariably attract other bears. Dr. Jaggar, whose camp was on Cache Creek just a short distance below where the streamlet entered it, noted unhappily that the streamlet "has its source far above the animals; indeed it trickles directly through the worm-eaten carcass of the cinnamon bear—a thought by no means comforting when we realized that the water supply for our camp was drawn from the Creek only a short dis-tance down the valley."

Chapter 25

Bears, Tourists, and Rangers/
The Eternal Triangle

 In 1953 a survey was conducted of Yellowstone's visitors. When asked "were you aware while you were in Yellowstone that bear feeding is prohibited?" 95% answered yes. Feeding by visitors was quite common at this time, common enough to keep dozens of black bears along the roads. There were probably two big reasons for the easy lawbreaking. First, feeding was being allowed because rangers were only occasionally enforcing the law. People have an astounding capacity for doing things for no better reason than that they can get away with it. The second reason was (and is, for people still do it at every opportunity) that they could not see what was wrong with feeding a "poor hungry bear." Most visitors apparently had no great sympathy for park ideals—if they even understood them—so they did not appreciate any distinction between a Yellowstone bear and a zoo bear.

Rangers have tried reasoning with visitors in many ways, but one of the most effective approaches to talking people out of bear-feeding (rather than fining them out of it) has been to make them realize that it hurts the bear. Pointing out to people that begging degrades the character (a wonderfully loaded expression) of a wild animal has worked. A report prepared for the United States National Park Service and the National Parks of Canada in 1969 summed up the power of this viewpoint:

> The public generally is opposed to pollution. The roadside bear, no less than the urban rat, is a direct result of environmental pollution. Once the public becomes aware of this fact, we anticipate the demand to see demoralized beggar bears will be replaced by a demand to clean up the park environment and restore the bear to its natural habitat and behavior patterns.

The comparison with the rat is the clincher. It is completely appropriate, and, once heard, is seldom forgotten. Bears, of course, have no "morals." The demoralization is actually our own, brought about by abuse of a valuable ethic.

Other more practical points can be made in the bear's behalf. Black bears managed to survive on their garbage-enhanced diets, except those that were hit by cars, pestered by people until they injured somebody and then were destroyed as "dangerous," or ingested too much harmful material. Bears feed by smell. If something smells interesting, or sweet, it will probably get eaten. Candy wrappers, broken pop bottles, and aluminum foil qualified, and were consumed in quantity. Glass, foil, cigarette butts, and film wrappers are not digestible, but they are all too common wherever people travel. Even feeding the bear "something good" was wrong, because it kept the bear there until it could be further abused.

Worse things than accidental mistreatment occurred. A black bear can be in a pretty mean mood if he's just been fed a firecracker. Some visitors are not at all concerned about the condition of the bear, they want only the chance to see it. I once explained to an apparently intelligent visitor that during the 1960s an average of twenty-four black bears were destroyed every year because of troubles with begging. The visitor's response was that it was worth it, that that was a reasonable price to pay, so that he could see bears.

Making people aware of the danger to the bear seems to be more useful than telling them bear feeding is dangerous to people. Even the parents of young children are willing to take horrible risks. Recounting a few injuries to them will make them cringe at the campfire program, and the family will walk very close together back to their tent afterwards, but in the brave morning light many will succumb. Visitors with children were responsible for some of the most outrageous behavior in the beggar-bear days. In the interests of photography children were told to go stand by the bear. Smaller children were placed on the bear's back, and even smeared with jelly so that the bear could be photographed licking it off.

There is no getting around the horror of such behavior, the hundreds of injuries, and the callous treatment of very vulnerable wild animals, but if the point has not been made by now there is no hope, for the readers or the bears. The story has a lighter side, and that side is the reason for this chapter.

Down in The Dumps

Running into a bear in Yellowstone has always been a most-remembered part of the visit. Many scratched fingers, fenders, and ice chests were proudly displayed back home. Paw-prints in the dust near a tent were photographed, and trees were examined for claw marks. Everybody wants a bear story.

The public feeding grounds were an endless source of yarns. Owen Wister, the author of *The Virginian* and other western novels, was a regular visitor to Yellowstone in the 1890s:

> I walked out once in the early evening at the Lake hotel and counted twenty-one bears feasting. I saw a bear march up to a tourist and accept candy from his hand, while his wife stood at a safe distance, protesting vainly, but I think rightly. I saw the twenty-one bears suddenly cease feasting and withdraw to a short distance. Out of the trees came a true grizzly, long-snouted and ugly; and while he selected his dinner with ostentatious care and began to enjoy it, a cinnamon bear stole discreetly, as if on tip-toe, toward the meal he had left behind him. He got pretty near it, when the grizzly paused in eating and merely swung his head at him—no more than that; in a flash the cinnamon had galloped humptily-dumptily off and sat down watching. He came back presently; and the scene was reenacted three times before I had enough of it and left; each time when the cinnamon had reached a certain point the grizzly swung his head, and this invariably sufficed. It is my notion that the cinnamon was a bit of a wag.

The proximity of the dumps, and therefore a lot of grizzlies, made life exciting for many people who were not even interested in the bears. Shortly after the turn of the century a stableman was searching for some stray horses not far from the Canyon hotel.

> As he entered a little glade, a big bull elk dashed through closely pursued by a grizzly. The stableman yelled, the grizzly stopped for a moment, and then started after him. As he put it, "I just natchully faded away. I reckon that atmosphere is all het up yet with the way I come through it."

It became apparent in the 1890s that a guard was needed at the dumps, so a soldier was stationed, rifle in hand. Later, after soldiers were replaced by rangers, it became tradition for the ranger, if asked about the danger of the bears, to exclaim that he wasn't there to protect the *people*; he was there to protect the *bears*!

Once formal educational programs were started by the Park Service, another feature was added, the mounted ranger who gave a talk on bears while the crowd watched the feast. One of the most famous of these rangers was Philip Martindale, who spoke of the coolness of his horse under considerable stress:

> The bear feeding grounds lecture stadium at Old Faithful seats now almost 2700 people and is usually crowded at the 7 o'clock lecture on wild animals. Most always certain loud noises, laughter, hand clapping etc. prevails during the lecture.
>
> It is only about 125 feet from the crowd behind the (cable) to the lunch counter or platform where the food is placed to attract the bears, and the horse (as a lecture platform) is backed up to within 30 feet of the platform which is in turn only about 50 feet from the woods.
>
> Training and confidence are responsible for the fact that the horse will not even turn when a grizzly comes in behind him, but this has taken time and patience.
>
> On a certain night early in August a grizzly came around the pit by mistake and came directly toward my horse, within 15 feet in fact. I waited for him to turn but finally decided and quickly that he did not see me. I made a noise and sudden motion which caused him to stand up on his hind legs and then he turned. Their eyesight is so unquestionably dull living as they do in deep timber.

The dumps were a grand show. Spectacular and bloody fights occurred between grizzlies over food, and once in a while an exceptionally bold black bear would join in. There is no denying the initial thrill of seeing several—to

Philip Martindale, astride an amazingly calm horse, giving his "bear-talk" at Old Faithful in the 1920s. N.P.S. photo.

BEARS, TOURISTS, RANGERS   207

say nothing of several dozen—adult grizzlies ponderously sorting through the piles of trash. First sight of a grizzly is a thrill under any conditions. But quickly one comes to realize that the scene is actually an ugly one, and wishes, with some selfish regret, that the bears were a little harder to see.

The Panhandlers

Most encounters, however, did not occur at the dumps. They took place between black bears and visitors along the roads and in the camps. Owen Wister described a campground scene of 1891 that remained part of the Yellowstone adventure for over half a century:

> One night in 1891 our sleep was murdered by sudden loud rattling and clashing of our tin plates and other hardware. We rushed out of the tent into silence and darkness. In the morning our sugar sack lay wounded but still with us. MacBeth while dragging at it had tumbled the hardware about him. He was not educated enough to stand that and had taken to the woods. Another bear took to a tree that week. As dusk was descending, campers found him in suspicious proximity to their provender and raised a shout. The shouting brought us and others not to the rescue, but to the highly entertaining spectacle of a tree surrounded by fascinated people waving their arms, and a bear sitting philosophically above their din. Night came on, the campers went to bed, and the bear went away.

Tourists and bears were constantly interested in each other: " 'Do you mean to tell me those cute creatures will harm anyone?' says a lady, 'Why they smile and wiggle their tails in the most cunning manner!' 'Yes lady,' replies the ranger, 'but you must not trust either end of a bear.' "

The "hold-up" bears that became famous gathered huge crowds. As the traffic backed up there was created, in ranger-parlance, a "bear-jam," as in "There's a godawful bear jam at Diamond Lil's station." Some store employees still remember visitors who, having overheard the term somewhere, asked where they could buy a jar of bear jam.

Sometimes the best performance was to the biggest crowd. One was reported by Horace Albright in the 1940s:

> I remember only one very sad case of a woman and a bear where mental torture and burning humiliation were doubtless a thousand times more terrible than the pain and the sting from a bear's tooth. In this case, the lady had a big bear on his hind legs up on the landing platform

On the steps of Roosevelt Lodge in the 1920s. N.P.S. photo.

at the Canyon Lodge. She had the bear reaching for food as dozens of shutters clicked, for some 500 tourists were being seated in open buses for the day's journey to Mammoth Hot Springs. Someone yelled at the "bear expert" doing the feeding and she turned around. The bear thinking the show was over and the food gone dropped to all-fours and in so doing caught his claw in the lady's shoulder straps and took off all her clothes except part of her girdle and her stockings, yet did not even give her a scratch. She wanted the bear killed, but after a full investigation we found the bear not guilty of any wrong-doing.

A more private embarrassment took place in a story less well substantiated but equally well known in the park. A couple was honeymooning in their tent in a park campground when a bear began to tear through the tent's doorway. According to oral tradition (the most colorful kind), the young husband whipped out a knife—at which point the wife can be imagined, hands clasped on breast, eyes full of pride, thinking "My hero!"—and cut a hole in the other end of the tent, making a swift getaway into the night. The tent collapsed on bear and spouse, who were extricated without harm by neighbors. On the subsequent success of the marriage, oral tradition has remained silent.

Another equally well circulated (and undocumented) incident involved a family asleep in their motor home. During the night they were awakened by a racket, and looked out to see a large bear annihilating their ice chest. The wife exclaimed, "Look, that bear has our ice chest!" The husband answered with knowing wisdom, "No, that's *his* ice chest. . . ."

In the late 1960s one of the oil companies concocted a scheme for advertising in which they distributed to all customers bright orange styrofoam balls with their emblem. These were to be attached to car antennas. A bear in the Sylvan Pass area took a shine to these, and tore off countless antennas to get them. The only reason anyone came up with at the time was that

N.P.S. photo.

someone had fed that particular bear an orange of exceptional quality, and the bear wanted more.

In earlier days, when cars were more often open or cloth-topped, bears found them easy pickings, ruining many a roadster. One incident, which was anything but amusing at the time but which now has a Keystone Kops air about it, took place in the vicinity of an Oldsmobile rumble seat about 1930:

> Mr. Anderson and his family were driving toward the Cooke entrance of the park and were beyond the Buffalo Ranch. In rounding a curve near the Devils Well, a female grizzly and her two cubs were seen feeding on a carcass near the road. There were two cars preceding the Anderson car and the road was muddy with considerable slush snow in it. As the cars approached, the mother grizzly charged and jumped down into the cut made by the snowplow in recently clearing the road, but for some reason, just before the cars reached her, she sprang back up on the snow bank at the side of the road. While she was in the cut, her cubs disappeared over the hill into Soda Butte Creek. When the mother regained the bank and failed to see her cubs, she immediately gave chase to the cars which were then about fifty yards ahead of her. A brother of Mr. Anderson, who was riding in the rumble seat of the six cylinder Oldsmobile, became alarmed and warned the Ranger by rapping on the rear window. Vigorously blowing the horn, the Ranger tried to get the cars ahead to speed up all that they could, but due to the condition of the road, much speed was impossible. The grizzly quickly overtook the cars, and then jumping up on the snow bank, lunged out and down at the car. Several attempts were made in this manner to catch the car, but the grizzly missed each try as she lost time in jumping up on the snow before leaping for the car. Needless to say, the Ranger's brother had crawled down into the back of the car and had closed the rumble cover! They were chased from Devils Well to Hoppe's Prairie, a distance of approximately two miles, and the maximum speed (remembering road conditions) was 28 miles per hour. The bear had just come out of hibernation, which must also be considered.

Presidents and Bears

A surprising number of chief executives have been interested and involved in the Yellowstone bear story. The most famous was Theodore Roosevelt, who, in fact, inspired the American toy, the "Teddy Bear," in 1902 when the cartoonist Clifford Berryman portrayed the sportsman-president with a

TEDDY BIDS THEM ALL GOOD BYE THIS MORNING.

Local newspaper cartoon at the close of Roosevelt's 1903 visit to Yellowstone.

small black bear in Mississippi. Roosevelt was unwilling to shoot that particular bear because the circumstances were unsporting, and the cub quickly became one of his symbols.

In 1903 Roosevelt visited Yellowstone on a two-week vacation jaunt. He expressed great interest in seeing the bears, which had already become famous because of their dump-feeding. It was early spring, with the snow still several feet deep over most of the park, so a call was made to the Lake Hotel to learn if any bears had yet appeared in that area. The winterkeeper at Lake said they were not out, but it was later learned that he simply did not want to be bothered with the presidential party. Roosevelt, an experienced bear hunter, found the park bears fascinating:

> It is curious to think that the descendants of the great grizzlies which were the dread of the early explorers and hunters should now be semi-domesticated creatures, boldly hanging around crowded hotels for the

Park superintendent Horace Albright, President Coolidge, and Mrs. Coolidge all seem much less concerned about the bears at Tower than do the President's bodyguards during this 1927 visit. N.P.S. photo.

sake of what they can pick up, and quite harmless so long as any reasonable precaution is exercised.

Both Presidents Harding and Coolidge saw and fed the beggar bears along park roads on their visits to the park in the 1920s (Harding had heard of Jesse James). After seeing the familiarity of all the park wildlife, Harding was moved to comment, "As I watched the wildlife of the Park today, unconcerned and unmindful of the human beings about them, manifesting their confidence in the security of the situation, I thought how helpful it would be to humankind if we could have a like confidence in one another in all the relations of life."

Another president had close and extended contact with the bears of

BEARS, TOURISTS, RANGERS   213

Yellowstone. In 1936, a clean-cut (weren't they all?) young ranger at Canyon found himself assigned to ride shotgun at the bear-feeding grounds. He could not have known that on his next visit to the park, in 1976, he would be president. Gerald Ford has fond memories of Yellowstone (during his years as president there was an oil-painting of Old Faithful in his office), and recalls with some relief that he never had to use the shotgun. Years after his Yellowstone summer, he was so fond of telling his children about his bear adventures that they asked him, "PLEASE, don't tell us the story about the bears again, Daddy!"

"Who's in charge of this bear?"

Park managers have faced some extravagant demands in their efforts to keep both bears and people happy in Yellowstone. In 1913 the secretary of the interior received a letter from the president of the American Humane Association, the latter having heard that Yellowstone's bears were not being properly cared for. He understood that they were fed well from the dumps during the summer, but that during the winter no food was provided them and that they became so hungry by spring that they "sometimes eat the flesh from their paws." Acting Superintendent Brett answered for the secretary, explaining about hibernation, and assuring the president that the bears were "thoroughly competent to look after themselves." One cannot help but wonder if Col. Brett, while he wrote this letter, was plagued by visions of his troopers, wading through the snow with sacks of food on their backs, searching for bear dens so they could waken the animals to feed them.

Soldiers and rangers have been expected to handle almost equally difficult situations over the years; "Get that bear out of my car! He's eating all the marshmallows I bought to feed him." "I chased the bear that tore my tent up this tree and kept him there until you got here. He's yours now." The following is taken from a report filed by Ranger Elbert Robinson in 1960. Hearing of a seriously injured bear near Firehole Cascades, he got his rifle and drove out to put the bear out of its misery. On the way he was stopped by another car:

> A young man about 20 to 24 years old approached with a tissue in his hand and carefully unfolded it and showed me a rusty nail about 2½ inches long. He proudly stated that he had removed the nail from a bear's foot, and acted as if he expected a compliment for his brave act . . . I told the boy that he did not realize how fortunate he was that he had

not been bitten, beaten, or clawed to pieces. He stated that the bear had his head in a garbage can and his foot was sticking out with the nail plainly visible and all he had done was reach over and pull the nail out.

This report has been prepared because of the unusual circumstances and to prove that the Good Lord still provides and watches over a certain class of people that need someone else to do their thinking for them.

The bear, whether black or grizzly, has an endless capacity for destruction. This, much more often than injury, has brought officers "to the rescue," looking for ways to move the bear away from the people with as little risk as possible.

Bear traps in Yellowstone are simple devices. The bait hangs on a cable far enough inside the culvert trap so that the entire bear is in it before he can reach the bait. When the bear pulls on the bait, a lever releases the heavy cage door behind him. Numerous bait recipes have been tried, incidentally. Peanut butter, honey, ham, bacon, and many others work. Often the ranger takes whatever leftovers are available at the local hotel. One troublesome young grizzly that was raiding some rabbit pens just north of the park was baited with a saucer of milk. The owners of the rabbits had noticed that their cat's milk bowl was always emptied when the bear visited, so milk was used to bait the trap.

Bears often become trap-wise, and so before drug-firing guns were developed rangers faced a ticklish problem: how to get the bear into the trap/ trailer for transportation to a remote area. Some bears could be lured in with different foods than they were accustomed to, and small ones could be netted (with a long-handled affair known as a "butterfly net"). Many smooth captures were made, but sometimes things went wrong, and this happened with depressing regularity in front of large crowds.

Dale Nuss, one of Yellowstone's most experienced bear-handlers, tells of a small yearling that was causing trouble in the early 1960s at Old Faithful. After repeated attempts by rangers to catch him, Nuss and one of his men set out with trap, cookies, butterfly net, and iron resolve, to get the bear. Locating him was easy — at the center of the "damndest bear jam you ever saw." They started with the net:

> One of us was throwing the cookies, the other was standing with the net. Of course all the people were watching. This little bear would sneak up, eyeball us, eyeball those cookies, and finally he'd make a pass at them and we'd make a pass at him with the net; we'd miss and of

course everybody would cheer. This went on about 45 minutes, until the bear decided he was smarter than we were and left.

They followed him to an empty picnic area, where he climbed a tree. Quickly setting up a cookie-baited rope snare at the foot of the tree, they took the other end of the rope and retreated to a nearby picnic table to wait. It was approaching noon, and soon a crowd had gathered, unaware of the bear, at the other picnic tables. At last the bear climbed down, and just as planned he stuck his head in the snare.

> I forget which one of us had the rope. Our plan was for him to go *that* way and we'd go *this* way; well, it didn't work that way. The bear came right after us... Whichever one of us was runnin' with the end of the rope, well, the *other* one finally got smart and grabbed the middle of the rope and took a dally around a tree. Then the other guy dropped the end of the rope and went over and grabbed the net, and we had him. Then after we had him, we didn't know what to *do* with him. He had arms and legs and heads and everything through that net. We couldn't get him out to get him in the trap, so finally we just shoved the whole damn thing in the trap and away we went.

As awkward as roping was, it had long been a staple of management technique. Roosevelt had mentioned that, as early as 1902, the bears "sometimes get tin cans stuck on their paws, and the result is painful... scouts in extreme cases rope the bear, tie him up, cut the tin can off his paw, and let him go again. It is not an easy feat, but the astonishing thing is that it should be done at all."

Capturing bears with drugs, though now developed to a fine sophistication, still involves many risks. Determining proper dosage is very difficult, since it can depend on the bear's age, sex, weight, degree of excitement, and general physical condition. Those are not things easy to judge from a distance. An overdose can be fatal (more than one ranger or researcher has administered mouth-to-mouth resuscitation to a bear that was having trouble breathing), but underdose can be dangerous to the trappers if the bear revives too quickly. More flexible drugs have been developed recently that give the trapper more leeway in estimating the proper dosage.

Most drugs are not instantaneous. The bear usually flees after being hit by the drug syringe (it has a long hypodermic point that is designed to penetrate the coat and the skin), and, as one ranger put it, "the bear always seems to run down a hill and across a muddy stream before it conks out, so that

Hypodermic dart and the weapon that fires it. N.P.S. photo.

you've got to drag it back through the mud and up the hill to the trap." Never dress up for a bear trapping.

Trapping is only one part of the acquaintance park residents have with bears. Having the bears of Yellowstone for neighbors, and even houseguests, is a story in itself.

Chapter 26

Living With Bears

 It is difficult for the visitor, and for the new employee, to realize just how much a part of daily life bears once were in Yellowstone. Before modern management got the bears out of the developments, one simply expected to see them, every day. Now, with strict regulation and sanitation, most bears are kept wild and free-roaming. A bear in a campground causes real concern. Then, with food available everywhere, bears were a regular thing—a matter of routine.

There are still residents who remember chasing bears from kitchens, or teaching their children to look around before going outside. Living in bear country, such caution is always a good idea. Interestingly, as they look back on it, some comment that it did not seem at all unusual at the time: "You often carried an axe handle if you went out at night around the camp. Nobody thought anything of it." Park personnel have rarely been injured, perhaps because they quickly became conditioned to be more careful.

Bears often damaged buildings in the park. In 1891, Elwood Hofer, who was trapping park animals for the National Zoo, wrote from Yancy's Hotel near Tower Junction about his bear problems:

> I had a splendid Grizzly or Roachback cub and was going to send him into the Springs (Park Headquarters) next morning the team was here, I heard a racket outside went out and found him dead an old bear that made a 9½ inch track had killed and partly eaten him. Last night another one came, one that broke Yancy up in the milk business. You know how the cabins stand here. There is a hitching post between the saloon and the old house, the little bear was killed there. In a creek close by was a milk house, last night another bear came there and smashed the whole thing up, leaving nothing but a few flattened buckets and pans

and boards... I don't care about the milk but the damn cuss dug up the remains of the cub I had buried... Bear are very thick in this part of the Park, and are getting very fresh.

In 1932 the superintendent reported "the interiors of three snowshoe cabins were wrecked by grizzly bears." These small backcountry cabins, used by ranger patrols, were especially vulnerable. Some were very sturdy, but they were no match for a bear. One destroyed in 1924 was described:

> The door had been opened by main force. The bedding, including the mattress, had been all taken outside and strewn on the snow for distances varying up to 100 feet. The bed itself (a large heavily built affair) had been moved two feet out from the wall; the stove had been moved from its place, the zinc-covered cupboard had been turned over, broken into and contents emptied, provisions all eaten or (such as pepper and cinnamon) at least bitten into, excepting one small specially resistant tin. Every frying pan, dish pan and kettle had been knocked from the walls. A sack of oats had been torn from its nail on the ceiling, and contents eaten.

One patrol cabin was so badly damaged in the 1960s that a new one was built to replace it. A large grizzly that wants to get into a small building may enter from almost anywhere. This particular bear, a sow with two cubs, had further distinguished herself by biting holes through a *cast iron* skillet.

Milton Skinner reported that at one of the small backcountry cabins in 1915 a solitary man spent most of a night keeping four grizzlies from digging through the roof. His only weapon was a pitchfork:

> The roof was of clay and sod and was still frozen, for there had been no fire under it, although the sun had melted the winter snow from the top. Still more fortunately the split poles supporting the earth were heavy and stronger than usual and overlaid with thin sheet iron, so that the bears had much more trouble than they would have had ordinarily. It was a difficult job but in time they got through the clay, bent back the sheet iron and began to spring the poles apart. Then began a long, hard fight. Whenever a crack showed, the pitchfork was jabbed up through, and whenever it struck a paw or the bear's underparts it brought snarls and "woofs." The paws were so tough, very little damage was done to them, but once in a while a fortunate jab brought blood from nose, breast, or belly. Occasionally a nose or paw came down through a crack, but a steady clubbing on them caused their withdrawal and more howls. The bears would not give up the contest, but now that the strong odor of

the ham, bacon and fresh meat came direct to their nostrils they redoubled their efforts. The poles were strong and the sheet iron protected the roof, but still it is likely they would have succeeded if they could have held out long enough, for George's violent efforts. . .were fast tiring him. There were many times during the long night when it seemed as if he must give up, but finally dawn began to break. At first the bears hardly noticed it, but after a time they became less active and shortly after sunrise they jumped down and retired, growling, to the woods. But the roof was a wreck.

Before modern maintenance equipment was available, many of the park's road crews were located at small camps along the roads. These camps, each with a small crew of men, had kitchens and storehouses, and were frequently under siege. Each seemed to have its resident bear(s). Some camps had specially built meathouses (there was no electrical refrigeration at the time, and this was in the early 1950s!), made of 3-inch planks with 3-inch steel bands circling them, and *spikes* in the door, but at night, as one worker recalls, "the grizzlies would come in and take that meathouse apart like a matchbox."

The problem was worst at the close of the season, as in 1927, when the following report was filed:

> After the close of the tourist season, the abundant supply of table scraps from the hotels being at an end, the bears usually become more bold and look to the road camps and woodcutter's camps for a larger part of their rations. . . Two of the woodcutter's camps at the Canyon were so infested with bears, especially grizzlies, that regular night guards were kept busy warding away the prowlers by means of Roman candles and other devices. . . As many as fourteen bears, together with an undetermined number of cubs, have been seen at one time about a given camp.

Many a bear has been made a "pet" by park personnel. This occasionally happened at the road camps. William Hape, park maintenance supervisor, remembers a small black bear cub that was accustomed to sleeping in the bunkhouse during the day and being sent out at night. It has been more common, and infinitely more dangerous, near the hotels. Hotel employees, many of whom are new to the park, have baited bears in (in no sense taming them) until the visitation was a nightly event. Much like the camper who leaves food out to attract a bear "so I can get a picture," they are playing a very dangerous game. The greatest risk is to the chance passer-by, who is not in on the plan, and who stumbles onto a bear where a bear ought not to have been.

Living with bears is easy if everybody cooperates. Living in a place like Yellowstone is a special experience in many ways, but knowing that one is surrounded by bear country is one of the finest rewards of all.

Chapter 27

Camping With Bears

 The most important thing about camping in bear country like Yellowstone, whether in a roadside campground or in the back-country, is to take the park regulations seriously. Bears are indi-viduals. No two will behave the same, therefore no precaution is foolproof. Vigilance and common sense, as represented by park regulations, are the best bet for a trouble-free camp, but there is no guarantee they will work every time.

In the Campground

Be careful with food. Do not leave any food or food container (full or empty) out any longer than you need to. There is no such thing as a bear-proof ice chest. Lock all food and food containers in the trunk of your car rather than taking them into your tent. If possible, avoid cooking strong-smelling foods. If you are sleeping in a tent or other soft-sided shelter, it is best not to sleep in the clothes you cooked in. If a bear passes through the campground and is not drawn to odors, it will move on.

Do not be afraid to be a little nosy to see that your neighbor is being careful too. If he gets a bear into the area, it could be some member of your party that ends up being hurt. Because you cannot be sure that everyone else has been careful, and because bears travel alot at night, carry a flashlight and make a little noise as you walk, for example, to the rest room.

These precautions are easy, and they only take a few minutes. If you have a family, explain to the children why they must be careful. They will probably help more if they know.

On the Trail

While hiking, stay alert by watching for bears and bear signs and listening for sounds of movement nearby. It is good to make noise as you travel, either by talking or wearing a bell or by carrying a can with a pebble in it.

But nobody's making you any promises. There's a new joke in bear country about the way to tell black bear and grizzly bear droppings from each other: grizzly bear droppings are the ones with little bells in them. Actually, a study done in Glacier showed the hikers wearing bear bells were charged by bears far less often. But a recent study with captive grizzlies had a different result: the bear being tested twice slept through the noise. The scientist making the test was Gary Miller, a biologist at the University of Montana in Missoula, and his conclusions were discouraging for bell-wearers:

> The bells were of the type sold to hikers in Glacier and Yellowstone National Parks to warn bears of the approaching hiker and thereby prevent an encounter. In these tests, the assistant, less than 6m from the bear, failed to arouse it. Warning bears before getting too close is a good strategy for preventing encounters, but the bells currently sold to hikers are inadequate.

"Bear repellents" are a hot topic in outdoor magazines these days, and you will see some advertised. Many have now been tested, and others are being considered. Charles Jonkel of the University of Montana has been a leader in experiments in aversive conditioning. The goal is to find some way of either making bears fear people or give people some way to ward off bears. A host of traditional and modern aversives has been studied by Jonkel and others over the past few years, everything from recordings of *bigger* bears broadcast to keep bears away from developments, to a wide assortment of sprays. Some of these sprays—recently those on, almost on, or on and then off the market have included "Halt," "Bear Skunker," and "Animal Alert"— have been shown to work, some of the time, under laboratory conditions or even in the field. Some of them are quite promising (to say nothing of the fascination they hold for anyone interested in the study of animal behavior), but no scientist is even close to saying that you can count on them. You may get a bear that happens to like the taste of skunks, or who just last week walked through an electrical fence and isn't going to mind having his eyes burn for a while, or who got sprayed twice last month and has figured out how to dodge it. In a moment I will look at some of the more traditionally touted bear repellents, but there is something more important for the new hiker to learn first, and that is that it's much better to avoid the bear in the first place than to be put in the position of trying to repel it.

As I was saying, making noise helps. A group of hikers is often safer than an individual partly because they make more noise as they go down the trail. Be especially careful in situations of limited visibility, or where a noisy stream or high winds might drown out your own noises.

Avoiding an encounter—surprising a bear at close quarters—is the big goal. If you hike wisely you will not surprise an animal. Once you have surprised a bear at close range, whatever happens to you as a human being, you are a failure as a hiker.

When you see a bear at a distance, say at 100 yards or more, keep that distance. There are options at this point that depend on your own judgment:

1. You can try to detour around the bear. This may not be possible, but if you try it keep upwind of the bear and at a good distance from it, so that it can scent you without feeling surprised. If you are not familiar with the country, or the trail does not allow you to circle,

2. you can wait, and enjoy the rare view, hoping that the bear might move off. Do not assume that just because it has moved out of sight that it is far away. It might have bedded down five feet from the trail.

3. You can go back the way you came until the bear is well out of sight, and then approach again making lots of noise. The warning noises might cause the bear to move off. Most hikers in Yellowstone who have logged many miles are familiar with the sound of something running off somewhere ahead of them. If you proceed at this point, do it loudly and alertly.

4. You can call your trip off. Never be afraid to do this for fear of ridicule. Though it is rarely necessary to call a trip off because of bears, the person who makes fun of someone who has been "bear-spooked" will be secretly wondering what he or she would have done under the same circumstances.

Now to the most often asked question—"What should I do if I *do* surprise a bear?" There is no easy answer to it. Each bear reacts according to its feelings at that moment, but experience has shown that some actions are better than others.

1. Do not run, since it will likely cause the bear to chase you. In some circles running or otherwise displaying great fear is known as "acting like

dinner." If the bear rears up on its hind legs, you will feel like fainting, but remember that this is an investigative position. It often means the bear has not decided what to do yet either.

2. Immediately, but without sudden motion, look for a tree that can get you at least twelve feet from the ground. Do not overestimate your ability to beat the bear to the tree. If you decide to go for the tree, drop something interesting, like your pack, to distract the bear for a moment. If you climb the tree, wait at least thirty minutes after the bear has left before climbing down. Bears can be surprisingly cagey and patient.

3. If there are no trees, and the bear seems uninterested, you might be able to quietly back away out of sight. Some authorities have recommended talking softly.

4. If there is no tree, you may have to take the hardest alternative of all. Play dead. Roll up in a ball with your hands covering the back of your neck, and act like you are invisible. The bear may come over and sniff at you, or even paw you around a little. If you yell or struggle the chances are greater that you will be injured.

These are generalizations. Hikers have also avoided injury by charging back at bears, but no authority recommends it. Others have pulled out their axes and gone at it with the bear, but few have survived. You cannot fight a bear with any hope of winning.

In Camp

While camping, your biggest risk is attracting a bear with odors. Why do some hikers insist on cooking foods like bacon and fish? Freeze-dried foods are much more convenient, and alot less smelly. Portable cookstoves are better than campfires, though many people do not want to give up that traditional wood fire. The small stoves also do you less harm; when you cook over a big blazing wood fire your clothes and hair will smell of whatever you cooked. Keep backpacks and other gear away from the smoke, too. Remember that when you get home, too—try not to hang your backpack next to the refrigerator.

Most parks with grizzlies warn menstruating women to stay out of the backcountry. Any sexual odor may attract or at least interest a bear. Cosmetics and deodorants are also strange and interesting odors to a bear.

Food storage should be systematic, as should all good packing. Keep all of your food in plastic bags, all bags in one container, and keep that container from contaminating anything else you carry with odors. At night suspend your pack (or at least that container) 20 or more feet from the ground, in a tree at least 100 yards from your camp. Flatten all empty food containers and keep them with the food. Do not use the fire pit as a garbage can. Carry out everything you brought in.

Sleep a good distance from the fire, because the fire pit will have lingering odors of food. Studies of bear-injured hikers have shown that hikers in tents are statistically less likely to be hurt by a bear than hikers sleeping only in a sleeping bag on the ground. You might locate your sleeping bag so that your head is pointed toward a tree.

These are basic guidelines, such as you will be presented with at a ranger station. As more research teaches us about bear behavior, some of them may become outdated. They are only the barest outline, in any case.

The Yellowstone Backcountry Permit System

Several years ago, because of increasing backcountry use, Yellowstone Park initiated a backcountry permit system. It works, at no charge, entirely to the advantage of the hiker. All overnight hikers are required by law to obtain the permit. As they receive it, they are made familiar with trail conditions, hiking opportunities, bear activity, and many other useful things. Day hikers, incidentally, are welcome to seek the same advice. The ranger station is the best place to find out about bears. If an unusual amount of bear activity has been reported for some area, it may be closed to hikers. For that same reason, you are not permitted to make your trip reservations weeks in advance; in the meantime a bear could move into your chosen area. Don't ever get smug about bears—"I'm an experienced hiker, and I don't need help." I have often encountered hikers, especially eastern hikers, who think they know "all about bears." Grizzly country is a whole new world to them. Nobody knows all about bears.

Some Dangerous Misconceptions About Bears

It is often said that you can outrun a bear by running downhill. This is not true.

It is said, though less and less often these days, that bears, even when they kill people, do not eat them. This is academic to the person, but bears,

Grizzly bear.

though they do not normally regard humans as a food source in the way they see berries or gophers, are meateaters. It may simply be that they have never learned to eat humans. In any case at least a few grizzlies have, undoubtedly, consumed human flesh.

It is generally said that adult grizzlies cannot climb trees, but even this rule has exceptions. Some have been known to haul themselves fifteen or more feet up a tree, climbing more or less like a black bear does. There are records, in Yellowstone and elsewhere, of large adult grizzlies climbing trees. If a tree has many ladder-like branches it will be easier for the bear to move up into it. A bear estimated at 500 pounds was observed to climb 21 feet into a large apple tree (a very good climbing-tree, as many children know) near Yellowstone's north boundary. Also, a scrambling leap can carry a grizzly some feet beyond its normal reach. If you choose to climb a tree, climb fast and climb high.

Black bear.

It is often said that dogs scare bears (in some states dog-packs are used to hunt bears). Dogs are illegal in Yellowstone on any trail, and must be leashed at all times even in developed areas. Indeed, during the army administration, it was illegal to bring one into the park. Your dog has probably never seen a bear, and you have no way of knowing what it will do. Dogs excite and frighten or anger bears, and may greatly increase the chance of attack. In some black bear country, a few hunters recommend always having a dog, but they are hunting, not hiking.

It is said that black bears, truly wild ones, are harmless to hikers; that they are terrified of people and always run away when approached. Any large wild animal is dangerous. In 1978 a black bear stalked and killed three boys in a park in eastern Canada.

It is said that grizzlies do not attack sleeping people. This is not true, though, as mentioned earlier, sleeping in a tent seems to be safer.

Back to bear repellents for a moment. A big disadvantage of them is that they often give the hiker a false sense of security that leads to carelessness: "I got my can of 'Bear-Raid,' so I'm ready for anything and don't have to worry until anything happens." Here are a few of the more traditional bear repellents that have been recommended for years. All but one of them involve very close-range action with the bear. They require the hiker to perform some last-minute maneuver with a bear that has been encountered at very close range, and, perhaps, is even charging. Keep in mind that hundreds of pounds of singleminded power is charging toward the hiker as he/she whips out (and it had better be handy—no burying it in the pack) the Wonder Weapon. A final all-out charge by a bear of firm convictions cannot be stopped by anything short of near-instant death.

1. Tear gas. At least two types were tested against Yellowstone black bears years ago, and neither was found effective. Assume that the grizzlies are stronger and better able to take such abuse. And what is the range of commercially available tear-gas weapons?

2. Airhorns. These are the obnoxious little cannisters used by the drunken alumnus sitting behind you at football games. They are advertised as being effective against dogs and wild animals, and have been recommended in major outdoor magazines as a good way to scare off bears. Loud noises were often used to drive bears out of campgrounds in the old days in the park—pots and pans were banged together, for example. I once participated in an informal test of such an airhorn on a sow grizzly with one yearling. The bears, feeding at a dump, were within thirty feet of the front of the patrol car, and, though facing away from the car when the airhorn was sounded, the bears were not frightened. They gave a bit of a start, as anyone would who was feeding quietly in the middle of the night if one of those things was blasted. They looked around for the source of the noise, and then resumed eating. A second, much longer blast on the airhorn produced a second little jump, and shortly after that the bears wandered away. If they experienced any emotion it was annoyance rather than fear.

3. Firearms. Firearms are illegal in the Yellowstone backcountry. Even park personnel, some of whom live back there, rarely carry them except

for law enforcement purposes. Practically no hiker of the 1970s has the combination of skill, discretion, and coolness to know when to use one. If you are of a mind to break that law, you will have to do it by concealing the weapon, and that will make it useless to you if you need it fast. More than any other device, firearms breed a false sense of security.

4. Mothballs. Here is an interesting one. It has been claimed that a few bags of mothballs (paradichlorobenzene) around camp will keep bears away. One article even said that they had been tested in Yellowstone, at the dumps. Former Yellowstone Resource Management Specialist Ted Bucknall agrees that there was such a test, but that the bears *ate* the paradichlorobenzene. Not very convincing proof of effectiveness, I'd say . . . One hiker, according to the above-mentioned article, carried mothballs with him during four years of hiking and had no trouble with bears, "which proved," according to the writer, "that grizzlies have a definite aversion to paradichlorobenzene." No, that is very muddy logic. All it proves is that the hiker, like countless others, hiked for four years without having any bear problems. For all we know it was pink shoelaces that kept the bears away. Mothballs, like many other chemical compounds, may be unpleasant to some animals, but scientific research has not yet shown them to be an effective repellent.

Research is being conducted into aversive agents of different kinds, and perhaps someday there will be something you wear, spray, eat, or sing that will guarantee your safety. In a way it would be a shame, since an important and humbling part of the grizzly country experience is that sharpening of senses—the tuning-in on one's surroundings—that it brings out. This point was most vividly brought home to me one rainy day in Glacier National Park. A party of hikers travelling the opposite direction on the trail had been fishing, and one of them was carrying a small trout. For at least 100 yards after passing them, the air was heavy with the smell of that one little fish. If my jaded senses could do that well with one trout, imagine what a grizzly can do.

A survey of grizzly-caused hiker injuries in national parks of the United States and Canada showed that sows with young were responsible for most. Old bears were also disproportionately represented in the totals, as were garbage-fed bears. There are so many variables, though, that each encounter is unique. A charge may be only a bluff, or a curious approach for a better look. There may be cubs hidden from view. There may be a carcass or a mate similarly hidden. Our best bet, as visitors in bear country, is to avoid the encounter in the first place, and not have to wonder.

In over a century, four people have been killed by bears in Yellowstone, and only one of those was in an area that could be defined as backcountry. It is all very well to tell an apprehensive hiker that the odds are very slim he will be hurt, but it rarely allays fears. It shouldn't, really, as long as the presence of grizzlies does not stop him from hiking. The bear is part of the experience, a very exciting dimension of wilderness hiking that few other places can provide. Many hikers prefer grizzly country for that reason.

We, as protectors of the bears, are the ones who must make the sacrifices if we are to coexist with them. They will only behave as they know how. This means there must be restrictions on people, and, in the future, the restrictions may become even greater. If restrictions on hiking in Yellowstone seem to limit your freedom too much (and hiking has a lot to do with freedom), try to think of it as cooperation. The bear's freedom is important, too. If that is not good enough for you, then you probably should not hike in Yellowstone.

Chapter 28

Bear Appreciation

 By now it should be clear that there are ways to improve your chances of seeing bears in Yellowstone. Their activity during daylight hours is often greatest at first and last light. They frequent meadows and forest edges, and find relatively little of value in dense stands of lodgepole forest. Their spring carrion feeding often exposes them to view. They are as independent and unpredictable as other wild animals, but they can be seen.

For over sixty years Yellowstone has meant bears, maybe even more than it has meant Old Faithful. The bears are still there, but Yellowstone must now mean other things, because bear sightings are no longer cheap or easy. Now they are challenging and depend upon your willingness to work—to get up early, to look hard, and to accept failure sportingly.

As the effort is greater, so is the reward. The skilled mountaineer seeks more challenging peaks; the skilled angler praises the "difficult fish" that is not easily taken; wild animal appreciation is, or should be, on the same plane. When you accept the challenge, you've won the battle whether you see the bear or not.

Bears, especially grizzlies, have been so encased in publicity and prejudgment that you might worry that when you finally do see one it will be a letdown. You do not have to fear that. The grizzly is all you could expect.

In 1931 Park Naturalist Dorr Yeager wrote a small book about Yellowstone's wildlife in which he said that the grizzly "is the finest, most lordly and most powerful of all our wilderness friends and he must be seen to be appreciated." We have learned, since those well-intentioned words were written, that if the grizzly is to survive in the company of man it will have to be on less selfish terms. If wild bears do not choose to be seen, then that is the way we must appreciate them.

For the first time in almost a century the bears of Yellowstone are living like wild bears. They feel no gratitude for this; it was entirely our choice to make it so. It does not matter one way or the other to the bear; he is just making the best of what he has. It does matter to us, though, because we have something very special in the bears of Yellowstone. We ought to make the best of it, too.

Appendix

Bear Statistics

There is an old saying, that "there are lies, damned lies, and statistics." I don't entirely agree with the sentiment, but I must warn you that the following numbers, and various interpretations of them, have generated even more emotion than they have mathematical confusion. Depending upon who was reading them, they were used to "prove" many things, some of which I believe, others of which still seem unproven to me.

I happen to like a good statistical table; it may oversimplify some things, but it does give you a tangible starting point. It even offers surprises. Consider the table of grizzly bear population estimates from 1971-1982. During this period, the Park Service was being roundly criticized in the press and by the Craigheads for its management program, and frequent cries were going up that the bear population was in decline; many people must have been frustrated that the Park Service was so slow to change its ways under such attacks. But look at what the scientists were saying. Only the Craigheads believed that the bear population between 1971 and 1982 was in any trouble; several independent authorities asserted that the population had been considerably larger than the Craigheads had supposed back in the 1960s, and even the scientists now in the field were hard pressed to find evidence that the Craigheads' gloomy 1974 estimate of 136 bears was anywhere near accurate. And then, in 1982, when the Interagency Study Team finally came up with a low estimate, it was still 50% higher than the Craigheads' 1974 estimate. But because it was lower than many previous estimates, it started a whole new round of controversy. I'm not sure what all that means, but it does suggest to me that there are several ways of looking at an issue, and that tables like these are enormously helpful when the rhetoric gets thick and the headlines heat up.

If you're not interested in numbers, then no encouragement from me will convince you to read these tables; but I hope you do.

I must also caution you that there are a lot of minor inconsistencies in the various publications—from all sources—that I used to obtain these statistics. I notice now and then that some scientific document will disagree with itself from one page to the next, or some government report will disagree with itself from one year to the next. In virtually all cases, these inconsistencies are insignificant. As far as I can trace most of them, they represent refinements in data sorting. For example, information on a "possible" mortality of a grizzly bear one year may surface the following year when the bear's carcass is found. Changes like those, and many others, gradually work their way into the literature.

What I will say, though, is that I have put in a lot of time—with help from others now and then—to make sure that at least these tables are internally consistent. If you find that some scientific reference disagrees with me in some place, you will usually find that the difference is only one or two bear mortalities, injuries, or whatever. The tables are as good as I can make them, and have their best use in revealing general trends rather than in any specifics anyway.

Numbers and ratios of female grizzlies to their cubs in observed family groups, 1959-1984.

Year	Females	Cubs	Ratio
1959-66 (avg.)	15	33	2.2
1972	11	22	2.0
1973[a]	15	27	1.8
1974	15	26	1.7
1975	4	6	1.5
1976	17	35	2.0
1977	13	25	1.9
1978	10	19	1.9
1979	13	26	2.0
1980	9	19	2.1
1981	13	22	1.7
1982	11	21	1.9
1983	13	25	1.9
1984[b]	16	29	1.8

[a]Cole, 1976, for all statistics before 1974.
[b]Knight, Blanchard, and Mattson, 1985, for all statistics 1974-1984.

Grizzly Bears in Yellowstone Park, 1920-1970; population estimates from various sources.

Year	Supt. Annual Reports	Annual Wildlife Census Reports[b]	Craighead Research Team Min. Counts	Year	Supt. Annual Reports	Annual Wildlife Census Reports[b]	Craighead Research Team Min. Counts
1920	40	—		1946	200	200	
1921	—	—		1947	200	200	
1922	—	—		1948	—	200	
1923	—	—		1949	200	200	
1924	—	—		1950	180	—	
1925	75	75		1951	—	—	
1926	80	80		1952	—	—	
1927	100	100		1953	—	150	
1928	140	140		1954	—	—	
1929	150	160		1955	—	"common"	
1930	167	167		1956	—	—	
1931	180	180		1957	—	—	
1932	213	—		1958	—	"common"	
1933	260[a]	260		1959	—	"common"	154
1934	250	310		1960	—	—	169
1935	250	335		1961	—	—	166
1936	286-300	286		1962	—	200	155
1937	290	290		1963	—	200	177
1938	270	270		1964	—	200	185
1939	300	300		1965	—	250	187
1940	320	320		1966	—	250	202
1941	300	300		1967	—	250	175
1942	—	—		1968	—	250	181
1943	—	—		1969	—	250	195
1944	300	300		1970	—	250[c]	179
1945	250	200					

[a]The Superintendent's annual reports issued before 1934 covered the period from October 1 to September 30 of each year. In 1934 that procedure was altered so that the 1934 Superintendent's Report covered only from October 1, 1933 to June 30, 1934 (June 30 was the end of the fiscal year). This change apparently misled some previous researchers (Craighead, 1967, and Bray and Barnes, 1967) and caused their reported population estimates to be one year out of kilter with the actual year being reported on by the Superintendent (Bray and Barnes, who reported on black bears, are one year off prior to 1934, and Craighead, who reported on both black and grizzly bears, are one year off after 1935).

[b]The Annual Wildlife Reports, on file in the Biologist Office, Yellowstone Park, have had several names. They should not be confused with the "Wildlife Inventory" done by the National Park Service. The "Wildlife Inventory" listed population estimates of various animals from many different National Park Service areas, and in the case of Yellowstone was directly derivative of the Annual Wildlife Reports. Note that in a few years before 1951 the Superintendent's Annual Reports and the Annual Wildlife Reports differ on the number of bears, and that the Superintendent's Annual Reports no longer carried bear population estimates after 1950.

[c]Figures in this column for the years 1959 to 1966 are from Craighead, 1967. Figures from 1967 to 1970 are from Craighead, 1974. In Craighead, 1967, it is stated that the figures given to that date are supposed to be almost all of the grizzlies in Yellowstone. In Craighead, 1974, these figures are apparently redefined to represent approximately 77.3% of the total population of grizzlies in the Yellowstone Ecosystem.

Black Bears in Yellowstone Park, 1920-1978, population estimates from various sources.[a]

Year	Supt. Annual Reports[b]	Annual Wildlife Census Reports	Research Biologist Reports	Year	Supt. Annual Reports[b]	Annual Wildlife Census Reports	Research Biologist Reports
1920	100	—	—	1950	360	—	—
1921	—	—	—	1951	—	—	—
1922	—	—	—	1952	—	—	—
1923	—	—	—	1953	—	360	—
1924	—	—	—	1954	—	—	—
1925	200	200	—	1955	—	"common"	—
1926	225	225	—	1956	—	—	—
1927	275	275	—	1957	—	—	—
1928	350	350	—	1958	—	"common"	—
1929	440	450	—	1959	—	"common"	—
1930	490	490	—	1960	—	—	—
1931	465	500	—	1961	—	—	—
1932	517	—	—	1962	—	500	—
1933	525	525	—	1963	—	500	—
1934	500	591	—	1964	—	500	—
1935	500	633	—	1965	—	500	—
1936	621	621	—	1966	—	500	—
1937	520	520	—	1967	—	500	—
1938	450	450	—	1968	—	500	—
1939	500	500	—	1969	—	500	—
1940	510	510	—	1970	—	500	—
1941	550	550	—	1971	—	500	—
1942	—	—	—	1972	—	500	—
1943	—	—	—	1973	—	500	—
1944	—	550	—	1974	—	500	—
1945	450	450	—	1975	—	500	—
1946	450	450	—	1976	—	—	650
1947	—	360	—	1977	—	650	—
1948	360	—	—	1978	—	650	—
1949	360	360	—				

[a]Note comments in text on the relative reliability/unreliability of the various early estimates. Most were crude, based in part on sighted animals.

[b]Footnote "a" in Grizzly Bear population estimates table explains discrepancies that have occurred in past reporting of these numbers from the Superintendent's Annual Reports.

Injuries caused by grizzly bears and grizzly bears killed in Yellowstone Park, 1930-1985.

Year	Number of Injuries	Number of Bears Killed for Control	Year	Number of Injuries	Number of Bears Killed for Control
1930	0	0	1959	1	6
1931	0	1	1960	1	4
1932	3	4	1961	2	1
1933	0	2	1962	2	4
1934	1	0	1963	8	2
1935	2	6	1964	2	2
1936	0	0	1965	8	2
1937	0	10	1966	2	3
1938	0	0	1967	3	4
1939	0	0	1968	2	5
1940	0	0	1969	6	10
1941	1	0	1970	3	12 (8 others
1942	3[a]	28			sent to zoos)
1943	0	0	1971	0	6
1944	0	3	1972	3[a]	8 (1 other
1945	0	0			sent to zoo)
1946	0	0	1973	0	0
1947	1	0	1974	0	2
1948	7	3	1975	2	0
1949	0	8	1976	4	1
1950	0	0	1977	1	1
1951	0	4	1978	0[b]	2
1952	0	1	1979	2	1
1953	1	1	1980	1	2
1954	0	5	1981	2	0
1955	1	5	1982	0	3
1956	0	0	1983	1	2
1957	2	1	1984	5[a]	3
1958	1	2	1985	0	0

[a]Includes one fatality.

[b]One serious backcountry injury was inflicted by a bear that may well have been a grizzly; it has been impossible to confirm the species either way, and so the injury is officially classified as caused by a bear of unknown species. This same situation was true in the 1942 death of Martha Hansen.

Statistics in this table are from Cole 1970 and Meagher 1978 for before 1978. Statistics from 1978-1985 are from bear management office records.

Injuries from black bears, control actions, and park visitors in Yellowstone Park, 1931-1984.

Years	Number of Injuries[a]	Number of Bears Removed[b]	Number of Captures & Transplants Per Year	Average Number of Park Visitors (Millions)
1930s	58(22-115)	33(2-66)	—	0.3
1940s	29(2-89)	15(2-55)	—	0.5
1950s	56(38-109)	19(6-40)	—	1.3
1960s	41(24-69)	31(4-85)	—	1.9
1931-69	46	24	?	1.0
1970	7	7(1)[c]	19	2.3
1971	9	4(2)	15	2.1
1972	5	11(3)	34	2.2
1973	5	3(0)	13	2.0
1974	7	3(2)	11	1.9
1975	1	1(1)	5	2.2
1976	4	4(1)	13	2.5
1977	2	7(3)	15	2.5
1978	1	1	0	2.6
1979	0	0	0	1.9
1980	0	1(1)	0	2.0
1981	1	0	2	2.5
1982	0	1(1)	0	2.4
1983	1	1(1)	3	2.4
1984[d]	0	1(1)	0	2.3

[a]Statistics given for before 1970 are averages for each decade, with range of yearly totals in parentheses.

[b]Statistics given are average for the decade, with range of yearly totals in parentheses.

[c]Statistics given include bears killed by human accidents, usually by being hit by cars. Number in parentheses is the non-management portion of the total.

[d]Statistics from before 1979 are from Meagher and Phillips, 1983. Statistics from 1979-1984 are from bear management office compilations.

Property damage cases due to bears, 1931-1984.

Year	Number[a]	Year	Number[a]
1931	209	1958	117
1932	451	1959	269
1933	146	1960	358
1934	38	1961	247
1935	141	1962	112
1936	34	1963	278
1937	81	1964	224
1938	81	1965	291
1939	92	1966	298
1940	75	1967	284
1941	102	1968[b]	240(55)
1942	118	1969	199(44)
1943	38	1970	88(16)
1944	18	1971	52(31)
1945	7	1972	87(26)
1946	20	1973	32(4)
1947	9	1974	52(6)
1948	27	1975	27(2)
1949	26	1976	27(4)
1950	48	1977	31(2)
1951	75	1978	13(2)
1952	84	1979	7(3)
1953	66	1980	12(6)
1954	115	1981	18(5)
1955	121	1982	50(15)
1956	106	1983	14(5)
1957	125	1984	0(0)

[a]1931-1967, the number is the total for both species of bears.

[b]1968-1984, the first number is the total, the number in parentheses is for grizzly bears.

Statistics for 1931-1967 from Superintendent's reports. Statistics for 1968-1984 from bear management office compilations.

Grizzly bears in Yellowstone Park and in the Yellowstone ecosystem — population estimates, 1971-1982.

Year	In Park	In Ecosystem
1971		175[a]
1972		
1973	250-300[b]	300-400[b]
1974	254-290[c]	319-364[c]
		136[d]
		234[e]
1975	250-320[f]	237-540[g]
		301[h]
1976		
1977		
1978		312[i]
1979		
1980		300-350[j]
1981		247[k]
1982		197[l]

[a]Craighead 1971.
[b]Cole 1973.
[c]Cole 1974.
[d]Craighead 1974.
[e]National Academy of Sciences 1974 — This was an estimate for the population during the period before 1970.
[f]Cole 1975.
[g]Knight 1975.
[h]Cowan 1975 — This was an estimate for the period 1959-1970.
[i]McCullough 1978 — This was an estimate for the period 1959-1970.
[j]Knight et al. 1980.
[k]Knight, Blanchard, and Kendall 1981.
[l]Knight, Blanchard, and Kendall 1982.

Total known grizzly bears removed from the Yellowstone Ecosystem, including natural deaths, 1970-1985.

Year	Known	Probable	Possible	Total	Portion of Total due to Park Service Management Actions
1970	43	0	1	44	20
1971	39	3	2	44	6
1972	24	0	0	24	9
1973	10	5	3	18	0
1974	15	0	1	16	2
1975	2	1	0	3	0
1976	5	1	0	6	1
1977	13	1	1	15	1
1978	5	2	3	10	2
1979	3	6	2	11	1
1980	7	0	0	7	2
1981	9	4	2	15	0
1982	17	0	0	17	3
1983	6	0	0	6	2
1984	10	0	0	10	3
1985	6	—	—	6	0

Note: "portion of total due to park management actions" includes deaths resulting from accidents during such actions as well as deaths resulting from accidents during research. It also includes bears sent to zoos.

Statistics for first four columns, 1970-1984, from Knight, Blanchard, and Mattson, 1985. Statistics for final column ("portion of total due to Park Service management actions") are from bear management office records. Statistics for 1985 are from bear management office records as of December 1985 and thus do not include probable and possible losses, which will be compiled later.

Acknowledgments

Many people have assisted with either this or the previous edition of this book. Here are those who helped with the first edition, published in 1980.

Dr. Mary Meagher, then Supervisory Research Biologist of Yellowstone Park, provided assistance in many ways, including access to various files and assistance in tracking down vagrant publications. Mary also read and commented on the manuscript.

Dr. Douglas Houston, then a Yellowstone research biologist and now a research biologist in Olympic National Park, took time to answer many questions relating to park wildlife, and read and commented on the manuscript.

Ila Jane Bucknall and her successors Val Black and Bev Whitman, all of the Yellowstone Park Reference Library, patiently assisted me with my research and frequently provided me with material when I was not able to visit the library.

Joan Oliver and Ruth James of the Research Office in Yellowstone responded promptly to many requests for reports and other documents. Sue Fullerton, of the same office, was a great help in sorting out statistical tangles relating to the tables in this book. Her patient examination of many earlier publications resulted in previously unachieved understanding of pre-1950 bear population estimates. Sue also helped me locate a number of elusive publications.

Dr. Richard Knight of the Interagency Grizzly Bear Study Team read and commented on Part I of the book, providing numerous useful suggestions.

In Yellowstone Park the manuscript was read by then Chief Park Naturalist Alan Mebane, then Resource Management Specialist Ted Bucknall, and Supervisory Rangers Jerry Mernin, Dale Nuss, and Jerry Phillips.

In the National Park Service Rocky Mountain Regional Office, Denver, the manuscript was read and commented on by Regional Publications Specialist Earle Kittlemans.

Dr. John Craighead provided me with a number of his publications, and also reviewed the events of the grizzly management controversy in detail for me, both in correspondence and in several hours of phone conversation. Others who either provided me with publications or answered specific questions were: Dr. Stephen Herrero, University of Calgary; Dr. Clifford Martinka, Glacier National Park; Jim Reid, Rocky Mountain Regional Office Regional Chief Scientist, National Park Service; and Charles Willey, Wildlife Biologist, State of Vermont Agency of Environmental Conservation.

A number of park employees shared their bear stories with me. I especially appreciated the willingness of Supervisory Ranger Dale Nuss and Maintenance Supervisor Bill Hape to tell stories, not only on the bears but on themselves.

I first wrote this book in 1978, after having moved from Yellowstone to Vermont. In Manchester, Vermont, the staff of the Mark Skinner Library, especially Assistant Librarian Esther Coburn, was very helpful with many interlibrary loan requests. Mrs. Anne Secor, Vice President of the Orvis Company, arranged for my use of office equipment, especially for photocopying, which made work much more convenient.

Others who helped or encouraged me with the first edition were Geri Hape, Les Inafuku, Cheryl Moore, Jeremy Schmidt, and Linda Green.

The second edition acknowledgments sound much less like an Academy Awards speech. The book was reread by Dick Knight and Mary Meagher, both of whom offered numerous suggestions for revision. Jon Swenson, Montana Department of Fish, Wildlife and Parks, read the book and made many valuable comments. Yellowstone Research Administrator John Varley provided me with a wealth of recently-published materials, as well as access to various files of relevant material.

Sandy Fowler in the Resource Management office at Yellowstone helped with updating statistical tables.

My wife Dianne Russell provided encouragement as well as help with various details of finishing up the revised manuscript.

Finally I am especially grateful to the National Park Foundation for their financial support of the revision of this book, and to my editor and publisher, Rick Rinehart, for his support and guidance with many related projects over the past eight years.

Bibliography

The literature of the bear is immense, and within the past twenty years even the technical literature of bear research has increased several times over. There are many thousands of titles now listed in master bibliographies published by the National Park Service; those lists cover bear-related publications the world over, but even in Yellowstone the list is very long. There have been, for example, many hundreds of articles in newspapers and magazines on just the one very narrow topic of the bear management controversy. If you like to read about the bears of Yellowstone, you may never run short of material.

The following list is not all that I consulted to write this book, but the information in the book could all have been derived from it. It includes a representative sampling of popular articles, but is far more inclusive in the case of technical publications, which are not only more reliable but also infinitely more informative. In the process of researching this book, both editions, I have been repeatedly struck by the often large gap between "nonfiction" and truth. You will have to make up your own mind about some things you read, whether they involve bear natural history, hiker safety, or the events of the bear management debates; my only recommendation is that whenever possible you rely on the original sources rather than on popular articles. That goes for my book as well; the next step is to read the scientists themselves. It's great fun, once you get used to the language, and bear research is exciting however you read about it.

This list will begin to be out of date by the time the book is published. The Interagency Study Team is continually refining their interpretations and publishing new findings. The story goes on, and we learn more all the time.

There are several other bear books that have appeared recently that deal all or in part with Yellowstone, or that should be of special interest to anyone who likes bear country. My favorite among them is Stephen Herrero's *Bear Attacks: Their Causes and Avoidance*. Steve is one of the leading bear biologists, and has done a masterful job of explaining bear behavior, natural history, and bear-human interactions. There are a number of less worthy, sensational books about bear attacks that have pretended to do what Steve has actually done. The complete references to Steve's book and the other books I will mention are in the bibliography. Frank Craighead's book *Track of the Grizzly* is both the most complete popular account of the Craighead study and the most comprehensive attack on the Park Service's management program. I have to say that I find him frequently guilty of selective memory, and that I know other participants in that controversy whose memories of the events he reports are quite different from his, but I also have to say that this book is a milestone in popular bear literature, and that if you are really going to pursue the Yellowstone bear in print, you must read it. Thomas McNamee, a New York writer, has written a book, *The Grizzly Bear*, about all the remaining bear populations in the lower forty-eight. Tom is an independent and conscientious writer who has consumed a huge volume of technical material and synthesized it very well. Tom and I seem to disagree on a point here and there, but, except for Steve Herrero's book, which I uniformly admire, I doubt that I (or *any* bear book author) entirely agrees with any other bear book author. Tom and I do seem to at least occupy the same version of reality; Frank Craighead and I do not. When I wrote the first edition of *The Bears of Yellowstone* I thought it would be nice to explore all of man's perceptions of bears someday; as I say in this book, the bear is our most complex animal idea. Eight or ten other book projects have kept me from doing it, though, and now it's been done by someone else. Shepard and Sanders' book *The Sacred Paw* will introduce you to the rich cultural heritage of bear worship, bear fear, and bear confusion, in an impressive search of the world's historical and modern bear literatures. There are other bear books in the works. Some years ago John Craighead told me that he was informally working on a book about his research experiences, and I know of others. I have one or two of my own I hope to get to some time. I'm sure the number of new ones will increase rather than decrease as more and more people discover what a wonder bears are.

If you want to graduate from popular writing, though, there is a series of volumes you must not miss. I have to introduce them here because I have taken certain liberties with their titles in the following bibliography. In order to save space, I have shortened the inordinately long titles of these volumes, whose full titles I will give you below. They are the proceedings of a series of bear biology symposia, and though bear research findings are being published in a host of journals and monographs, these volumes are the mother lode for the newcomer. Each contains dozens of papers detailing the findings of bear research in all parts of the world. It is a feast. In each of the following references, I will give you first the abbreviated designation of the volumes as I use it in the bibliography. Then I will give you the full reference. Here they are:

Bears, I.U.C.N., 1972—Stephen Herrero, ed., *Bears,—their biology and management.* Papers and proceedings of the International Conference on Bear Research and Management, Calgary, Alberta, Canada, 6-9 November, 1979. Morges, Switzerland: International Union for the Conservation of Nature and Natural Resources.

Bears, I.U.C.N., 1976—Michael Pelton, Jack Lentfer, and G. Edgar Folk, eds., *Bears—their biology and management.* Papers and proceedings of the Third International Conference on Bear Research and Management, Binghampton, New York, U.S.A. and Moscow, U.S.S.R. June 1974. Morges, Switzerland: International Union for the Conservation of Nature and Natural Resources.

Bears, B.B.A., 1980. Clifford Martinka and Katherine McArthur, eds., *Bears—their biology and management.* A selection of papers from the Fourth International Conference on Bear Research and Management, Kalispell, Montana, U.S.A., February 1977. Washington, D.C.: Bear Biology Association/ Government Printing Office.

Bears, B.B.A., 1983—E. Charles Meslow, *Bears—their biology and management.* A selection of papers from the conference held at Madison, Wisconsin, U.S.A., February 1980. No location: International Association for Bear Research and Management.

A sixth international conference was held at the Grand Canyon in 1983. I have used manuscripts of several articles that will appear in that volume; these are listed as such, in press, though they may be published by the time this book is out. The seventh international conference is scheduled for early in 1986 in Virginia. I recommend it as enthusiastically as I recommend the others.

Abbie, L. 1942. Grizzly and bull elk battle. *Yellowstone Nature Notes* (May-June).

Adams, C. C. 1925. The relation of wild life to the public in national and state parks. *Roosevelt Wildlife Bulletin* 2 (4): 371–402.

Albright, H. 1931. Letter to Joseph Dixon, November 9. Yellowstone Archives. Yellowstone National Park, Wyoming.

————. 1945. New orders for national park bears. *The Backlog: A Bulletin of the Camp Fire Club of America:* 6–7.

————. 1928. *Oh ranger.* New York: Dodd Mead.

————. 1972. Memories of the great and near-great in Yellowstone. *Montana, The Magazine of Western History* 22 (3): 80–89.

Amstrup, S., and J. Beecham. 1976. Activity patterns of radio-collared black bears in Idaho. *Journal of Wildlife Management* 30 (2): 340–348.

Anderson, Jack. 1970. Letter to John Craighead, July 9. Yellowstone Files. Yellowstone National Park, Wyoming.

————. 1971a. Letter to John Craighead, July 20. Yellowstone Files. Yellowstone National Park, Wyoming.

————. 1971b. Letter to John Craighead, August 3. Yellowstone Files. Yellowstone National Park, Wyoming.

————. 1971c. Letter to John Craighead, February 9. Yellowstone Files. Yellowstone National Park, Wyoming.

Anonymous. 1916. A grizzly attack in Yellowstone National Park. *Outdoor Life* (October): 373–374.

————. 1916. The late grizzly bear attacks in Yellowstone National Park. *Outdoor Life* (December): 583–584.

————. 1924. Grizzly visits snowshoe cabin. *Yellowstone Nature Notes* (November 20).

————. 1970. Noted bear expert challenges Yellowstone Park bear policy. *Cody Enterprise:* 7 October.

————. 1970. Official bemoans grizzly slaughter. *Jackson Hole News:* 12 November.

————. 1978. Bear feeding would lessen maulings, Craighead agrees. *Jackson Hole Guide:* 29 June.

Arnold, B. 1930. Cannibal bear. *Yellowstone Nature Notes* 7 (8): 54.

Bacon, E. S. 1977. Curiosity in the American black bear. In *Bears,* B.B.A., ed. C. J. Martinka and K. L. McArthur, 153–157.

Bacon, E. S., and Burghardt. 1976a. Ingestive behaviors of the American black bear. *Bears,* IUCN, 13–26.

————. 1976b. Learning and color discrimination in the American black bear. *Bears,* IUCN, 27–36.

Baggley, G. 1932. Outline of method for bear control. Yellowstone Park Work Plan. Mimeographed.

Bailey, V. 1930. *Animal Life of Yellowstone National Park.* Baltimore: Charles C. Thomas.

Ball, R. E. 1976. The use of time-lapse cameras in destruction and population studies of grizzly bears (*Ursus arctos*) in the Shoshone National Forest, Park County, Wyoming. M.S. Thesis, University of Wyoming.

Barbee, R. 1985. Comments on proposed forest plan – Gallatin National Forest. Yellowstone Park files. Mimeographed.

Barmore, W. 1967. Bear management recommendations by John and Frank Craighead. Memorandum to Yellowstone Park Superintendent, July 13. Yellowstone Files. Yellowstone National Park, Wyoming.

Barnes, V. G. 1967. *Activities of black bears in Yellowstone National Park.* M.S. Thesis, Colorado State University.

Barnes, V. G., and O. E. Bray. 1966. Black bears use drainage culverts for winter dens. *Journal of Mammalogy* 47 (4): 712–713.

————. 1967. *Population characteristics and activities of black bears in Yellowstone National Park.* Final Report. Colorado Cooperative Wildlife Research Unit, Colorado State University.

Bartlett, R. 1974. *Nature's Yellowstone.* Norman: University of Oklahoma Press.

Basile, J. V. 1982. Grizzly bear distribution in the Yellowstone area, 1973-79. USDA-FS, Intermtn For. and Range Exp. Sta. Research Note INT-321.

Beal, M. 1951. Bear caves in Norris geyser basin. *Yellowstone Nature Notes* (November-December).

————. 1960. *The story of man in Yellowstone.* Yellowstone Park: Yellowstone Library and Museum Association.

Bean, M. 1978. *The evolution of national wildlife law.* Washington: U.S. Government Printing Office.

Beck, M., and D. Junkin. 1984. Whose park is it, anyway? *Newsweek,* June 25, 33.

Beeman and Pelton. 1976. Homing of black bears in the Great Smoky Mountains. In *Bears,* IUCN, 87–96.

Bennett, L. J., P. F. English, and R. L. Watts. 1943. The food habits of the black bear in Pennsylvania. *Journal of Mammalogy* 24 (1): 25–31.

Bieberdorf, F. W., Mrs. 1940. Bruin takes a Turkish bath. *Yellowstone Nature Notes* (May-June).

Blanchard, B. 1978. *Grizzly bear distribution in relation to habitat areas and recreational use: Cabin Creek–Hilgard Mountains.* M.S. Thesis, Montana State University.

———. 1983. Grizzly bear-habitat relationships in the Yellowstone area. In *Bears*, B.B.A., 118–123.

Blanchard, B., and R. Knight. 1980. Status of grizzly bears in the Yellowstone system. Proc. 45th North Am. Wildl. Conf.: 263–267.

Bock, D. 1953. A survey of public opinion concerning the Yellowstone bear feeding problem. Research Project, Colorado A & M School of Forestry.

Bray, O. E., and V. G. Barnes. 1967. *A literature review on black bear populations and activities.* National Park Service and Colorado Cooperative Wildlife Research Unit.

Bromely, G. 1965. *The bears of the southern far east of USSR.* Canadian Wildlife Service translation of Russian.

Bucknall, E. 1972. Annual Wildlife Report, May 1, 1971 to April 30, 1972. Yellowstone Park Files. Mimeographed.

Bunnell, F. L., D. S. Eastman, and J. M. Peek, eds. 1978. Symposium on natural regulation of wildlife populations. In Proceedings of the Northwest Section, The Wildlife Society, No. 14, University of Idaho.

Burghardt, G. M., and L. D. Burghardt. 1972. Notes on the behavioral development of two black bear cubs: the first eight months. In *Bears*, IUCN, 207–220.

Burst, T. L., and M. R. Pelton. 1983. Black bear mark trees in the Smoky Mountains. In *Bears*, B.B.A., 45–53.

Burt, W. H., and R. P. Grossenheider. 1952. *A field guide to the mammals.* New York: Houghton Mifflin.

Cahalane, V. H. 1947. *Mammals of North America.* New York: MacMillan.

Cahn, R. 1976. The future of the parks: II. In *Research in the Parks: transactions of the National Park Centennial Symposium.* Washington DC: U.S. Government Printing Office, 213–220.

Cauble, C. 1977. The great grizzly grapple. *Natural History* (August-September).

Chase, A. 1983. The last bears of Yellowstone. *The Atlantic* (February): 63–73.

———. 1986. The grizzly and the Juggernaut. *Outside* (January).

Childs, F. 1934. Additional notes on the hibernation habits of the black bear (*Euarctos americanus*), from observations taken in Yellowstone National Park, 1933–1934. Yellowstone Files. Mimeographed.

Cole, G. 1967. Research goals, Yellowstone National Park. Yellowstone Park files. Mimeographed.

———. 1967. Craighead report on Yellowstone bears. Memorandum to Deputy Chief Scientist, National Park Service. Yellowstone Park files.

———. 1969a. Elk and the Yellowstone ecosystem. Yellowstone Research Note no. 1. Mimeographed.

———. 1969b. Grizzly bears. Memorandum to the Superintendent. Yellowstone Park files.

———. 1971. Preservation and management of grizzly bears in Yellowstone National Park. *Bioscience* 21: 858–863.

———. 1972a. Grizzly bear-elk relationships in Yellowstone National Park. *Journal of Wildlife Management* 36 (2): 556–561.

———. 1972b. Preservation and management of grizzly bears in Yellowstone National Park. In *Bears*, IUCN, 274–288.

———. 1973a. Management involving grizzly bears in Yellowstone National Park, 1970-1972. Natural Resources Report no. 7, National Park Service.

———. 1973b. Management involving grizzly bears and humans in Yellowstone National Park, 1970-1973. *Bioscience* 24: 335–338.

———. 1974. Comments on National Academy of Sciences Report. Memorandum to Files. Yellowstone Park Files, September 11.

———. 1975a. Management involving grizzly bears in Yellowstone National Park, 1970-1974. Paper presented at 26th Annual A.I.B.S. Meeting of Biological Sciences at Oregon State University.

————. 1975b. Natural vs. man-caused deaths of wild animals in national parks. Yellowstone Park Information Paper no. 26.

————. 1975c. Population regulation and the consequences of artificially feeding wild animals. Yellowstone Park Information Paper no. 27.

————. 1976. Management involving grizzly and black bears in Yellowstone National Park, 1970-1975. Natural Resources Report no. 9, National Park Service.

————. 1978. A naturally regulated elk population. Research Report, Yellowstone National Park.

Condon, D. 1956. The Yellowstone grizzly. Yellowstone Park Files. Mimeographed.

Cottam, C., A. I. Nelson, and T. E. Clarke. 1939. Notes on early winter food habits of the black bear in George Washington National Forest. *Journal of Mammalogy* 20 (3): 310-314.

Cottrell, L. Black bear abroad in February. *Yellowstone Nature Notes* 2 (1): 6.

Cowan, I. M. 1975. Letter to Glen Cole, April 29. Yellowstone Park Files. Photocopied.

Craighead, F. 1969. Increasing concern over grizzly bear survival. *Jackson Hole Guide*: 6 November.

————. 1970. Grizzlies may be endangered. *High Country News*: 5 October.

————. 1973. They're killing Yellowstone's grizzlies. *National Wildlife* (October-November): 4–9.

————. 1976. Grizzly bear ranges and movements as determined by radiotracking. In *Bears*, IUCN, 97–110.

Craighead, J. 1960. Proposal for research on ecology of the grizzly bear (*Ursus horribilis*) initiated by the Montana Cooperative Wildlife Research Unit. Submitted to the National Science Foundation and the National Academy of Sciences.

————. 1969a. Letter to Jack Anderson, April 14. Yellowstone Park Files.

————. 1969b. Investigator's Annual Report. Yellowstone Park Files, 14 January.

————. 1971. Letter to Jack Anderson, April. Yellowstone Park Files.

Craighead, J., and F. Craighead. 1967. *Management of bears in Yellowstone National Park.* Unpublished report.

————. 1971. Grizzly bear-man relationships in Yellowstone National Park. *Bioscience* 21 (16): 845–857.

————. 1972. Grizzly bear prehibernation and denning activities as determined by radiotracking. *Wildlife Monographs*, no. 32.

Craighead, J., F. Craighead, and M. Hornocker. 1961. *An ecological study of the grizzly bear, third annual report, summary of work accomplished, 1959–1961.* Montana Cooperative Wildlife Research Unit.

Craighead, J., F. Craighead, and H. McCutcheon. 1970. Age determination of grizzly bears from fourth premolar tooth sections. *Journal of Wildlife Management* 34 (2): 353–363.

Craighead, J., F. Craighead, and J. Sumner. 1976. Reproductive cycles and rates in the grizzly bear, *Ursus arctos horribilis*, of the Yellowstone ecosystem. In *Bears*, IUCN, 337–356.

Craighead, J., M. Hornocker, and F. Craighead. 1969. Reproductive biology of young female grizzly bears. *Journal of Reprod. Fert., Suppl.* 6: 447–475.

Craighead, J., J. S. Sumner, and G. B. Scaggs. 1982. *A definitive system for analysis of grizzly bear habitat and other wilderness resources.* University of Montana: Wildlife-Wildlands Institute Monograph Series no. 2.

Craighead, J., J. Varney, and F. Craighead. 1973. *A Computer analysis of the Yellowstone grizzly bear population.* Unpublished mimeographed report.

————. 1974. A population analysis of the Yellowstone grizzly bears. Bulletin 40, Montana Forest and Conservation Experiment Station, University of Montana.

————. 1976. Telemetry experiments with a hibernating black bear. In *Bears*, IUCN, 357–372.

Craighead, J., et al. 1971. Satellite monitoring of black bear. *Bioscience* 21 (24): 1206–1213.

————. 1960. Trapping, immobilizing and color-marking grizzly bears. In *Transactions of the Twenty-fifth North American Wildlife Conference, March 7, 8, and 9,* 347–363.

Crocker, F. C. 1893. After wapiti in Wyoming. In *American Big Game Hunting*, ed. T. Roosevelt and G. B. Grinnell, 140–154. New York: Forest and Stream Publishing Co.

Curry-Lindahl, K. 1972. The brown bear in Europe: decline, present distribution, biology, and ecology. In *Bears*, IUCN, 74–80.

Darling, F. F., and N. Eichorn. 1969. *Man and nature in the national parks.* Washington, D.C.: The Conservation Foundation.

Despain, D. 1972. Fire as an ecological force in Yellowstone ecosystems. Yellowstone Information Paper no. 16.

————. 1973. Major vegetation zones of Yellowstone National Park. Yellowstone Information Paper no. 19.

Dinkel, T. R., and M. Y. Su. 1974. Aerial detection of grizzly bears in Yellowstone National Park. Final Report, National Park Service Science Center.

Dixon, J. 1929. Report of the bear situation in Yellowstone. Yellowstone Park Special Research Report. Mimeographed.

Doane, G. 1970. *Battle drums and geysers, the journals of Gustavus Doane.* Chicago: Swallow Press.

Dole, R. 1914. Report on sanitary conditions in Yellowstone Park. Yellowstone Park Archives, type-script. Yellowstone National Park, Wyoming.

Dood, A. R., R. D. Brannon, and R. D. Mace. 1985. *Grizzly bear environmental impact statement, preliminary draft.* Helena: Montana Department of Fish, Wildlife, and Parks.

Douglas, J. 1925. Black bear and cub under Lake Hotel. *Yellowstone Nature Notes,* 18 March.

East, B. 1978. Disney beast or mankiller. *Outdoor Life* (October).

Egbert and Stokes. 1976. The social behavior of brown bears on an Alaskan salmon stream. In *Bears,* IUCN, 41–56.

Erickson, A. 1959. The age of self-sufficiency in the black bear. *Journal of Wildlife Management* 23 (4): 401–405.

Erickson, A., J. Nellor, and G. A. Petrides. 1964. *The Black Bear in Michigan.* Research Bulletin 4, Michigan State University Agricultural Experiment Station.

Folk, G. E., M. A. Folk, and J. G. Minor. 1972. Physiological condition of three species of bears in winter dens. In *Bears,* IUCN, 107–125.

Folk, Larson, and Folk. 1972. Physiological condition of three species of bears in winter dens. In *Bears,* IUCN, 107–125.

Franklin, W. S. 1913. The Yellowstone Park. *Science* 38 (969): 127–129.

Frome, M. 1974. Do grizzlies face a grisly future? *Field and Stream* (January).

Fund for Animals. 1974. News releases concerning Yellowstone bear management and Fund for Animals Lawsuit. February.

Gilbert, B. 1976. The great grizzly controversy. *Audubon* (January): 62–92.

Glen, et al. 1976. Reproductive biology of female brown bears, *Ursus arctos,* McNeil River, Alaska. In *Bears,* IUCN, 381–390.

Graber, D. M., and M. White. 1983. Parks and bears: the ecological consequences of recreation. Paper presented at the Sixth International Conference on Bear Research and Management, Grand Canyon, Arizona.

Graham, D. 1978. *Grizzly bear distribution, use of habitats, food habits and habitat characterization in Pelican and Hayden Valleys, Yellowstone National Park.* M.S. Thesis, Montana State University.

Greer, K. 1972. Grizzly bear mortality studies in Montana. In *Bears,* IUCN, 53–66.

————. 1976. Managing Montana's grizzlies for the grizzlies! In *Bears,* IUCN, 177–190.

Gresswell, R. 1977. Personal communication.

Griffel, D. E., and J. V. Basile. 1981. Identifying sheep killed by bears. USDA-FS, Intermtn. For. & Range Exp. Sta. Research Note INT-313.

Grimm, R. 1938. A climbing grizzly. *Yellowstone Nature Notes* (November-December).

Grinnell, G. B. 1885. Report on the park. *Forest and Stream* (June 11): 1.

Grinnell, J., and T. Storer. 1916. Animal life as an asset of national parks. *Science* 1 (44): 375–380.

Gross, J. 1973. A computer re-analysis of a computer analysis of the Yellowstone grizzly bear population by Craighead, Varney, and Craighead. Photocopied.

Haines, A. 1977. *The Yellowstone story.* Boulder: Colorado Associated University Press.

Hamer, Herrero, and Ogilvie. 1977. *Ecological studies of the Banff National Park grizzly bear, Cut-head/Wignore region, 1976.* Parks Canada.

Hampton, H. D. 1971. *How the U.S. cavalry saved our national parks.* Bloomington: Indiana University Press.

Hanley, W. 1977. *Natural history in America*. New York: Massachusetts Audubon Society and the *New York Times*.

Hanna, W. 1978. *The grizzlies of Glacier*. Missoula: Mountain Press.

Hape, W. 1978. Personal communication.

Haroldson, M., and D. Mattson. 1985. Response of grizzly bears to backcountry human use in Yellowstone National Park. Yellowstone Park Files. Mimeographed.

Harrison, G. 1979. Are we creating killer bears? *Sports Afield* (February).

Harting, A. L. 1985. *Relationships between activity patterns and foraging strategies of Yellowstone grizzly bears*. M.S. Thesis, Montana State University.

Haynes, B. D., and E. Haynes. 1966. *The grizzly bear: portraits from life*. Norman: University of Oklahoma Press.

Heller, E. 1925. The big game animals of Yellowstone National Park. *Roosevelt Wildlife Bulletin* 2 (4): 404–467.

Henderson, A. B. undated. Journal of the Yellowstone expedition of 1866 under Jeff Standifer, also the diaries kept by Henderson during his prospecting journeys in the Snake, Wind River, and Yellowstone country during the years 1866–1872. Yellowstone Park Files. Typescript.

Hensel, Troyer, and Erickson. 1969. Reproduction in the female brown bear. *Journal of Wildlife Management* 33 (2): 357–365.

Herrero, S. 1972. Aspects of evolution and adaptation in American black bears (*Ursus americanus* Pallas) and brown and grizzly bears (*U. arctos* Linne) of North America. In *Bears*, IUCN, 221–231.

———. 1976. Conflicts between man and grizzly bears in the national parks of North America. In *Bears*, IUCN, 121–146.

———. 1985. *Bear attacks: their causes and avoidance*. New York: Nick Lyons Books/Schocken.

Herrero and Hamer. 1977. Courtship and copulation of a pair of grizzly bears, with comments on reproductive plasticity and strategy. *Journal of Mammalogy* 58 (3): 441–444.

Holzworth, J. M. 1930. *The wild grizzlies of Alaska*. New York: G. P. Putnam's Sons.

Hornaday, W. 1922. *The minds and manners of wild animals*. New York: Charles Scribner's Sons.

Hornocker, M. 1962. *Population characteristics and social and reproductive behavior of the grizzly bear in Yellowstone National Park*. M.S. Thesis, Montana State University.

Houston, D. B. 1971. Ecosystems of national parks. *Science* (14 May 1971): 648–651.

———. 1973. Wildfires in northern Yellowstone National Park. *Ecology* 54 (5): 1111–1117.

———. 1977. Elk as winter-spring food for carnivores in northern Yellowstone Park. Paper presented at the American Association for the Advancement of Science Annual Meeting, February.

———. 1977-1979. Personal communication.

———. 1982. *The northern Yellowstone elk: ecology and management*. New York: Macmillan.

Howell, A. B. 1921. The black bear as a destroyer of game. *Journal of Mammalogy* 2 (1): 36.

Hubbard, W. P., Harris, and Seale. 1960. *Notorious grizzly bears*. Chicago: Swallow Press.

Jaggar, T. A. 1899. Death Gulch, a natural bear-trap. *Appleton's Popular Science Monthly* (February).

Jenness, Erickson, and Craighead. 1972. Some comparative aspects of milk from four species of bears. *Journal of Mammalogy* 53 (1): 34–47.

Johnson, A. 1973. Yellowstone grizzlies: endangered or prospering? *Defenders of Wildlife News* (October): 557–568.

Johnson, F. 1900. Bear in Yellowstone Park. *Recreation* 12 (1).

Johnston, F. 1950. History of the Yellowstone bear problem. Memorandum from Acting Superintendent to Regional Director. Yellowstone Park Files.

Jonkel, C. 1975. Of bears and people. *Western Wildlands* (Winter): 30–37.

———. 1978. Black, brown (grizzly), and polar bears. In *Big Game of North America*, ed. J. L. Schmidt and D. L. Gilbert, 227–248. Harrisburg: Stackpole Books.

Jonkel, C. and I. Cowan. 1971. The black bear in the spruce-fir forest. *Wildlife Monograph* no. 27.

Jope, K. L. 1985. Implications of grizzly bear habituation to hikers. *Wildlife Society Bulletin* 13: 32–37.

Jordan, R. 1976. Threat behavior of the black bear, *Ursus americanus*. In *Bears*, IUCN, 57–64.

Judd, S. L., R. Knight, and B. Blanchard. 1983. Denning of grizzly bears in the Yellowstone area. 6th Int. Conf. on Bear Res. and Manage., Grand Canyon, Arizona. (In press)

Kearns, W. 1937. The speed of grizzly bears. *Yellowstone Nature Notes* (January-February).

Kendall, K. C. 1980. Bear use of pine nuts. In *Bears*, B.B.A., 166–173.

Knight, R., and B. Blanchard. 1983. Report of the Interagency Study Team, 1981. USDI-NPS.

Knight, R., B. Blanchard, and K. Kendall. 1981. Report of the Interagency Study Team, 1980. USDI-NPS.

———. 1982. Report of the Interagency Study Team, 1981. USDI-NPS.

Knight, R., B. Blanchard, and D. Mattson. 1985. Report of the Interagency Study Team, 1983 and 1984. USDI-NPS.

Knight, R., and L. L. Eberhardt. 1984. Projected future abundance of the Yellowstone grizzly bear. *Journal of Wildlife Management* 48 (4): 1434–1438.

———. 1985. Population dynamics of Yellowstone grizzly bears. *Ecology* 66 (2): 323–334.

Knight, R., and S. L. Judd. 1983. Grizzly bears that kill livestock. In *Bears*, B.B.A., 186–190.

Knight, R., D. J. Mattson, and B. Blanchard. 1984. Movements and habitat use of the Yellowstone grizzly bear. Mimeographed.

Knight, R., et al. 1974. Grizzly bear study team, first interim report. USDI-NPS.

———. 1975. Yellowstone grizzly bear investigations: annual report of the Interagency Study Team. USDI-NPS.

———. 1976. Yellowstone grizzly bear investigations: annual report of the Interagency Study Team, 1976. USDI-NPS.

———. 1977. Yellowstone grizzly bear investigations: annual report of the Interagency Study Team. USDI-NPS.

———. 1980. Yellowstone grizzly bear investigations: report of the Interagency Study Team. USDI-NPS.

———. 1983. Final Report of the ad hoc Committee to Investigate the Need and Feasibility of the Supplemental Feeding of Yellowstone Grizzly Bears. Yellowstone National Park. Mimeographed.

Kurten, B. 1976. *The cave bear story.* New York: Columbia University Press.

Langford, N. 1972. *The discovery of Yellowstone Park,* ed. Aubrey Haines. Lincoln: University of Nebraska Press.

Lentfer, et al. 1972. Remarks on denning habits of Alaska brown bears. In *Bears*, IUCN, 125–132.

Leopold, A. S. 1970. Weaning grizzly bears. *Natural History* (January): 94–101.

———. 1975. Letter to William Spivak, February 10.

———. 1978. Letter to Mary Meagher, May 11.

Leopold, et al. 1963. Wildlife management in the national parks—report to the Secretary. USDI-NPS.

———. 1969. A bear management program and policy for Yellowstone National Park. Report to the Director by the Natural Sciences Advisory Committee of the National Park Service. USDI-NPS.

Lindzey and Meslow. 1976. Winter dormancy in black bears in southwestern Washington. *Journal of Wildlife Management* 40 (3): 408–415.

Linn, R. 1968. Memorandum to the Associate Director of the Bureau of Sport Fisheries and Wildlife, May 21.

Little, J. R. 1974. Memorandum from Acting Regional Solicitor, NPS to Associate Solicitor, Conservation and Wildlife. Yellowstone Park Files.

Ludlow, J. 1976. Observations on the breeding of captive black bears, *Ursus americanus.* In *Bears*, IUCN, 65–70.

Luque and Stokes. 1976. Fishing behavior of Alaska brown bear. In *Bears*, IUCN, 71–78.

Marti, J. 1984. CBS News gets mauled. *High Country News:* 29 October.

Martindale, P. 1926. Bears still out. *Yellowstone Nature Notes* 3 (2).

———. c. 1920. Close contact with grizzly bears. Yellowstone Park Files. Handwritten report.

———. 1931. Bears during the so-called hibernation state. Yellowstone Park Files. Typescript.

Martinka, C. J. 1971. Status and management of grizzly bears in Glacier National Park, Montana. Transactions of the North American Wildlife and Natural Resource Conference, vol. 36, 312–322.

———. 1974. Population characteristics of grizzly bears in Glacier National Park, Montana. *Journal of Mammalogy* 55: 21–29.

———. ed. 1978. Fourth international conference on bear research and management, abstracts.

Matson, J. R. 1946. Notes on dormancy in the black bear. *Journal of Mammalogy* 27 (3): 203–212.

——. 1952. Litter size in the black bear. *Journal of Mammalogy* 33 (2): 246–247.

——. 1954. Observations on the dormant phase of a female black bear. *Journal of Mammalogy* 35 (1): 28–35.

Mattson, D. J. 1984. *Classification and environmental relationships of wetland vegetation in central Yellowstone National Park.* M.S. Thesis, University of Idaho.

Mattson, D. J., R. Knight, and B. Blanchard. 1985. Derivation of habitat component values for the Yellowstone grizzly bear. Paper presented at the Grizzly Bear Habitat Symposium, Missoula, Montana, April 30–May 2.

McCracken, H. 1955. *The beast that walks like man.* New York: Hanover House.

McCullough, D. 1978. Population dynamics of the Yellowstone grizzly bear. Paper presented for the International Symposium on Population Dynamics of Large Mammals, Logan, Utah, May 25–27. Photocopied.

——. 1982. Behavior, bears, and humans. *Wildlife Society Bulletin* 10: 27–33.

——. 1983. Interpretation of the Craigheads' data on Yellowstone grizzly bear populations. 6th Int. Conf. on Bear Res. and Manage., Grand Canyon, Arizona. (In press)

McGee, G. 1977. Senate Hearing before the Committee on Appropriations: proposed critical habitat area for grizzly bears. Fiscal Year 1977. 94th Congress, 2nd sess. Washington, D.C.: U.S. Government Printing Office.

McGuire, J. A. 1911. Camping in the Yellowstone. *Outdoor Life* (May): 479–485.

McNamee, T. 1984. *The grizzly bear.* New York: Knopf.

Meagher, M. 1973. *The bison of Yellowstone National Park.* Washington D.C.: U.S. Government Printing Office.

——. 1976. Summary of 1974 National Academy of Sciences recommendations and measures taken as of November, 1976. Yellowstone Park Files. Photocopied.

——. 1977. Evaluation of bear management in Yellowstone National Park, 1976. Yellowstone Research Note no. 7. Yellowstone Park Files.

——. 1978. Evaluation of bear management in Yellowstone National Park, 1977. Yellowstone Research Note no. 8. Yellowstone Park Files.

——. 1977-1979. Personal communication.

Meagher, M. and J. R. Phillips. 1983. Restoration of natural populations of grizzly and black bears in Yellowstone National Park. In *Bears*, B.B.A., 152–158.

Mealey, S. P. 1975. *The natural food habits of free ranging grizzly bears in Yellowstone National Park, 1973–1974.* M.S. Thesis, Montana State University.

——. 1979. *Guidelines for management involving grizzly bears in the greater Yellowstone area.* USDA-FS.

Miller, G. D. 1983. Responses of captive grizzly and polar bears to potential repellents. In *Bears*, B.B.A., 275–279.

Miller, L. 1955. Color change in the black bear. *Journal of Mammalogy* 36 (3): 460.

Miller, T. S. 1963. Weights and color phases of black bear cubs. *Journal of Mammalogy* 44 (1): 129.

Mills, E. 1919. *The grizzly: our greatest wild animal.* New York: Houghton Mifflin.

Mitchell, J. 1976. Bear at the brink. *Sports Afield* (January and February).

Moment, G. 1968. Bears: the need for a new sanity in wildlife conservation. *Bioscience* (December): 1105–1108.

——. 1969. Bears and conservation: realities and recommendations. *Bioscience* (November): 1019–1020.

——. 1970. Man-grizzly problems—past and present. *Bioscience* (November): 1142–1144.

Moore, B. 1925. Importance of natural conditions in national parks. In *Hunting and Conservation: The Book of the Boone and Crockett Club*, ed. George Bird Grinnell and Charles Sheldon, 340–355. New Haven: Yale University Press.

Moore, S. 1970. Grizzly bear study ends. *Livingston Enterprise*: January 19.

Moorman, E. J. 1963. Memoirs of E. H. Moorman. *Livingston Enterprise*: February.

Morrison, E. E. 1976. *Guardian of the forest: a history of the Smokey Bear program.* New York: Vantage Press.

Morse, M. 1936. Hibernation and breeding of the black bear. *Journal of Mammalogy* 18 (4): 460–465.

Mundy, K. R. D., and D. R. Flook. 1973. *Background for managing grizzly bears in the national parks of Canada*. Canadian Wildlife Service Report Series 22.

Murie, A. 1937. Some food habits of the black bear. *Journal of Mammalogy* 18 (2): 238–240.

———. 1940. *Ecology of the coyote in the Yellowstone*. Washington D.C.: U.S. Government Printing Office.

———. 1961. *A naturalist in Alaska*. New York: Devin-Adair.

Murie, O. J. 1944. Progress report on the Yellowstone bear study. Yellowstone Park Files. Mimeographed.

———. 1954. *A field guide to animal tracks*. Boston: Houghton Mifflin.

National Academy of Sciences. 1974. *Report of the Committee on the Yellowstone grizzlies*. Mimeographed.

National Park Service. 1971a. Memorandum of understanding between the National Park Service and the Bureau of Sport Fisheries and Wildlife providing for research on the grizzly bear, *Ursus arctos*, in Yellowstone National Park by the Montana Cooperative Wildlife Research Unit. Yellowstone Park Files.

———. 1971b. Wilderness study, Yellowstone National Park. Yellowstone Park Files.

———. 1972. Draft environmental statement, proposed Yellowstone Master Plan. Yellowstone Park Files. Mimeographed.

———. 1973. Yellowstone National Park: Master Plan. Yellowstone Park Files.

———. 1975. Grizzly bear management program, Yellowstone National Park, Wyoming, Idaho, Montana. Yellowstone Park Files. Mimeographed.

———. 1984. Board of Inquiry into the death of Brigitta Fredenhagen. Yellowstone Park Files. Mimeographed.

———. 1985. Response to Chase article "the grizzly and the Juggernaut." Photocopy.

Netherby, S. 1974. Detente with ursus. *Field and Stream* (June).

Nuss, D. 1978–1979. Personal communication.

Panel Discussions. 1972. In *Bears*, IUCN,

Pearson, A. M. 1972. Population characteristics of northern interior grizzly bears in the Yukon Territory, Canada. In *Bears*, IUCN, 32–35.

———. 1975. *The northern interior grizzly bear (Ursus arctos L.)*. Canadian Wildlife Service Report Series, no. 34.

Pelton, M., et al. 1976. Attitudes and opinions of persons experiencing property damage and/or injury by black bears in the Great Smoky Mountains National Park. In *Bears*, IUCN, 157–168.

Peterson, S. 1973. Comments on the Craighead Computer Evaluation. . . Yellowstone Park Files. Photocopied.

Picton, H. 1978. Climate and reproduction of grizzly bears in Yellowstone National Park. *Nature* (August): 888–89.

Picton, H. D., and R. Knight. 1980. Obtaining biological information from grizzly bear (*Ursus arctos horribilis*) hair. Proceedings of the Northwest Section of the Wildlife Society, Banff, Canada.

———. 1983. Using climate data to predict grizzly bear litter size. 6th Int. Conf. on Bear Res. and Manage., Grand Canyon, Arizona. (In press)

Poelker and Hartwell. 1973. *Black bear of Washington, its biology, natural history and relationship to forest regeneration*. Washington State Game Department Biological Bulletin no. 4.

Pope, S. 1923. *Hunting with bow and arrow*. San Francisco: G.P. Putnam's Sons.

Pruitt, C. 1976. Play and agonistic behavior in captive black bears. In *Bears*, IUCN, 79–86.

Rausch, R. L. 1963. Geographic variation in size in North American brown bears, *Ursus arctos* L., as indicated by condylobasal length. *Canadian Journal of Zoology* 41: 33–45.

Reed, N. 1974. The grizzly debate, a response from Interior. *National Wildlife* (December-January): 16.

———. 1971. Letter to Senator Lee Metcalf, June 2.

———. 1973. Letter to Stephen Seater, June 1.

Reese, R. 1984. *Greater Yellowstone: the national park and adjacent wildlands*. Helena: Montana Magazine, Inc.

Regenstein, L. 1973. Letter to Nathaniel Reed, August 23.

Reid and Learmonth. 1969. Bear management in national parks, prepared for Joint Committee United States and Canadian National Parks, by Neil Reid (NPS) and Donald Learmonth (Parks Canada). Yellowstone Park Files. Mimeographed.

Reiger, J. 1975. *American sportsmen and the origins of conservation.* New York: Winchester Press.

Replogle, W. 1939. Marathon swimming for black bear. *Yellowstone Nature Notes* (September-October).

Reynolds, Curatolo, and Quimby. 1976. Denning ecology of grizzly bears in northeastern Alaska. In *Bears,* IUCN, 403–410.

Robertson, E. 1960. Memorandum to West District Ranger, entitled Bears and people. Yellowstone Park Files.

Robbins, W. J., et al. 1963. *A report by the Advisory Committee to the National Park Service on research of the National Academy of Sciences-National Research Council.* National Academy of Sciences.

Rogers, L. 1974. Shedding of foot pads by black bears during denning. *Journal of Mammalogy* 55 (3): 672–674.

———. 1976. Effects of mast and berry crop failures on survival, growth, and reproductive success of black bears. In Transactions of the 41st North American Wildlife and Natural Resources Conference, published by the Wildlife Management Institute, Washington D.C.

Rogers, L., et al. 1976. Characteristics and management of black bears that feed in garbage dumps, campgrounds, or residential areas. In *Bears,* IUCN, 169–176.

Roop, L. 1975. Grizzly bear progress report. Wyoming Game and Fish Department.

———. 1977. Grizzly bear progress report. Wyoming Game and Fish Department.

———. 1978. Grizzly bear progress report. Wyoming Game and Fish Department.

Roosevelt, T. 1893. *The wilderness hunter.* New York: G.P. Putnam's Sons.

———. 1925. *Outdoor pastimes of an American Hunter.* New York: Charles Scribner's Sons.

Rowan, W. 1947. A case of six cubs in the common black bear. *Journal of Mammalogy* 28 (4): 404–405.

Rush, W. 1928. How fast does a black bear climb? *Journal of Mammalogy* 9 (4): 335–336.

———. 1939. *Wild animals of the Rockies, adventures of a forest ranger.* Garden City: Halcyon House.

Russell, A. 1967. *Grizzly country.* New York: Knopf.

Russell, C. P. 1933. A concise history of science and scientific investigations in Yellowstone National Park. Yellowstone Park Files. Mimeographed.

Schleyer, B. 1983. *Activity patterns of grizzly bears in the Yellowstone ecosystem and their reproductive behavior, predation and the use of carrion.* M.A. Thesis, Montana State University.

Schnoes, R., and E. Starkey. 1978. Bear management in the national park system. National Park Service Oregon Cooperative Park Studies Unit, School of Forestry, Oregon State University.

Schoonmaker, W. J. 1968. *The world of the grizzly bear.* New York: Lippincott.

Schullery, P. 1975. *The Yellowstone archives: past, present, and future.* M.A. Thesis, Ohio University.

———. 1976. "Buffalo" Jones and the bison herd in Yellowstone: another look. *Montana, The Magazine of Western History* (Summer): 40–51.

———. 1978. A partnership in conservation . . . Roosevelt and Yellowstone. *Montana, The Magazine of Western History* (Summer): 2–15.

———. 1984a. Bear myths. *Field and Stream* 89 (8).

———. 1984b. Securing the grizzly's small portion. *National Parks* 58 (7–8): 27–32.

———. 1984c. *Mountain time.* New York: Nick Lyons Books/Schocken.

———. 1985. Reflections on bear stories. *Safari Magazine* 11 (6): 78–83.

———, ed. 1979. *Old Yellowstone days.* Boulder: Colorado Associated University Press.

———, ed. 1983. *American bears: selections from the writings of Theodore Roosevelt.* Boulder: Colorado Associated University Press.

Schullery, P., et al. 1984. *Fishing Bridge and the Yellowstone ecosystem: A report to the Director.* USDI-NPS.

Seater, S. 1973. Letter to Secretary of the Interior Morton, April 23.

———. 1975. Grizzly at bay. *The Environmental Journal* (November): 11–16.

Servheen, C. 1982. A national plan of recovery. *Western Wildlands* 8 (1): 13–15.

Seton, E. T. 1899. *The biography of a grizzly.* New York: The Century Company.

———. 1909. *Lives of game animals.* New York: Doubleday, Doran and Company.

———. 1913. *Wild animals at home.* New York: Grosset and Dunlap.

Shaffer, M. L. 1981. Minimum population sizes for species conservation. *Bioscience* 31 (2): 131–134.

———. 1983. Determining minimum viable population sizes for the grizzly bear. In *Bears,* B.B.A., 133–139.

Shepard, P., and B. Sanders. 1985. *The sacred paw: the bear in nature, myth, and literature*. New York: Viking.

Skinner, C. 1932. Some notes on the black bear (*Euarctos americanus*) from observations at Old Faithful, Yellowstone National Park. Yellowstone Park Files. Typescript.

Skinner, Milton. 1925a. *Bears in the Yellowstone*. Chicago: A.C. McClurg and Company.

————. 1925b. *The Yellowstone nature book*. Chicago: A.C. McClurg and Company.

————. 1927. The predatory and fur-bearing animals of Yellowstone Park. *Roosevelt Wildlife Bulletin* 4 (2): 163–282.

Smith, F. D. 1909. *Book of a hundred bears*. Chicago: Rand McNally.

Smith, J. 1913. The Yellowstone Park. *Science* (June 20): 941.

Sparrowe, R. 1968. Sexual behavior of grizzly bears. *The American Midland Naturalist* 80 (2): 570–572.

Spencer, H. F., Jr. 1955. *The black bear and its status in Maine*. Maine Department of Inland Fisheries and Game, Division Bulletin 4.

Stebler, A. M. 1972. Conservation of the grizzly—ecological and cultural considerations. In *Bears*, IUCN, 297–303.

Stokes, A. W. 1970. An ethologist's views on managing grizzly bears. *Bioscience* 20 (21): 1154–1157.

Stonorov, D., and A. W. Stokes. 1972. Social behavior of the Alaska brown bear. In *Bears*, IUCN, 232–242.

Storer and Tevis. 1955. *California grizzly*. Berkeley: University of California Press.

Suchy, W. J., et al. New estimates of minimum viable population sizes for grizzly bears of the Yellowstone ecosystem. *Wildlife Society Bulletin* 13 (3): 225–227.

Thompson, B. 1934. Letter to Max Bauer, Yellowstone Naturalist, September 3.

Thompson, T. 1942. Grizzly bears get food. *Yellowstone Nature Notes* (May-June).

Tisch, E. L. 1961. Seasonal food habit of the black bear in the Whitefish Range of northwestern Montana. M.S. Thesis, Montana State University.

Trefethen, James. 1975. *An American crusade for wildlife*. New York: Winchester Press and the Boone and Crockett Club.

U.S. Executive Order 11507. 1970. Prevention, control, and abatement of air and water pollution at federal facilities. February 4.

U.S. Fish and Wildlife Service. 1982. *Grizzly bear recovery plan*. USDI-FWS.

Van Wormer, J. 1966. *The world of the black bear*. Philadelphia: Lippincott.

Walker, R. 1975. Memorandum to Director, U.S. Fish and Wildlife Service, entitled Grizzly bear management program Yellowstone National Park. Yellowstone Park Files.

Weaver, J. 1978. The wolves of Yellowstone. Natural Resources Report no. 14. National Park Service.

Wilber, C. 1970. Incompatible species. *Bioscience* 20 (6): 326. Letter to the Editor.

Willey, C. 1978. *The Vermont black bear*. Vermont Fish and Game Department.

Wills, L. 1975. Two agencies criticized about grizzly bear kills. *Bozeman Daily Chronicle*: November 2.

Wister, O. 1936. Old Yellowstone days. *Harper's Magazine* (March 1).

Wooldridge, D. R. 1980. Chemical aversion conditioning of polar and black bears. In *Bears*, B.B.A., 167–173.

Worley, et al. 1976. Helminth and arthropod parasites of grizzly and black bears in Montana and adjacent ranges. In *Bears*, IUCN, 455–464.

Wright, G., J. Dixon, and B. Thompson. 1933. *Fauna of the national parks of the United States*. Washington D.C.: U.S. Government Printing Office.

Wright, G., and B. Thompson. 1935. Fauna of the national parks of the United States: wildlife management in the national parks. Washington D.C.: U.S. Government Printing Office.

Wright, W. 1910a. *Ben, the black bear*. New York: Charles Scribner's Sons.

————. 1910b. *The grizzly bear*. New York: Charles Scribner's Sons.

Yeager, D. 1931. *Our wilderness neighbors*. Chicago: A.C. McClurg Company.

————. 1933. Bringing up Barney. *Nature Magazine* 21 (1): 27–30.

Yellowstone Archives. Especially pre-1916 records, and Law Enforcement and Research sections of post-1916 records. Only those referred to are listed, but many other reports, files, and volumes were consulted.

Yellowstone Park. 1970. Proposed criteria for transplant or disposal of problem bears. Yellowstone Park Management Plan. Photocopied.

———. 1977. Bear management operational plan. Yellowstone Park Files. Photocopied.

———. 1982. Final environmental impact statement – grizzly bear management program. USDI-NPS.

Yellowstone Park Biologist Office. Bear files and correspondence files, as referred to or quoted. This material is available under the terms of the Freedom of Information Act.

Yellowstone Park Superintendent's Reports. All were consulted. Several are referred to or quoted in the book.

Zunino, F. 1981. Dilemma of the Abruzzo bears. *Oryx* 16 (2): 153–156.

Index

About the Author

Since 1972 Paul Schullery has worked at various times in Yellowstone as a ranger-naturalist, as park historian, and as a research consultant. His M.A. Thesis (Ohio University, 1975) was an archival study of Yellowstone's historic administrative record collection, and he has published numerous articles and reports about park history and wildlife. He is author, co-author, or editor, of many books about national parks and nature, and his other Yellowstone books are *Old Yellowstone Days* (1979), *Freshwater Wilderness: Yellowstone Fishes and Their World* (with John D. Varley, 1983), and *Mountain Time* (1984). He has written on nature, conservation, and sport for many magazines, including *Country Journal, The New York Times Book Review, Newsweek, Field & Stream, National Parks,* and *Outdoor Life.* He lives in Livingston, Montana, where he works as a writer and research consultant.